T5-BQA-345

BRITAIN: PROGRESS AND DECLINE

TULANE STUDIES in
POLITICAL SCIENCE

Volume XVII

Tulane Studies in Political Science

TULANE STUDIES IN POLITICAL SCIENCE are published under the editorial direction of the Department of Political Science of Tulane University. Volumes may be ordered through the Department of Political Science, Tulane University, New Orleans, Louisiana 70118.

Volume I – L. Vaughan Howard and David R. Deener, *Presidential Politics in Louisiana, 1952*

Volume II – Leonard Reissman, K. H. Silvert and Cliff W. Wing, Jr., *The New Orleans Voter: A Handbook of Political Description* and Kenneth N. Vines, *Republicanism in New Orleans*

Volume III – L. Vaughan Howard, *Civil Service Development in Louisiana*

Volume IV – *International Law and the Middle East Crisis: A Symposium*

Volume V – Henry L. Mason, *Toynbee's Approach to World Politics*

Volume VI – L. Vaughan Howard and Robert S. Friedman, *Government in Metropolitan New Orleans*

Volume VII – Philip B. Taylor, Jr., *Government and Politics of Uruguay* (out of print)

Volume VIII – Kenneth N. Vines and Herbert Jacob, *Studies in Judicial Politics* (out of print)

Volume IX – William B. Gwyn, *The Meaning of the Separation of Powers*

Volume X – Henry L. Mason, *Mass Demonstrations against Foreign Regimes: A Study of Five Crises*

Volume XI – Alex B. Lacy, Jr., editor, *Power in American State Legislatures*

Volume XII – James D. Cochrane, *The Politics of Regional Integration: The Central American Case*

Volume XIV – Henry L. Mason, *College and University Government: A Handbook of Principle and Practice*

Volume XV – William B. Gwyn and George C. Edwards, III, *Perspectives on Public Policy-Making*

Volume XVI – Robert S. Robins, editor, *Psychopathology and Political Leadership*

Volume XVII – William B. Gwyn and Richard Rose, editors, *Britain: Progress and Decline*

BRITAIN: PROGRESS AND DECLINE

Edited by

William B. Gwyn and Richard Rose
for the British Politics Group

TULANE UNIVERSITY
NEW ORLEANS
1980

First published 1980 in the UK by
THE MACMILLAN PRESS LTD
London and Basingstoke
First published in the USA
by the Tulane University Press

ISBN 0-930598-18-0

Printed in Great Britain

Contents

Preface vii

Notes on the Contributors xii

1 Jeremiahs and Pragmatists: Perceptions of British Decline 1
William B. Gwyn

2 The British Economy and its Problems 26
Alan Peacock

3 Welfare: Progress and Stagnation 39
Hugh Heclo

4 Westminster and Whitehall 57
Anthony H. Birch

5 From Gentlemen to Players: Changes in Political Leadership 73
Dennis Kavanagh

6 The Impact of Organised Interests 94
Graham Wootton

7 Immigration and Racial Change 111
Donley T. Studlar

8 From Steady State to Fluid State: the United Kingdom Today 129
Richard Rose

Index 155

Preface

Britain has changed greatly in the lifetime of the average adult. Anyone who doubts this can turn to the files of a popular magazine such as *Picture Post* and view the record of bomb damage and shortages in the austerity state of immediate post-war Britain. The story of change is told more precisely and equally convincingly in official statistics. If comparison is pushed back to 1939, the extent of change is even greater.

The story of Britain since 1945 has been a record of both progress *and* decline. The same evidence can be cited as proof of each of these judgments because absolute progress can be combined with relative decline. The mixed economy welfare state provides a far higher standard of living than was available before 1939. Yet the welfare state has failed to meet the expectations of those who wished to abolish poverty completely, or dreamed of a new, classless society. The British economy produced historically unparalleled national wealth. But when its achievements are compared with those of European neighbours, the economy is seen to be declining vis-à-vis its major competitors. There are also events – such as the Nationalist challenge to the unity of the United Kingdom – that are controversial; they are regarded by some as evidence of decline and by others as a sign of progress.

The purpose of this book is two-fold. The first task is to describe the major changes that have been taking place under the auspices of British government since the creation of the mixed economy welfare state in the crucible of war and reconstruction in the 1940s. The second object is to evaluate these changes. The contributors write without any *a priori* commitment to the belief that England is the victim of an incurable (and perhaps contagious) disease, nor do they suffer from the belief that there is a divine providence that protects the British people from the mistakes of government. The past two decades have produced more than enough simplistic polemics about what's wrong or what's right with Britain. As Chapter 1 demonstrates, jeremiahs have not seen these prophecies of doom fulfilled, but pragmatists have also failed to show that their remedies will work a cure for the troubles they diagnose.

The simplest changes to describe are those that can be measured in quantitative terms: growth in the economy, in average earnings, and in such conditions of individual well-being as life expectancy, education and health. Comparison with conditions twenty or forty years ago almost invariably emphasises the progressive improvement in living conditions. But a failure to make cross-national comparisons can lead to an over-generous evaluation of material progress. For example, an author writing in praise of the presumed preference of English people for leisure as against work (whether on or off the job is not made clear) ignores the fact that the average Briton's working week is 44 hours. British workers accept or seek at least four hours overtime work a week. Therefore, the average work week in Britain is longer than that in the European Community as a whole. Germans work fewer hours a week on average than British workmen; they also work more effectively.[1]

Many of the most important changes in society are qualitative, not quantitative. The second task of this book is to evaluate changes in Britain. Comparison is the basic tool of evaluation. By examining trends over the years, we can see how much change (or, from a reformist perspective, failure to change) there has been. By comparing conditions in Britain with other major Western nations, we can assess relative as well as absolute progress. The fact that this volume is the product of a bi-national team of authors – mixing Americans resident in Britain and Britons resident in America as well as seasoned travellers living in their native land – makes it practicable to view insular anxieties and complacencies with detachment.

Among those working in British government, diplomatists are most sensitive to the country's relative standing in the world today. It is therefore specially noteworthy that men expected to put the best face on the condition of England are among those most gloomy about the country's present and future prospects. Shortly before being appointed HM Ambassador to Washington in 1977, Peter Jay wrote, 'We in Britain are a confused and unhappy people.'[2] Two years later, in a characteristic stream of multiple negatives, Sir Nicholas Henderson wrote from the Paris Embassy, shortly before moving to Washington, 'Today we are not only no longer a world power, but we are not in the first rank even as a European one. . . . You only have to move about Western Europe nowadays to realise how poor and unproud the British have become in relation to their neighbours.'[3]

One may object that such criticisms tend to reflect an excessive materialism. Peter Jay's forecasts of doom are derived from an economistic model of human behaviour, and the worst of his warnings have yet to be realised, perhaps because ordinary British people are not so much at home with logical reasoning as Jay himself. As Gwyn's chapter shows, some even regard material progress as evidence of a decline in the quality of life in Britain. Yet the derisory vote for Ecology candidates at the 1979 general election shows how narrow is popular support for such a view. Moreover, Fabian Socialists have always presupposed that the state would have the material means to achieve the ends they wished. The 1964–70 Labour government, and even more, its 1974–9 successor, provided ample evidence to the contrary.[4]

At a minimum, politicians must take responsibility for their own style of leadership, and the way in which they manage and change institutions of government in Whitehall. Westminster and Whitehall have talked much about reforming their own institutions in the past two decades, and produced many reports canvassing change. Yet the substance of change is little, as Anthony Birch notes, and the chief conclusion one might draw from the record is that political reformers cannot even reform the institutions that they themselves control. Dennis Kavanagh's study of the changing social character of leadership emphasises the extent of change from an era in which Sir Winston Churchill (Harrow and the Hussars) faced Clement Attlee (Haileybury and Oxford) in the House of Commons. Kavanagh concludes that broadening the social recruitment of politicians has not, *ipso facto*, made for better governance of those whom they represent. Rose's study of the 'cracking of the cake of custom' that held together the United Kingdom emphasises that change has occurred, but leaves open the direction of change. In Northern Ireland, change has led to more rather than less dissension.

The great bulk of public policies are co-operative. In a free society, and Britain remains pre-eminently that, government depends upon the co-operation of masses of interest groups and millions of citizens to achieve its intentions. Economists disagree about the extent to which government initiatives can improve the performance of the economy, as against reliance upon market choices. Alan Peacock makes clear that whether British government be accused of too much or too little direction of the economy the record is poor by European comparison. Graham Wootton's analysis of interest groups argues that the blame for this condition cannot simply be laid upon trade unions.

In a non-totalitarian society, there is a limit to which government can be responsible for the collective welfare of its people. While social relations are not controlled by government, the contemporary welfare state has been important in providing a material basis for individual life satisfaction. Yet Hugh Heclo argues that, by failing to include economic policy, the welfare state has not gone far enough. Because trade unions as well as employers have opposed intervention with free market bargaining about wages, both Labour and Conservative governments have found it electorally expedient to avoid the issue of a 'fair wage' until an economic crisis strikes. Immigration similarly raises a question about the extent to which government can influence mass attitudes. Donley Studlar shows that as Britain made the sea change from an all-white to a multi-racial society, government policy was lagging rather than leading on this issue.

The 1979 British general election gave both politicians and ordinary voters an opportunity to review the condition of England as it approached the 1980s. By polling day, the choice before the electorate was defined as whether the country wished (or, more significantly, could risk) change. Imitating Stanley Baldwin, James Callaghan campaigned on a 'safety first' line, arguing that a Conservative government was 'too big a gamble for the country to take'.[5] Echoing Labour's 1964 campaign against 13 wasted years, Conservatives out of office for 11 of the previous 15 years advertised, 'It's time for a change. Don't just hope for a better life. Vote for one.'

A pro-Labour *Guardian* leader described the electoral choice as 'dismaying'. 'The party of change and reform has become the party of benevolent immobilism. The party of resistance to change has sought to become the party of (at least rhetorical) revolution.'[6] The best the *Guardian* could say for Labour's economic record was that it was 'attempting (often inadequately) to cope'. The Conservative writer Peregrine Worsthorne also emphasised that the Conservatives had become identified, first under Edward Heath and then under Margaret Thatcher, as a party of change. Moreover, Worsthorne assumed that the British electorate today is afraid of change, perhaps because they regard it as an harbinger of decline, not progress. In arguing 'Why Labour voters should take a chance on Mrs T', this anti-Socialist author was reduced to saying, 'Whatever happens in the election is not going to make all that much difference.'[7]

The electorate's own verdict on the state of Britain today was to give a mild two cheers for the two parties governing it alternately since 1945. The Conservative party won an absolute majority in the House of Commons in 1979, gaining more seats but fewer votes than Edward Heath won for his programme of 'action not words' in 1970. The Labour party polled its worst vote since 1931, notwithstanding the appeal that its leader made to the putative 'conservative consensus' in the country.

The chapters that follow are not concerned with the ephemera of elections, but with the inertia of continuing events. Each was initially drafted for presentation at a conference at Tulane University, New Orleans, between 8–10 November 1978, sponsored jointly by the University and the British Politics Group, an Anglo-American society of social scientists wishing to promote a better understanding of contemporary British politics. The editors are particularly indebted to Robert Stevens, then Provost of Tulane University, and Jorgen S. Rasmussen, Secretary of the British Politics Group, for assistance with the conference. It was made possible by grants from James J. Coleman Jr, Honorary British Consul for Louisiana, and the Nuffield Foundation. The papers were revised, and edited to include references as appropriate to political events occurring up to the general election of 3 May 1979.

The past is a very uncertain prelude to the future; it provides a basis for reflection rather than a guide to specific policies. Public figures often draw misleading conclusions about the future in the flux of the present. For example, in 1959, just before the British economy entered a lengthy period of great difficulties, Lord Cromer, a leading banker and Britain's economic minister in Washington, announced proudly to the world, 'Two years ago, in the summer of 1959, British economic fortunes were again at a low ebb. Less than two years later, the British economy emerges as one of the strongest in the Western world and the pound sterling is a highly sought after currency.'[8] The ups and downs – principally downs – of sterling since have shown how temporary can be generalisations from a single point in time.

The pages that follow present a mixed record. They show the many positive achievements of British government since 1945, but they also record many disappointments. There is a peculiarly English tendency to regard setbacks as harbingers of good fortune; for example, Dunkirk is often cited as a British triumph, when in fact it marked the end of a disastrous military campaign. The fact that Britain has faced and overcome dire conditions previously is a caution against 'doom-mongering'. But it should not become an excuse for over-confidence. There is no ground for complaçency in the pages that follow. To believe that Britain will 'muddle through' is inadequate as explanation or analysis. Progress, and even stability, are not inevitable. The history books are littered with the stories of empires that did decline, and whose glory is no more.

WILLIAM B. GWYN   RICHARD ROSE

NOTES

1. Cf. Bernard D. Nossiter, *Britain – a Future that Works* (Boston: Houghton Mifflin, 1978) ch. 3; and *Social Trends*, vol. VIII (London: HMSO, 1977) Table 5.5.
2. See Peter Jay, 'Englanditis', in R. Emmett Tyrrell Jr. (ed.), *The Future that Doesn't Work: Social Democracy's Failures in Britain* (Garden City, NY: Doubleday, 1977) p. 167.
3. Sir Nicholas Henderson's confidential report, 'Britain's Decline: Its Causes and Consequences', printed in *The Economist*, 2 June 1979.
4. Cf. Wilfred Beckerman (ed.), *The Labour Government's Economic Record, 1964–1970* (London: Duckworth, 1972).
5. 'Casting her Net for Floating, Undecided and Tactical Voters', *Guardian*, 2 May 1979.
6. 'A Faith that Curled at the Edges', *Guardian*, 2 May 1979.
7. *Sunday Telegraph*, 29 Apr 1979.
8. Lord Cromer, 'The British Economy since 1957', *British Affairs*, June 1959, p. 60.

Notes on the Contributors

ANTHONY H. BIRCH, B.Sc. (Econ.), Ph.D (London). Professor of Political Science, University of Victoria, British Columbia, since 1977. Formerly, Professor of Politics, Universities of Hull and Exeter. Author of *Small-Town Politics, Representative and Responsible Government, The British System of Government, Political Integration and Disintegration in the British Isles*, etc.

WILLIAM B. GWYN, BA, MA (Virginia), Ph.D. (London). Professor of Political Science, Tulane University, since 1969. Author of *Democracy and the Cost of Politics in Britain, The Meaning of the Separation of Powers* and co-editor of *Perspectives on Public Policy-Making.*

HUGH HECLO, BA (George Washington), MA (Manchester), Ph.D (Yale). Professor of Government, Harvard University, since 1978. Formerly, Senior Fellow, the Brookings Institution. Author of *Modern Social Politics in Britain and Sweden* and *A Government of Strangers*; co-author of *The Private Government of Public Money.*

DENNIS KAVANAGH, BA, MA (Manchester). Senior Lecturer in Government, University of Manchester since 1974. Author of *Constituency Electioneering in Britain, Political Culture*, and Nuffield studies of the two 1974 and 1979 British general elections with D. E. Butler, and co-editor of *New Trends in British Politics.*

ALAN PEACOCK, MA (St Andrews), Principal of University College at Buckingham since 1980. Formerly, Professor of Economics, York and Edinburgh. Chief Economic Adviser, Departments of Industry and Trade from 1973 to 1976. Author or co-author of *The Growth of Public Expenditure in the United Kingdom, 1890–1955, Economic Theory of Fiscal Policy, The Composer in the Market Place, Welfare Economics: A Liberal Re-interpretation*, etc.

RICHARD ROSE, BA (Johns Hopkins), D.Phil. (Oxon). Director of the Centre for the Study of Public Policy and, since 1966, Professor of Politics, University of Strathclyde. Author of *Politics in England Today, Influencing Voters, Governing without Consensus, The Problem of Party Government*, etc. Editor or co-editor of *Studies in British Politics, Policy-Making in Britain, New Trends in British Politics, Presidents and Prime Ministers*, etc.

Donley T. Studlar, BA (Texas Tech.), Ph.D. (Indiana). Assistant Professor of Political Science, Centre College, Kentucky, since 1976. Thesis on British attitudes to immigration winner of the first Samuel Beer prize of the British Politics Group. Contributor of articles on immigration politics to journals in Britain and America.

Graham Wootton, BSc. (Econ.), Ph.D. (London). Professor of Political Science, Tufts University, since 1967. Formerly, Historical Section, Cabinet Office, and Senior Staff Tutor, Delegacy for Extra-Mural Studies, Oxford University. Author of *The Politics of Influence, Workers, Unions and The State Interest Groups, Pressure Groups in Britain 1720–1970*, and *Pressure Politics in Contemporary Britain.*

1 Jeremiahs and Pragmatists: Perceptions of British Decline

William B. Gwyn

In every society, there are always some people who believe it declining, and others who see progress. Disagreement as to whether change should be interpreted as progress towards a superior condition or decline into an inferior one can result from examining different areas of change, or perceiving a given change differently, or applying different standards to evaluate change, or some combination of these. While there is never complete agreement about whether a society or a significant aspect of it is declining or progressing, historically there have been occasions when large numbers of people have shared such a view. During the first century, people often wrote of Roman decline, usually attributing it to moral decadence. Following its Golden Age, Spain from the seventeenth century was frequently described as a kingdom in decline. During the nineteenth century, it was very common to refer to the Ottoman Empire as 'the sick man of Europe', while between the 1920s and the 1960s France was often pictured as a nation in decline. Mid-Victorian Britain, by contrast, was frequently described by Britons and foreigners alike as a flourishing, progressing society. As late as 1876, *The Times*, in evaluating the preceding quarter of a century, could declare confidently, 'Upon the whole, Englishmen must regard it as one continued triumph of progress, though not always in the way that had been expected'.[1]

For the past two decades, the dominant perception of Britain has been one of decline rather than progress or even stability, although there is disagreement about the rate and extent of decline and which aspects of British society are languishing. The United Kingdom has now become in many people's eyes the sick man of Europe and 'the British disease', or 'English sickness', is something other countries fret about contracting. 'State of Britain' inquiries are frequently published in newspapers and magazines or delivered over radio and television, and national decline appears as significant themes in British novels.[2]

It is difficult to date with precision the beginning of this pessimistic mood. After the depression of the 1930s, the dislocation and deprivation of the war years, and the austerity and controls imposed by the post-war Labour governments of 1945–51, the 1950s were seen by most Britons as 'an age of prosperity and achievement'.[3] Angry Young Men and others might raise their voices against the materialism of the 1950s and the continued predominance of an upper class establishment, but on the whole the language of national decline was rare. As G. D. H. Cole noted in the 1956 edition of his survey of the condition of Britain, the first edition of 1937 had been 'written in a prevailing atmosphere of national pessimism, which the course of events was making deeper year to year'. In the mid-1950s, however, he was able to record:

> not only in many respects, a great and unmistakable improvement over pre-war conditions, but also, despite Great Britain's serious difficulties over the balance of payments, a more favourable economic outlook than that of the 1930s, and, therewith, I believe, a much more optimistic temper among the people despite the appalling possibilities of destruction involved in a war waged with atomic weapons.[4]

1956 was also the year in which Anthony Crosland published his influential *The Future of Socialism*, which emphasised the declining importance of economic problems in a Britain entering an age of affluence. While recognising a need to give 'a reasonably high priority to economic growth', he observed that it was not 'an over-riding priority; for we already enjoy a rapid growth rate in Britain, and one almost adequate to accommodate [valid claims on the country's resources] within a reasonable space of time'. A high rate of growth was believed by Crosland to be entirely compatible with the ideals of socialism. As proof he pointed to Britain, one of the least competitive of nations, which nevertheless would double its living standard in 25 years if it maintained its current rate of growth.[5] In a 1958 review of J. K. Galbraith's *The Affluent Society*, a book which enjoyed a considerable vogue among British socialists at the time, Crosland could still quote from his book a passage that Britain in a couple of decades could 'stop worrying about hard work and economic matters',[6] and even as late as March 1960 he can be found calling upon his party to adapt itself to the abundant society created by a mixed economy. The only thing said to be wrong with the British economy was the fairness with which the wealth it produced was distributed.[7]

Sometime during 1960–1, optimism gave way to pessimism. 'It is nearly fashionable', wrote the sociologist Donald MacRae in the autumn of 1961, 'to accept, almost voluptuously, public despair'. Two years later, the political scientist Brian Chapman observed that 'over the last few years the Cassandras in Britain have become more numerous, their prophecies more woeful, their pessimism more justified by events'.[8] Those who did not accept the widely articulated view of British decline attacked it as a kind of mental illness afflicting British society. The journalist Henry Fairlie deplored 'The ceaseless articles, books, and special numbers about "the state of

England"' and their preoccupation with 'decline' and 'crisis'. 'What ought to be matters of interest change their character when they become obsessions. Problems which are real and manageable become part of a Problem which can never be tackled but only constantly written about'. The historian Marcus Cuncliffe came to much the same conclusion. Englishmen were suffering from national hypochondria.

> We have frightened ourselves unnecessarily as hypochondriacs do. Much in English life is unlikeable and unsatisfactory, but there is nothing hopelessly wrong with us. In comparison with most societies of the world we are extremely well off—economically, politically, socially. The point is that where we once exaggerated our prowess, our freedom of will, we now exaggerate our incapacity, our predestined downfall.[9]

No one can deny that Britain in the 1960s and 1970s faced many problems, some quite serious. Such problems, however, have been perceived in Britain in two significantly different ways. The 'jeremiahs', as I shall call them, view these problems as reflecting a long-term downward trend in vitally important aspects of British society, which can be reversed only by eliminating certain deep-seated characteristics of that society and which, if not reversed, will lead to increasingly unsatisfactory, perhaps disastrous, consequences for the British people. By contrast, 'pragmatists' are inclined to view Britain's problems severally and not as evidence of national decline. Post-war Britain is perceived instead in terms of stability or progress. Policy-makers sharing this point of view are inclined to tackle public problems piece-meal and to tinker with society rather than introduce the radical changes recommended by the jeremiahs. The latter accuse the pragmatists of dealing only with the symptoms of decline and ignoring its real causes.

Jeremiahs do not agree about what is declining in Britain. During the past 20 years or so, a number of institutions and aspects of society have been described as being in that state: Parliament, the Cabinet, the capability of the civil service, political leadership, governmental authority, law and order, civic-mindedness, civil liberty, racial purity, morality, the quality of the welfare state, the aristocracy, the middle class, architecture, village life, etc. What most people who have lamented British decline during the 1960s and 1970s have had in mind is, however, economic decline or, most frequently in the 1960s, a combination of economic decline and decline in the country's power and influence in the international political system. Often economic and international decline are seen as causally related – sometimes mutually so – or as both being the result of the same cause or causes. As British people gradually adjust to accepting something less than major power status,[10] economic decline has in the 1970s become the main subject for concern, with a number of the other possible types of decline sometimes mentioned as causes or effects. The popular expression 'the English disease' refers to weaknesses in Britain's economy which prevent it from achieving adequate levels of production and overseas trade and which promote unacceptable levels of inflation and unemployment.[11]

During the 1960s, concern about the economy focused especially on complaints about Britain's economic growth and productivity and the decline in its share of overseas trade, while in the 1970s inflation and unemployment have come into the limelight. This shift of emphasis reflects not an objective improvement in production and trade but a worsening of inflation and unemployment. Various consequences have been attributed to economic decline, ranging from the country's becoming a relatively comfortable backwater[12] to the breakup of the United Kingdom[13] or 'eventual social and political upheaval'.[14]

Concern about production, productivity, and foreign trade arose when comparisons with the performance of other highly industrialised countries indicated that, while Britain during the 1950s might have been performing in absolute terms well above her pre-war achievement, relatively she was slipping behind other modern nations. For a people who for generations had recognised as a fact of life that national prosperity and even survival depended on their success in foreign trade, it could be a chilling experience to be told that between 1951 and 1962 while the British share of world trade declined from 22 to 15 per cent, West Germany's had expanded from 10 to 20 per cent, or that during roughly the same period, British exports increased by 30 per cent as compared to a 190 per cent increase in the exports from the Common Market countries.[15] It was equally upsetting to learn that, while the country in 1950 had been one of the wealthiest in Europe, surpassed only by Sweden and Switzerland, by the early 1960s the United Kingdom had been caught up by West Germany and France. The reason for Britain's relative decline of wealth was, of course, her having one of the lowest rates of economic growth in Western Europe.[16] Despite efforts to improve productivity and trade during the 1960s, the situation continued to deteriorate. The British share of world trade continued to dwindle for a time until it stabilised at about West Germany's 1951 share. The British annual rate of economic growth remained on average about at the level of the 1950s; however, with the continuing higher rates on the Continent, by the early 1970s British GNP per capita was lower than that of all the more highly industrialised Western European countries.[17] During the 1970s, the United Kingdom encountered two new frightening occurrences. Full employment was no longer so full as in the 1950s and 1960s and inflation reached a double-digit figure. Both of these developments, viewed comparatively, indicated that British experience was worsening relatively to that of other Western nations.[18]

Reactions to the United Kingdom's economic performance have varied considerably. During the 1950s and early 1960s, when they were not ignored altogether, the relatively low growth rates were often perceived as temporary, the result of Britain's being the oldest industrial country ('All growth rates will in time drop to our level') or of the Continental countries' making up ground they had lost during the depression or the war ('Germany, France, and Italy can't keep it up and will soon sink to our levels'). Still another soothing idea was that comparative data about growth was very inexact and that growth rates varied according to the starting dates for calculating them. Unfortunately all available data and the use of a variety of starting dates leave Britain near the very bottom of the Western European growth league. Such attempts to explain away the unpleasant facts of British economic life moved Arthur Koestler to characterise the average Englishman as, except in emergencies, an ostrich who 'buries his head in the sand with the tranquil conviction that Reality is a nasty word invented by foreigners'.[19] As the alarming growth pattern persisted through the 1960s and into the 1970s, Britons found it increasingly difficult to maintain this 'struthonian' (ostrich-like) attitude.

Those who recognised that Britain was falling behind other industrial nations in production and foreign trade, held very different attitudes toward the phenomenon. The country's few revolutionary Marxists were delighted that such conditions would before long destroy capitalism. Another small but articulate minority also concluded that economic decline was a good thing: to allow growth to continue would cause a serious decline in the quality of British life. Most persons aware of the relative decline of the country's growth rate and exports were, however, convinced that this was a dangerous state of affairs requiring remedying if more unfortunate consequences were not to follow. Members of this much larger collection of people tend to fall into one of two groups with respect to their diagnoses and remedies for Britain's economic problems.[20]

The pragmatists viewed economic problems mainly as the result of incorrect government policies. Recognising no strong long-term downward trend in the economy arising from deeply ingrained characteristics of British society, they perceived economic problems as a puzzle to be solved by the government's adopting the correct type and mixture of policies to determine the proper level of demand, investment, etc. Probably a sizeable majority of professional economists and most politicians have followed this line of thinking. Although pragmatists have disagreed among themselves about the causes of Britain's economic difficulties and the public policies required to eliminate or greatly lessen them,[21] they do agree that some economic policies are what is chiefly needed to produce a satisfactory economy and that deep-seated characteristics of British society unrelated directly with economic activity are not the major source of difficulty. Jeremiahs, on the other hand, take the opposite point of view. Britain can only overcome its economic problems by radically changing certain aspects of its culture and society.

I Jeremiahs and British Economic Decline

Institutional Explanations

While some jeremiahs agree with the pragmatists that Britain's economic decline is mainly caused by incorrect public policies, they attribute the choice of such policies to certain characteristics of the political system that greatly lessen the likelihood of correct policies being adopted.

One type of institutional explanation of hyper-inflation perceives Britain as having an advanced case of a disease afflicting all representative democracies. Perhaps the two best known British exponents of this position are the economic writers and journalists Samuel Brittan and Peter Jay, both of whom have acknowledged their theoretical indebtedness to the Austrian economist Joseph Schumpeter. Both also appear to have been considerably influenced by recent so-called 'economic' theories of democracy.[22] Brittan argues that liberal democracies cannot avoid several weaknesses. Firstly, by bidding for votes, politicians generate excessive popular expectations about the economic benefits of government action and an under-estimation of the costs. Secondly, trade unionists in a free collective bargaining system make claims upon the economy beyond its productive capacity, causing cycles of unemployment and inflation. Thirdly, people in modern democracies are afflicted by an excessive egalitarianism which leads them to judge their present material well-being not by comparison with their past circumstances but by envious comparison with the well-being of others. This envy influences them to make exorbitant demands on the economic product of their societies. Peter Jay, before he became Ambassador to the United States in 1977, summarised his rather similar theory as follows:

> The operation of free democracy appears to force governments into positions (the commitment to full employment) that prevents them from taking steps (fiscal and monetary restraint) that are necessary to arrest the menace (accelerated inflation) that threatens to undermine the condition (stable prosperity) on which political stability and therefore liberal democracy depend.

Under conditions of full employment, unions in collective bargaining are uninhibited from pressing for higher and higher wages. Because there is not a corresponding increase in output, prices will rise, in turn prompting unions to make further pay claims. Both Brittan and Jay are pessimistic about the continuation of representative democracies because of these destructive tendencies, and they are especially gloomy about such an advanced case as Britain's.[23]

Other institutional explanations of the United Kingdom's economic decline as well as other problems have stressed weaknesses not in representative government generally but in British political institutions in particular. One version of this viewpoint is very critical of the policy-making capabilities of the country's governmental institutions. Brian Chapman's *British Government Observed* is a good example of this argument during the early 1960s, while Richard Rose's characterisation of policy-making in Britain as 'directionless consensus' is another good example from a few years later.[24] Often such criticism has sought out the senior civil service for especially severe censure. In a very influential essay of the late 1950s, Thomas Balogh warned, 'Britain's power has been declining at a rate unparalleled since the crash of the Spanish Empire.' He attributed this decline largely to defects in civil service policy-making: 'What makes a review of policy-making machinery imperative is that all these acute crises and this creeping paralysis [since the war] share in having taken the authorities unawares, though they were predictable and predicted by the critics of the policies pursued.'[25]

Events of the 1970s suggested to some observers that the weakness of British public policy-making was not so much in the governmental institutions themselves but was the result of constraints put on the government by organised labour. In one of his last publications Arnold Toynbee wrote that, because the government could no longer impose its will on the unions, there was no longer a single sovereign in Britain, which meant that the country had 'reverted politically to the situation of England before the reign of Henry VII'. This condition of 'a state within the state' could lead to excessive inflation and then military dictatorship, although Toynbee thought it more likely that Britain would follow the ancient Roman pattern in which the tribunes of the plebs were co-opted into a 'plebeian–patrician "establishment"' with the tribunes functioning 'as constitutional agents for keeping the mass of the plebs under control'.[26]

The analogy between trade unions and medieval barons has been carried even further by other writers. The late Labour MP John Mackintosh observed that medieval English kings achieved legitimacy and support for their policies from powerful barons by calling them together in Parliament. 'It was this desire to legitimise policies and laws by getting the prior consent from the most powerful men in the country that led to the creation of the Houses of Lords which were, in practice, the most important chambers in medieval parliaments.' After describing the recent experience of certain Continental countries in bringing powerful labour and management groups within the public policy-making process, Mackintosh recommended that the House of Lords, while retaining its current limited powers, be reconstructed as a functional chamber with most of its representatives nominated by trade unions, industry, and other pressure groups.[27]

The non-partisan character of this line of thinking is indicated by the fact that a similar proposal based on the same analogy has been made recently by a banker and former conservative political adviser. According to Brendon Sewill, the health of the British economy could be restored only if 'the unions were prepared to give up their bargaining power based on the strike weapon'. For this to occur, a Council of the Nation, containing representatives of the unions, management, and Parliament, should meet to negotiate a 'New Concordat', under which unions would forgo strikes and co-operate in raising productivity, management would agree to share control with employees, and the Government would introduce policies to accomplish full employment, price stability, and increased productivity, while also replacing the House of Lords with a Senate based on regional and functional representation. Containing substantial union representation and having co-ordinate authority with the House of Commons, the Senate would become 'the main forum of economic debate'. In Sewill's opinion, this new Magna Carta could succeed only if the initiative came from the unions. 'It must be their plan. They alone have the industrial strength to force it through.'[28]

For those who see union power as a major cause of economic decline, some form of corporatism is likely to seem the best remedy. There has been a good deal of talk in recent years of the need for 'tripartism' or 'concertation' as the structural arrangements most likely to succeed in governing a neo-feudal society.[29] The more old fashioned, confrontation point of view also continues to be heard. Representative of this latter approach is Professor Hayek's call in 1977 for the revocation of the special privileges granted to British unions by the Trades Dispute Act of 1906. 'There can be little doubt to a detached observer that the privileges then granted to the trade unions have become the chief source of Britain's economic decline.'[30]

Ideological Explanations

Many Conservatives and exponents of a 'free market economy' are inclined to blame economic decline on socialism and the extensive government economic management and welfare state activity that they associate with that ideology. This is very much the position of Margaret Thatcher, the present British Prime Minister, and her staunch ally Sir Keith Joseph. It has also been the position for many years of the Institute of Economic Affairs, which has published some 250 papers to promote the return to a market economy largely free of governmental intervention. The causes for Britain's post-war economic failure have been catalogued by Ralph Harris, the Institute's director, as:

> the suppression of prices, profits, and other incentives to the economy; the spawning of subsidies (cars, shipbuilding), politicised monopolies (steel, nuclear power), 'free' services (welfare, transport) and similar incitements to prodigality; the central planning of industries, regions, employments, and other distortionary, disruptive, doomed endeavours.

All of these activities, in Harris's opinion, have been motivated by a 'reigning intellectual consensus' which has been created in Britain by a group of intellectuals he calls 'Keynesian-collectivists'. Included in this category are mostly socialist writers – e.g. Anthony Crosland, Richard Crossman, Nicholas Kaldor, Richard Titmuss and the Fabians generally – while Keynes is depicted not so much as an early member than as the intellectual stimulus behind the group's erroneous thinking. Having no doubt that the Keynesian – collectivist arguments have been thoroughly discredited, Harris explains the failure of British government to embrace the wisdom of the market economists in terms of Keynes's own argument that public policy-makers tend to rely on outmoded ideas. 'It is mostly the Bourbons of the Keynesian inheritance, now in their 50s and 60s, who still rule the roost in government, bureaucracies, academia, media, and the church.'[31]

Harris is not alone among right-wing intellectuals in blaming his counterparts on the left for Britain's economic decline. Colin Welch, the Deputy Editor of the *Daily Telegraph*, has declared, 'If our country is (relatively) poorer, less free, more equal, and less competitive, it is probable that the teachings of such intellectuals have powerfully contributed to the developments.' In Samuel Brittan's opinion, the United Kingdom's economic problems are more severe than those of other modern democracies because her intellectuals, by so strongly emphasising inequality in British society, have reinforced 'envious, self-defeating attitudes'. The concept of equality, he concludes, 'has done immense harm to my country'.[32]

Cultural Explanations

Blaming the United Kingdom's economic decline on a dominant collectivist ideology is one type of cultural explanation. Not surprisingly, jeremiahs frequently find the cause of Britain's economic problems in certain cultural conditions. Thus in a 1963 inquiry into the state of Britain, Arthur Koestler wrote, 'We hold that psychological factors and cultural attitudes are at the root of the economic evils.' Eleven years later, the Hudson Institute's report on Britain came to the same conclusion: the country's economic decline was ultimately the result of 'aspects of British culture and an inheritance of a particular British historical experience'. Consequently, 'no specific remedies will work for Britain if there is not a shift, a deep shift, in psychology, in will – in short, in style'.[33]

Occasionally, cultural explanations are little more than simple moralistic assertions that the character of the British people has deteriorated. The economist Paul Einzig has written an entire book on this theme. In the tradition of the early Roman Empire and seventeenth and eighteenth century republicanism, he attributed all of Britain's problems to its people putting their private interests ahead of the public interest. 'While before and during the War the British were probably the most public spirited in the world, today they probably rank among the least public spirited.' Similarly,

Alastair Burnet believes that a major cause of the failure of the British economy is the country's ungovernable propensity to consume. 'No other advanced industrial country has chosen to consume in public spending and in private, so much of its gross national product, or to invest so little, or to borrow so readily abroad whenever the consequences have got a trifle uncomfortable.'[34] The most popular cultural explanation, however, has been concerned mainly with the subject of economic growth, which is related to certain attitudes, values, and beliefs said to have carried over from the country's agricultural and early industrial past into its highly industrialised and urbanised present. These cultural traits, which are seen as particularly English, are believed to affect economic production adversely with regard to the efficiency of both management and labour.[35]

The aspects of English economic culture most frequently condemned by this school of thought are those associated with the expression 'the cult of the amateur'. As the sociologist Donald MacRae put it in 1961, 'The ethos of our culture, with its contempt for the rational, the applied sciences, and technology, its faith in established ways – never in fact established – its primitive wisdom and inspired amateurism has become less and less appropriate to our condition.'[36] According to this perception, British managers have absorbed the pre-industrial aristocratic notion that the inspired and gifted amateur is to be preferred to the theoretically trained professional expert. One result has been the inadequate training and use within the economy of applied scientific, technological and business specialists. Another is the fact that many discoveries by British scientists have been first exploited commercially by rival economies, notably those of the United States and Germany. The tendency in Britain too often has been to follow old methods rather than to promote more effective new ones.[37]

A second debilitating aspect of English economic culture is said to be the prejudice among middle and upper middle class people against business and industrial careers. This prejudice is often explained in terms of Victorian educational innovations which aimed at producing gentlemen with a humanistic education to govern the British Empire rather than business men and manufacturers, who came to be seen as pursuing inferior careers. This disdain for industry and commerce is further strengthened by nostalgia for an aristocratic, agricultural society which influences Englishmen to adopt pre-industrial lifestyles.

A third frequently mentioned aspect of English economic culture is the enmity and distrust British workmen feel for their middle class managers and workers' obsession with economic security. The social class system is seen as producing a 'cloth-cap mentality' which inhibits British workmen from readily accepting changes in working methods in order to achieve higher productivity and incomes. It would seem that Marx was correct in predicting proletarian revolt in Britain: what he did not foresee was that it would take the form not of violent revolution but of a prolonged and economically harmful cold war.

The inclination of British workmen to prefer security to prosperity is part of a broader characteristic ascribed to the country's economic culture. The British people generally do not rank economic growth and its attendant prosperity as highly as other values, which themselves have the effect of reducing the growth rate. In the opinion of a 1960 PEP study of the United Kingdom's growth problems:

> It is probably true that the chief impediment to a faster growth of the British economy is that we do not want it enough. Both management and labour and, more widely, people in general, do not attach such a priority to material progress as might lead them to great enough efforts to achieve the economic results of the United States, or West Germany, or the Soviet Union.[38]

It was not, the authors observed, that the British people did not want more material goods but that they were not willing to run the risks or make the necessary efforts to achieve them. Security and leisure were simply preferred by many Englishmen to prosperity. Occasionally rather more laudable values have been seen as inhibiting economic growth. Michael Shanks has observed that British economic leadership was weakened because of the fear that someone might be hurt by effective policies:

> The issues that really arouse the British people are not issues of national efficiency but issues of 'social justice' or 'fair play'. . . . The very niceness of the British, the national desire to 'do the decent thing', uninformed by any rational calculus of what constitutes the common interest, has become an enormous force for *immobilisme*. . . . This is in many ways an admirable trait, but it is a sure recipe for national decay.[39]

Such a trait had inhibited effective tax reform and income policies and had influenced Governments to subsidise unproductive ailing industries.

Most people who explain Britain's post-war economic decline in terms of economic culture are probably aware that they are not the first to describe certain English traits as economically dysfunctional. Indeed, they interpret the similarity of their diagnoses with others dating back well over a century as indications that the relative decline of British industry and its cultural causes extend back at least to the middle of the nineteenth century. As the historian Corelli Barnett sees it, '"The English disease" is not the novelty of the past 10 or 20 years . . . , but a phenomenon dating back more than a century'.[40] Criticisms of the cult of the amateur date back at least to 1900 when British setbacks in the Boer War suggested that something was very wrong not simply in the army but in other institutions including the civil service, Parliament, education and commerce. 'The same amateur spirit which cripples the Army', wrote George Brodrick in 1900, 'pervades nearly the whole of what is called the professional and public life of this country.' It was a spirit originating in the English aristocracy which had infected all but the working class.[41] Much the same point was to be made by Harold Laski in 1932 in his well known and amusing essay 'The Danger of Being a Gentleman'.[42]

Concern over signs of American and German industrial production overtaking the British goes back to the middle of the nineteenth century when the superiority of technical education on the Continent and in America was often stressed as accounting for Britain's falling behind. For example, following the Paris Exhibition of 1867, the chemist and educational reformer Dr Lyon Playfair reported that out of ninety classes of industry represented there, Britain had pre-eminence in scarcely a dozen. From conversations with British participants at the conference, he concluded that there were two causes for the relative lack of progress in British industry. First, there was almost unanimous mention of the superior 'industrial education' for managers on the Continent; secondly, many had also observed 'that we had suffered from that want of cordiality between employers of labour and workmen, engendered by numerous strikes, and more particularly by that rule of many Trades' Unions, that men shall work upon an average ability, without giving free scope to the skill and ability which they may individually possess'.[43] Such warnings were not exceptional. Especially after the long industrial and commercial depression got underway in 1873, there spread 'a querying of the basis of Britain's industrial growth and supremacy. The tone of the eighties was set: it was a time of questioning and misgiving.'[44]

Although economic historians are not agreed that the British economic growth rate was surpassed by that of Germany and the United States during the last decades of the nineteenth century, by and large over the past century British industrial production has expanded at a slower rate than that of industrial states such as the United States, Germany and Sweden. In a careful comparative analysis Professor E. H. Phelps Brown has concluded that this poorer British performance is mainly the result of the relative inefficiency with which labour and capital are used, an inefficiency determined by 'the culture of managers and workers – their culture in the sense of habits of mind, the values and expectations, and ways of perceiving the working life, in which they were reared, and which were linked with socially sanctioned norms of behaviour'.[45] The culture he then describes is very much like that described in the accounts we have been analysing. Richard Rose has characterised Britain's political culture as 'traditionally modern'.[46] The expression can be applied equally well to the country's economic culture. Traditional along with transition class-war elements within it may be a major cause for Britain's economic growth failing to keep up with that of major competitors.

II Jeremiahs and the Decline of the Quality of British Life

Far from perceiving the low rate of economic growth in Britain in terms of decline, one small but influential body of opinion would like to see it stop altogether. According to this view, a continued rapid rate of economic growth will deplete the world's national resources, pollute the environment, and generally lead to a decline in the quality of people's lives. Such arguments are heard, of course, not only in Britain but in North America and Continental Europe as well; however, in Britain they are especially prominent because of a long intellectual tradition of which they are merely the latest formulation.

The Industrial Revolution stimulated a body of thought, articulated mainly but not entirely by literary figures, which was sharply critical of certain aspects of the new economic system and the type of society it was producing.[47]. Industrial society was perceived as exalting the pursuit of material wealth as the highest goal in life, rather than the true goal, which Matthew Arnold described as 'a *harmonious* perfection, developing all sides of our humanity, and . . . a *general* perfection, developing all parts of our society'.[48] Industrialism was said to sacrifice creativity and imagination to rational calculation and altruistic service to the community to individual self-seeking. Relationships among men and women were reduced to the cash nexus. The beauty and wholesomeness of the rural countryside was replaced by the squalid ugliness, filth, disease and crime of the manufacturing cities. The Industrial Revolution had led not only to the neglect, deprivation, and degradation of the working classes but to the intellectual, emotional, moral and aesthetic impoverishment of both workers and those who own and manage the economy. Men in industrial society came to worship Mammon partly because their work provided them with so little satisfaction. Critics of industrialism shared with Marx a deep aversion for the division of labour, which, as Ruskin put it, turns men into 'machines' or 'tools', divides them 'into mere segments of men'.

The *bête noire* of those sharing this anti-industrial, humanistic, quality-of-life tradition was another intellectual product of the Industrial Revolution, the political economists, of whom during the early nineteenth century Malthus and Ricardo were the best known representatives. Of Ricardo it has been written, perhaps with some exaggeration, 'Maximum outputs was for him the overriding economic objective, which was not so much subordinate to, as the expression in the field of economic policy of, the great overriding (Benthamite) principle of utility.'[49] In this respect he was much like some of his professional descendents in the 1960s and 1970s. The nineteenth century humanists sharply criticised the political economists for conceiving of man as an idle self-seeking creature motivated only by wages and profits. Yet, because industrialism was actually producing such creatures, *laissez faire* notions were said to be wrong in holding that, if left alone, men would work for the well-being of society. Finally, the humanists criticised the economists' conception of wealth as the price people will pay for the goods and services offered for sale at any time to a society. In Ruskin's striking expression, much of what political economists called wealth was really 'illth', which frustrates rather than achieves human fulfilment.

Since Edmund Burke, quality-of-life jeremiahs have frequently opposed the fragmented, individualistic industrial society with the ideal of an 'organic society', a term which connotes the inter-relatedness, inter-dependence, and continuity of the members of a healthy community. According to Raymond Williams, 'The contrast between "grows" and "made" was to become the contrast between "organic" and "mechanical" which lies at the very center of a tradition which has continued to our own day.' The term 'organic', Williams observes, has taken on a wide range of meanings, two of which are very relevant to current discussion of British decline: it is used 'to reject "mechanist" and "materialist" versions of society' and 'to criticize industrialism, in favor of a society "in close touch with natural processes" (i.e., agriculture)'.[50] During the nineteenth century, the ideal organic society was frequently projected back to the Middle Ages, while twentieth century critics of industrial society find it existing in rural areas as late as the eighteenth century. In either case, an agricultural golden age is contrasted with a much inferior industrial society, and contemporary history is thus perceived in terms of a decline in the quality of life, which can be reversed only by eradicating the detrimental characteristics of industrial society.

Here, then, is a British intellectual tradition dating back to the end of the eighteenth century which describes and evaluates trends in society very differently from those people who fret today over the economic decline of the United Kingdom. Politically the tradition cuts across party and left/right ideological lines. It is well represented by socialist ideologists such as William Morris, G. D. H. Cole, George Orwell and R. H. Tawney, while Burke, Coleridge and Southey in the past and T. S. Eliot in this century represent its right wing.

That the tradition was very much alive in the late 1950s and early 1960s is illustrated by the famous Snow–Leavis controversy. Alarmed by the effect he believed the tradition was having on inhibiting scientific and economic development, C. P. Snow elaborated in 1959 his well-known two cultures thesis, which led the late literary critic F. R. Leavis in 1962 to flay Snow and everything he believed Snow stood for. Snow deplored the deep divide between British scientists with their optimism about improving social conditions through scientific methods and literary intellectuals who were pessimistic about the future and who 'have never tried, wanted, or been able to understand the industrial revolution, much less accept it'.[51] British intellectuals were, in short, 'natural Luddities'. Leavis's furious response suggests that, while Snow's thesis was perhaps formulated too simply, he was on the right track. Leavis drew fully on the anti-industrial quality of life tradition when describing the culture to which he assigned Snow.

> It is the world in which, even at the level of the intellectual weeklies, 'standard of living' is the ultimate criterion, its raising an ultimate aim, a matter of wages and salaries and what you can buy with them, reduced hours of work, and the technological resources that make your increasing leisure worth having; so that productivity – the extremely important thing – must be kept on the rise, at whatever cost to protesting conservative habit.

In Leavis's view, Snow's world was leading Britain into the horrors already existing in the United States: 'the energy, the triumphant technology, the productivity, the high standard of living and the life impoverishment – the human emptiness; emptiness and boredom craving alcohol – of one kind or another'.[52]

Although the anti-industrial tradition has been to a large degree the creation of literary men and women, it has been incorporated to some extent into the thinking of a variety of other sorts of people, including, since John Stuart Mill, that of some well known English economists.[53] The first British economist to attempt to base his thinking mainly on the tradition was John A. Hobson, who after systematising Ruskin's social thought in 1898, spent the next four decades elaborating what he deemed 'the humanist approach to economic life'.[54] During the 1960s and 1970s, the pure version of the anti-industrial humanist tradition has surfaced again in the arguments put forward by those economists and ecologists calling for an end to economic growth. Only the argument that further economic growth will soon become impossible because of the exhaustion of energy sources is somewhat new, and even that was anticipated to some extent by T. S. Eliot in 1938.[55]. Although current forms of pollution could not, of course, have been foreseen during the nineteenth century, the pollution theme was an important part of the anti-industrial position. It is difficult to improve upon Cobbett's analogy of urban areas as wens on the body of the English countryside.

The most prominent exponent of the no-growth position in Britain today is the economist Ezra Mishan, who has been described as 'the father of modern anti-growthman'.[56] Mishan's hostility toward industrialism and technology and his longing for a simpler world destroyed by them is as strong as that of any of his nineteenth century predecessors. He firmly rejects the idea that the proper goal of an economic system is to cater to choices people happen to make. The modern industrial society fails to provide the essentials for 'the good life', and if the majority of people do not realise this, so much the worse for them. 'If one is seriously concerned with social welfare, the effects of existing economic systems on the standard of taste or, for that matter, on the very character of people, are of primary importance.'[57] Although such questions may not be susceptible to quantitative analysis, Mishan believes them to be of the greatest importance and chides fellow economists for largely ignoring them.

When Mishan considers the immeasurable deleterious consequences of economic growth, he makes no claim to originality. 'Reflections of a similar kind, though more subtly or more forcefully expressed, may be found in memoirs, novels, essays and in literary journals.'[58] He puts forward a variety of 'ways in which the organized pursuit and realization of technological progress themselves act to destroy the chief ingredients that contribute to men's well-being'.[59] In order of increasing importance, these include the following grim catalogue.

1. Rapid technological change causes great anxiety among both professionals and workmen because of the obsolescence of their skills and experience, while consumers are made restless and discontented by the barrage of advertising aimed at selling them new and useless products.
2. Rapid mass transportation destroys areas of natural beauty and the ability to escape crowds and causes local and regional differences to give way to an ugly and uniform world culture.[60]
3. Science and technology have destroyed religious faith and the solace and altruism it brings to people.
4. Men are becoming increasingly the slaves of science and its machines. 'If machines are becoming like men, men are no less determined to become like machines in a most literal sense.'
5. The 'ceaseless search for profits in a wealthy economy' requires the elimination of traditional standards of excellence and propriety and 'the continuous creation of new dissatisfactions'. 'Taste becomes the slave of fashion, and fashion the creature of profits.'
6. Commercialism is the chief motive behind 'the movement for the abolition of all forms of censorships', which in turn is leading to an 'all permissive society'.
7. For Mishan the worst effects of industrialism have been the way it has frustrated the satisfaction of certain human needs which he believes to have been far better fulfilled in pre-industrial times.

Although some conditions of work may have improved under industrialism, two centuries of technological innovation have changed workmen from craftsmen and artisans into 'machine-readers and dial-readers' with a resulting loss of aesthetic and creative gratification. Division of labour is a major cause of this loss. 'We are far removed from the state of society in which craftsmen worked with their tools in transforming the material into the finished product.' Not only, however, did the craftsman experience creative satisfaction but he was also given self-respect by social recognition of the importance of his work. In treating workmen like machines to be organised in a manner to provide maximum efficiency, the industrial economy denies them both types of satisfaction. Also lost are mutual trust, human contact, and a sense of community, qualities 'nurtured in the small agrarian society based on mutual dependence'.

Where Mishan and other quality of life advocates[61] differ from the majority of jeremiahs is in their passionate conviction that the costs of industrialisation far outrun the benefits and that the only way to prevent further decline is either to stop further economic growth or actually to reverse it and return to a largely rural past. Mishan himself would settle for 'a stable or steady state economy within which there is explicit consideration of the factors that enhance the quality of life'.[62] Others, such as the British ecologist Edward Goldsmith, believe in more radical solutions which would create a society in Britain remarkably like that existing before the Industrial Revolution, indeed one reminiscent of the Middle Ages. The population of the country 'must be reduced probably at least by half', as also must energy consumption be greatly reduced. Society should be decentralised both politically and economically into 'small self-regulating communities'. The agricultural sector of the economy must be much expanded, using traditional and not modern methods of husbandry. Instead of modern manufacturing which employs machines to turn out masses of worthless things, there should be 'the construction of beautiful buildings, the manufacture of fine furniture, the development of local arts and crafts, the revival of local festivities and religious ceremonies'.[63] Goldsmith is not at all optimistic that medieval England can actually be revived. Like Mishan and E. F. Schumacher, he acknowledges that such changes cannot take place without there first occurring certain profound alterations in British culture. In this respect, ironically, the quality-of-life jeremiahs are identical with many of the jeremiahs who worry about the British economy not growing fast enough. Where they differ is in prescribing radically different changes in the attitudes and values of the British people.

III Concluding Comments

A major purpose of this paper has been to analyse what people mean when they say the United Kingdom is declining. The term 'decline' is generally used in such a context to refer to a long-term harmful downward trend in one or more important aspects of society that can be reversed only by changing certain fundamental conditions of that society. People who perceive social problems in this way I have called jeremiahs to distinguish them from pragmatists who do not relate social problems to the idea of long-term decline and who see them as soluble without the need for radical structural or cultural alterations in society. It has not been my purpose to test empirically the validity of the diagnoses and remedies articulated by pragmatists and jeremiahs. Existing social science theory and the lack of success of pragmatic solutions do, however, suggest that at least some of the jeremiahs should be taken seriously by politicians and social scientists.

What has been most frequently alleged to be declining in Britain during the 1960s and 1970s has been the economy. Various aspects of the economy have been criticised in this regard. In recent years, the causes and effects of the high rate of inflation have been much discussed, with jeremiahs attributing inflation to defects both in the structure of the political system and in British culture. However, the economic problem which has most exercised jeremiahs has been Britain's economic growth record. If one concentrates on comparing the country's post-war record with its pre-war performance, it is difficult to see any problem and impossible to describe the post-war growth rate in terms of decline. This is a point worth remembering when trying to understand why so many people are not alarmed by their country's growth rate as jeremiahs feel they should be. Jeremiahs, as well as many pragmatists, judge Britain's economic growth and productivity in relation to the performance of other industrial countries and in doing so are able to demonstrate a pattern of economic decline relative to those countries.

Even among jeremiahs, however, there has been profound disagreement in evaluating Britain's post-war economic growth. While one group laments the relative decline of the country's GNP per capita, another is equally if not more vexed that there has been any growth at all. We have seen that this disagreement between humanists and 'political economists' stretches back to the early decades of the nineteenth century and involves controversies over both facts and values, with the former being much influenced by the latter. Each side to this disagreement is very inclined to exaggerate the advantages and minimise the disadvantages of the type of society which they believe will best achieve their values. Each also perceives the other's arguments as evidence of what is currently wrong with British culture. Undoubtedly, the latter is much more of a mixture than either side appears to realise.[64]

We have seen that part of the critique of British economic culture by jeremiahs favouring economic growth is that British people simply are not as highly motivated economically as other people. Quality-of-life jeremiahs view such low economic motivation as a virtue. As a leader in *The Times* asserted in 1971, 'It is doubtful whether the British will ever come to regard wealth, as such, as being worth the supreme effort.' Instead of deploring this conclusion, the newspaper declared, in the spirit of humanist anti-industrialism, 'The secret hope of Britain is indeed that the monetary obsession has penetrated our society less deeply than it has others. There are probably still more people in Britain who will give total effort for reasons of idealism than for reasons of gain.'[65] One does not have to accept the self-congratulations of the last statement in order to take seriously the earlier ones. Survey data have become available which lend some support to them. In March 1977, the following question was asked in a survey: 'Do you think it is best for people to work as hard as they can for as much money as they can get, or for people to work only as much as they need in order to live a pleasant life?'[66] Of the respondents 59 per cent opted for a pleasant life as compared to 32 per cent for hard work and much money. Unfortunately, no comparison was made with opinion outside Great Britain, but the fact that the percentages of Scottish money-grubbers and life enjoyers were respectively 17 points above and 13 points below the percentages for the entire country does suggest that it would be useful to make further international comparisons with regard to this and certain other aspects of English economic culture. We may well find that jeremiahs have been offering more satisfactory explanations of British economic decline than the pragmatists.

Whether, as the quality-of-life jeremiahs believe, the British people would really find life more enjoyable in a relatively impoverished country remains to be seen. At present, the standard of living has not fallen appreciably behind that of Western Europe generally and a large majority of British people appear to be satisfied with the quality of their lives.[67]

NOTES

1. *The Times*, 1 Jan 1876. In its summary of progress, the newspaper related that 'the country has seen an extension of our manufactures, trade, and commerce beyond all anticipation; it has seen discoveries and inventions which it takes volumes even to enumerate. . . . It has seen the working classes, whether in country or in town receive their full share of national gains.'
2. E.g. Margaret Drabble, *The Ice Age* (London: Weidenfeld & Nicolson, 1977); John Fowles, *Daniel Martin* (London: Jonathan Cape, 1977). Drabble's novel contains a very perceptive account of the interaction of feelings of national and personal decline.
3. Introduction to Vernon Bogdanor and Robert Skidelsky (eds), *The Age of Affluence, 1951–1964* (London: Macmillan, 1970) p. 7.
4. G. D. H. Cole, *The Post War Condition of Britain* (London: Routledge & Kegan Paul, 1956) p. xxi. In an account of British intellectuals, the sociologist Edward Shils similarly contrasted their hostility to many aspects of British society during the two inter-war decades with their satisfaction with it after the Second World War. 'How rare has become the deeply critical voice. . . . Who criticizes Britain now in any fundamental sense, except for a few Communists and a few Bevanite irreconcilables? There are complaints here and there and on many specific issues, but – in the main – scarcely anyone in Great Britain seems any longer to feel that there is anything fundamentally wrong' – E. Shils, 'British Intellectuals', *Encounter*, IV (Apr 1955) 5–16. For another optimistic account of the 1950s by a well informed American, see Drew Middleton, *The British* (London: Secker & Warburg, 1957).
5. C. A. R. Crosland, *The Future of Socialism* (London: Jonathan Cape, 1956) Ch. 18.
6. C. A. R. Crosland, 'Production in the Age of Affluence', *The Listener*, 25 Sept 1958, pp. 447–9.
7. C. A. R. Crosland, 'The Future of the Left', *Encounter*, XIV (Mar 1960) 3–12. The following month Crosland's essay was attacked by R. H. S. Crossman for watering down socialist policies during 'a period of complacent prosperity'. While criticising Crosland's optimism about British productivity, Crossman did so by comparing it not with that of other mixed economies but with the productivity of the 'socialist economies' of the Communist world, which he

believed demonstrated their superiority over 'free enterprise' – R. H. S. Crossman, 'Spectre of Revisionism', *Encounter*, XIV (Apr 1960) 24–8. Subsequent events were to prove Crossman no more correct than Crosland.

8. Donald MacRae, 'Britain's Long Decline', *The Listener*, 66, 23 Nov 1961, 844; Brian Chapman, *British Government Observed* (London: Allen & Unwin, 1963) p. 9.
9. Henry Fairlie, 'On the Comforts of Anger', *Encounter*, XXI (July 1963) 9; Marcus Cunliffe, 'The Comforts of the Sick-Bay', ibid., 98–9.
10. Between 1965 and 1975, the percentage of Gallup poll respondents agreeing that it was important for their country to retain major power status fell from 55 to 30 per cent, while the percentage of those who agreed that they would like to see their country become more like Sweden or Switzerland rose from 26 to 52 per cent. George H. Gallup (ed.), *The Gallup International Public Opinion Polls: Great Britain, 1937–1975* (New York: Random House, 1975), vol. II, pp. 790, 869, 1150 and 1231.
11. The expression appears to have been coined in West Germany in the early 1960s when fuller employment there seemed to be leading to a decline in the productivity of German workers, who were alleged to be becoming like British workers in their slackness, restrictive practices, absenteeism, and wild-cat strikes. Paul Einzig, *Decline and Fall?* (London: Macmillan, 1969) p. 74. It was not long before the words came to be used more generally to refer to a variety of alleged weaknesses in the British economy. By the later 1970s they were sometimes applied even more broadly. According to Patrick Hutber, City Editor of the *Sunday Telegraph*, '"The English sickness" is a phrase that evokes instant recognition and it is no longer used exclusively in an economic context' – P. Hutber (ed.), *What's Wrong with Britain*? (London: Sphere Books, 1978) p. 11.
12. E.g. 'A lotus island of easy, tolerant ways, bathed in the afterglow of an imperial sunset, shielded from discontent by a threadbare welfare state and an accepted genteel society' – Michael Shanks, *The Stagnant Society: A Warning* (Harmondsworth: Penguin, 1961) p. 232. Donald MacRae's prediction is similar in 'Britain's Long Decline', *The Listener*, 23 Nov 1961, p. 845. Jeremiahs, these examples make clear, do not always predict the total collapse of Britain.
13. See especially Tom Nairn, 'The Twilight of the British State', *New Left Review*, Feb–Apr 1977, pp. 3–61. Conservatives have also observed a connection between economic decline and the strength of nationalistic movements. See Alastair Burnet, *Is Britain Governable?* (London: Conservative Political Centre, 1975) p. 8.
14. The Hudson Institute, *The United Kingdom in 1980* (London: Associated Business Programmes, 1974) p. 7. See also Peter Jay as quoted in Richard Rose and Guy Peters, *Can Governments Go Bankrupt?* (New York: Basic Books, 1978) p. 14; and various Marxist writers in the *New Left Review*. The latter, of course, see 'the crisis of British capitalism' in terms not of decline but of the progress of the proletarian cause.
15. Arthur Koestler, 'The Lion and the Ostrich', *Encounter*, XXI (July 1963) 6–7.
16. One of the earliest British publications to draw attention to this state of affairs was the PEP report *Growth in the British Economy* (London: Allen & Unwin, 1960). About the same time, Anthony Crosland appears to have first taken public notice of it. Between 1950–1960, the annual growth rate of total output

in the United Kingdom was 2.6 per cent compared to 7.6 per cent in West Germany, 5.9 per cent in Italy, 4.4 per cent in France, 3.3 per cent in Sweden and 3.2 per cent in the United States. See G. A. Phillips and P. T. Maddock, *The Growth of the British Economy, 1918–1968* (London: Allen & Unwin, 1973) p. 23.

17. *The United Kingdom in 1980*, ch. 2. Because of the continuing expansion of economic growth and the standard of living throughout the 1960s and into the 1970s, Daniel Bell has rejected the arguments of those who condemn British economic decline during the 1960s. While noting their roots in Britain's past, Bell dates Britain's serious economic problems from the increase of inflation in the early 1970s. See Daniel Bell, 'The Future that Never Was', *The Public Interest*, Spring 1978, pp. 35–73. Graham Wootton takes a similar position in his contribution to this volume.
18. See the tables in Alan Peacock's contribution to the present volume.
19. Koestler, in *Encounter*, XXI, 5.
20. My analysis here is similar to that of P. D. Henderson *Economic Growth in Britain* (London: Weidenfeld & Nicolson, 1966) pp. 15–17.
21. See *The Times* analysis of the views of sixteen economists on 31 Jan 1975, and the survey of economists' and politicians' economic thinking in Samuel Brittan, *Is There an Economic Consensus? An Attitude Survey* (London: Macmillan, 1973) p. 30. Brittan did find certain ways in which the economists as a group differed from the politicians, the most interesting being stated as follows: 'Most economists have some sort of intellectual commitment to the price mechanism, at least as a tool of economic policy, even when they are strong opponents of laissez faire. Politicians on the other hand, do not have any particular sympathy for prices as an allocative device and, like the general public, have some difficulty in distinguishing between relative prices and the general price level.'
22. See Joseph A. Schumpeter, *Capitalism, Socialism, and Democracy*, 3rd ed. (New York: Harper, 1950); and Anthony Downs, *An Economic Theory of Democracy* (New York: Harper, 1957).
23. Samuel Brittan, 'The Economic Tensions of British Democracy', and Peter Jay, 'Englanditis', in R. Emmett Tyrrell, Jr. (ed.), *The Future That Doesn't Work: Social Democracy's Failure in Britain* (Garden City, NY: Doubleday, 1977) pp. 126–43, 167–85. For a fuller exposition of this type of argument, see Rose and Peters, *Can Governments Go Bankrupt?*
24. Richard Rose, 'The Variability of Party Government', *Political Studies*, XVII (Dec 1969) 413–45. Taking much the same position as Rose but expressly critical of British governments is Michael P. Gordon, 'Civil Servants, Politicians, and Parties', *Comparative Politics*, IV (Oct 1971) 29–58. See also Ian Gilmour, *The Body Politic*, rev. ed. (London: Hutchinson, 1971), which carries the attack back to pre-war policy-making. Max Nicholson goes back even further and traces the cause of Britain's relative economic stagnation to a transformation of governmental, financial and business institutions which took place in the middle of the nineteenth century. See Max Nicholson, *The System: The Misgovernment of Modern Britain* (London: Hodder & Stoughton, 1967) pp. 47–54.
25. Thomas Balogh, 'The Apothesis of the Dilettante', in Hugh Thomas (ed.), *The Establishment* (London: Anthony Blond, 1959) p. 99. Such criticism led to the Fulton Report of 1968, which is discussed by Anthony Birch in his essay for the present volume.

26. Arnold Toynbee, 'A State within the State', *The Observer*, 26 Oct 1975.
27. *Reshaping Britain: A Programme of Economic and Social Reform* (London: PEP, Dec 1974) ch. 5. The contents of this chapter, written by Mackintosh, were approved by the report's four other authors.
28. Brendon Sewill, 'How to End the British Disease', *Sunday Times*, 20 Aug 1978. For an excellent analysis of the baronial analogy by a leading authority on British interest groups, see S. E. Finer, 'The Political Power of Organized Labour', *Government and Opposition*, 8 (Autumn 1973) 393–4.
29. See Wyn Grant, 'Corporatism and Pressure Groups', in Dennis Kavanagh and Richard Rose (eds), *New Trends in British Politics* (London: Sage, 1977) 167–90: and Norman H. Keehn, 'Great Britain: The Illusion of Governmental Authority', *World Politics*, XXX (July 1978) 538–62.
30. F. A. Hayek, Letter to *The Times*, 21 July 1977. The privilege Hayek finds most harmful is union exemption from liability for damages for torts.
31. Ralph Harris, 'Come Back Adam Smith, All is Forgiven', *Sunday Times*, 20 Aug 1978. See also Sir Keith Joseph, 'Proclaim the Message: Keynes is Dead!' in Hutber, *What's Wrong with Britain?*, pp. 99–106. For a brief account of the Institute of Economic Affairs, see T. W. Hutchinson, *Half a Century of Hobarts* (London: IEA, 1970). It has published papers by just about all prominent market economists, including Professors Milton Friedman, F. A. Hayek and John Jewkes.
32. Colin Welch, 'Intellectuals Have Consequences', and Samuel Brittan, 'The Economic Tensions of Democracy', in Tyrrell, *The Future that Doesn't Work*. pp. 55, 142–3.
33. Koestler, in *Encounter*, XXI, 8; *The United Kingdom in 1980*, pp. 7, 113. For similar remarks, see also Sir Frank McFadzean, 'The British Public as Victims', in Hutber, *What's Wrong with Britain?*, p. 38.
34. Einzig, *Decline and Fall?*, pp. 29–30; Burnet, *Is Britain Governable?*, p. 8. See also Lord George-Brown, 'If Winston Could See Britain Now', *Sunday Express*, 3 Dec 1978.
35. The account that follows is based on a number of publications, including the discussions on 'The State of the Nation' in *The Listener*, 5, 12, 19 and 26 July 1962; 'Suicide of a Nation?', a special number of *Encounter*, XXI (July 1963); the discussion paper *Industry, Education and Management* (London: Department of Industry, 1977); and Hutber (ed.), *What's Wrong with Britain?*
36. MacRae, in *The Listener*, 23 Nov 1961, p. 844.
37. See the PEP report 'Thrusters and Sleepers', completed in 1964 and republished as *Attitudes in British Management* (Harmondsworth: Penguin, 1966), which concluded that many of the firms in the six industries investigated did not apply even comparatively simple techniques that should contribute to high productivity. . . . It seems that indifference to modern practices for improving productivity and efficiency is widespread within certain strata of British industry', p. 13. More recently, the economist Sir Alec Cairncross has emphasised managerial slowness in applying new technology as the major cause for British economic growth lagging behind that of other modern economies – A. Cairncross, *Inflation, Growth and International Finance* (Albany, NY: State University of New York Press, 1975) ch. 3.
38. *Growth in the British Economy*, p. xi.
39. Michael Shanks, 'The Comforts of Stagnation', *Encounter*, XXI (July 1963) 31. A

similar point is made in *The Times* leader of 10 April 1963 entitled 'The Kindly Dinosaur'; the 1974 Hudson Report, p. 66; and Ian Fraser, 'False Compassion Has to Go' in Hutber, *What's Wrong with Britain?*, pp. 81–5.

40. Corelli Barnett, 'Obsolescence – and Dr. Arnold', *Sunday Telegraph*, 26 Jan 1975. Repr. along with other articles in this series in Hutber, *What's Wrong with Britain?* For a careful comparison of diagnoses of weaknesses in the British economy written at the beginning of the century and in the 1960s which comes to much the same conclusion, see E. H. Phelps Brown, 'Then and Now: The British Problem of Sustaining Development, 1900s and 1960s', in Maurice Peston and Bernard Corry (eds), *Essays in Honour of Lord Robbins* (London: Weidenfeld & Nicolson, 1972) pp. 187–210.
41. George C. Brodrick, 'A Nation of Amateurs', *Nineteenth Century*, XLVIII (Oct 1900) 521–35. See also Henry Birchenough, 'Lord Rosebery and The Dangers to British Trade', *ibid.*, (Dec 1900) 1064–70, which perceived such dangers as being mainly 'in our national character' and describes the most serious of all as a prejudice against 'systematic professional training'.
42. Harold J. Laski, *The Danger of Being a Gentleman and Other Essays* (New York: Viking Press, 1940) pp. 13–32. 'It is significant', wrote Laski, 'that the foreign challenge to English industrial supremacy became effective at the moment when the alliance between the aristocracy and the middle class became an essential feature of English life.'
43. Letter from Dr Lyon Playfair to the Rt Hon Lord Taunton, 7 June 1867, reproduced as an appendix to Sir Eric Ashby, *Technology and the Academics* (London: Macmillan, 1959) pp. 111–13. For extensive complaints about the go-slow practices of British workmen, see the series of eleven articles in *The Times*, beginning on 18 Nov 1901 and concluding on 16 Jan 1902. Charges of the detrimental effects of trade unions on industry were summed up in the 1894 *Report of the Royal Commission on Labour* and are reproduced in Herman Ausubel, *The Late Victorians* (New York: Van Nostrand, 1955) pp. 123–5.
44. S. G. Checkland, *The Rise of Industrial Society in England, 1815–1885* (London: Longman, 1964) p. 54. See also Ausubel, *The Late Victorians*, pp. 18–27, 111–15.
45. E. H. Phelps Brown, 'Labour Policies: Productivity, Industrial Relations, Cost Inflation', in Sir Alec Cairncross (ed.), *Britain's Economic Prospects Reconsidered* (London: Allen & Unwin, 1971) p. 117. For an analysis similar to that of Phelps Brown, see Michael Fores, 'Britain's Economic Growth and the 1870 Watershed', *Lloyds Bank Review* (Jan 1971) pp. 27–41. The Cairncross volume grew out of a conference on the much discussed Brookings study, Richard E. Caves and Associates, *Britain's Economic Prospects* (London: Allen & Unwin, 1968), in which Edward F. Denison in chapter 6, 'Economic Growth', concluded from his elaborate comparative quantitative analysis of the United Kingdom with the United States and seven industrialised Western European countries that '(1) There are important characteristics of the British economy that have not been isolated that are seriously adverse to high productivity, but (2) these are characteristics of long standing that did not cause further deterioration of the British position, compared to that of most other countries, during the period from 1950 to 1962.' (p. 263). The characteristics of residual efficiency, as Denison calls them, include such immeasurable phenomena as the skills and initiative of managers, the effort made by workers, and legal and other

institutional obstacles to the efficient use of resources. The way Britain can achieve rapid economic growth, according to Denison, is to increase her 'residual efficiency', an injunction not incompatible with the arguments stressing cultural and political limitations on economic growth.

46. Richard Rose, 'England: A Traditionally Modern Political Culture', in Lucian Pye and Sidney Verba (eds), *Political Culture and Political Development* (Princeton, NJ: Princeton University Press, 1965) pp. 83–129.
47. Raymond Williams, *Culture and Society: 1780–1950* (New York: Harper Torchbook, 1958). The key term in this tradition, according to Williams, is 'culture', which came into use in England during the Industrial Revolution, referring sometimes to art and poetry as the highest human endeavours and at other times to 'a whole way of life' perfecting human nature. Either version was a basis for criticising industrialism. Among those who took a major part in formulating and perpetuating the tradition in the nineteenth century were the political writers Burke and Cobbett, the Romantic poets Coleridge, Byron, Wordsworth, Keats, Shelley and Southey; novelists such as Dickens, Kingsley and Mrs Gaskell and literary and artistic figures such as Newman, Matthew Arnold, John Ruskin and William Morris. See also Bernard N. Schilling, *Human Dignity and the Great Victorians* (New York: Columbia University Press, 1946).
48. Matthew Arnold, *Culture Anarchy* (New York: Macmillan, 1897) p. xiv.
49. T. W. Hutchinson, *'Positive Economics' and Policy Objectives* (Cambridge, Mass.: Harvard University Press, 1964) p. 134.
50. R. Williams, *Culture and Society*, pp. 37, 264.
51. C. P. Snow, *The Two Cultures and a Second Look* (Cambridge: Cambridge University Press, 1963) p. 22.
52. Leavis is commenting here on Snow's argument that the Third World needs an 'industrial–scientific revolution'. F. R. Leavis, 'The Significance of C. P. Snow', *Spectator*, CCVIII (9 Mar 1962) 302–3. In a letter to *The Times* of 2 Nov 1971, Leavis describes Britain as far into decline: 'The civilization that dooms masses to "jobs" with no human meaning but for the pay they bring, "jobs" made sufferable only by the prospect of leisure, is precarious, sick, and far advanced on a path to death.' Lionel Trilling has pointed out that except for its bad temper, the Snow–Leavis controversy was very much a re-run of the debate between Matthew Arnold and T. H. Huxley during the 1880s over whether science or the humanities should be most stressed in education. See Lionel Trilling, 'Science, Literature and Culture: A Comment on the Leavis–Snow Controversy', *Commentary*, June 1962, pp. 461–77; repr. in the useful collection D. K. Cornelius and E. St Vincent (eds), *Cultures in Conflict: Perspectives on the Snow–Leavis Controversy* (Chicago: Scott, Foresman, 1964) pp. 37–54.
53. After referring to the criticisms of Carlyle and Ruskin, an English economist noted in 1964, 'Today it is the economists themselves who are making the charge of "materialism" – or, at any rate, a rather similar charge – against their own colleagues' – Hutchinson, *Positive Economics*, p. 155.
54. A very neglected writer today and underrated by most professional economists in his own time, Hobson not only anticipated much of Keynesian economics and provided Lenin with his analysis of imperialism but also elaborated the humanist position more thoroughly than his more emotional and radical successors in the 1960s and 1970s. See especially his *Confessions of an Economic Heretic* (London: Allen & Unwin, 1938); *John Ruskin: Social Reformer*, 3rd ed. (London: Nisbet,

1904); and *Health and Life* (London: Macmillan, 1929).

55. T. S. Eliot, *The Idea of a Christian Society*, as quoted in Williams, *Growth and Society*, p. 229.
56. Mancur Olson and Hans H. Landsberg (eds), *The No-Growth Society* (New York: Norton, 1973) p. 235.
57. E. J. Mishan, *Growth: The Price We Pay* (London: Staples Press, 1969), p. xviii. This book is a shorter, more popular version of his *The Costs of Economic Growth* (London: Staples Press, 1967). For briefer statements of Mishan's position, see his contributions to Olson and Landsberg, *The No-Growth Society*, and to Edward Goldsmith (ed.), *Can Britain Survive?* (London: Tom Stacey, 1971), as well as his article 'Economic Growth: The Need for Scepticism', *Lloyds Bank Review*, Oct 1978, pp. 1–26.
58. Mishan, *Growth: The Price We Pay*, p. 197.
59. Ibid., Part V.
60. Mishan ranks the automobile as 'one of the great disasters to have befallen the human race' (ibid., p. 162), and 'the greatest of man-made plagues' ('The Wages of Growth', in Olson and Landsberg, *The No-Growth Society*, p. 77).
61. In Britain, see especially the economist E. F. Schumacher, *Small is Beautiful: Economics as if People Really Mattered* (New York: Harper Torchbooks, 1973). Schumacher, who has been deemed by an American admirer 'the Keynes of post-industrial society' (Theodore Roszak's introduction to the American edition of *Small is Beautiful*), claims to have found his major inspiration in Eastern and particularly Gandhian and Buddhist thinking. What he calls 'Buddhist economics', however, would have been highly commended by all of the nineteenth century quality-of-life jeremiahs. See also Lincoln Allison, 'The English Cultural Movement', *New Society*, 16 Feb 1978, pp. 358–60.
62. E. J. Mishan, 'The Wages of Growth', in his *Growth: The Price We Pay*, p. 81.
63. Edward Goldsmith, *Can Britain Survive?*, p. 251.
64. Survey data suggest that people consistently articulating quality of life opinions constituted during the 1970s about 8 per cent of the British population while consistent 'materialists' made up slightly over a third. Most people have a mixture of the two types of attitudes. Ronald Inglehart, *The Silent Revolution: Changed Values and Political Styles Among Western Publics* (Princeton; N J: Princeton University Press, 1977) p. 104.
65. 'What is the British Disease?', *The Times*, 20 Apr 1971, which in its first two parts strongly reflects the anti-industrial humanistic tradition.
66. Tom Forester, 'Do the British Sincerely Want to be Rich?', *New Society*, 23 Apr 1977, pp. 158–61. Forester interprets the data from the survey generally by observing that the British 'are remarkably unambitious in a material sense. Very few sincerely want to be rich. Most people in Britain neither want nor expect a great deal of money. Even if they could get it, the vast majority do not seem prepared to work harder for it'.
67. In the spring of 1977, 82 per cent of British respondents in an EEC poll declared themselves either very satisfied or fairly satisfied with the lives they led. This percentage was similar to that of West Germany and well above that of France (68 per cent) and Italy (59 per cent). *World Opinion Update*, II (Jan 1978) 10.

2 The British Economy and its Problems

Alan Peacock*

I Introduction

There is an almost obsessive interest shown in the British economy by economists and politicians in other industrial countries. True, apart from any loss of utility suffered by those who have a sympathetic concern for Britain, at one extreme, and those who might obtain utility gains from *Schadenfreude* at the other, British economic conditions clearly affect the 'utility functions' of governments in other countries. Economic objectives sought by the EEC, for example, mean that the flow of revenue and expenditure of the EEC budget and thus the 'fiscal residuum' experienced by individual members is closely tied to relative economic prosperity of its members. Further, governments are acutely aware of possible 'demonstration effects', if pressure groups such as trade unions succeed in their objectives in one country, it can affect the strategy of their counterparts in other countries. Events in the United Kingdom, therefore, are sometimes seen as a foretaste of what could happen elsewhere, unless appropriate action is taken.

In this paper I offer a *vade mecum* for those interested in what has become known as 'the British disease', which is particularly associated with a relatively poor record in economic growth. I shall first of all provide the barest minimum of statistical comparison to give a broad idea of recent movements in the British economy compared with other economies. Secondly, I shall try to summarise the debate among economists about our poor economic performance with particular reference to the rate of economic growth. Some reference then becomes necessary to the economic policies which successive governments have tried to devise to cure our ills. Finally, I shall try to take a view of the future of the British economy; particularly in the light of its role as an oil-producing country.

* This paper draws on my experiences as Chief Economic Adviser of the Department of Trade, Industry and Prices and Consumer Protection, United Kingdom Government from 1973 to 1976, but commits officialdom in no way whatsoever.

II The Symptoms of 'The British Disease'

Table 2.1 shows movements in basic indicators of economic performance. British growth is relatively poor both during the pre- and post-oil crisis period. Employment over the last two decades is no more than respectable and gives the impression of deteriorating. Its economic stability (as measured by the rate of inflation) was relatively poor before the mid-1970s and since then has been worse than any major industrial country except Italy.

With growing internationalisation of trade, as reflected in the more rapid rate of growth of the volume of world trade as compared with the growth in the volume of production, much is made of the fact that relatively poor growth and rising industrial unemployment is associated with a falling share in world trade and growing import penetration. Certainly this is true of Britain where the share of world trade in manufactures declined in value terms from 10 per cent in 1955 to 8.8 per cent in 1974, stabilising somewhat since at about 9.5 per cent. The proportion of imports to home sales (a measure of import penetration) rose from 9.5 per cent in 1961 to nearly 25 per cent in 1975. As we shall see later, much of the policy debate about Britain's poor growth performance hinges on what to do about import penetration.

We must always be careful in making comparisons, so let me mention qualifications, if only because they are constantly being deployed in British economic debate:

1. Other indicators may be considered relevant in trying to arrive at some judgement of economic performance. Thus *fluctuations* in GDP and in employment, as measured by the amplitude of the business cycles, have been less in the United Kingdom than in most major industrial countries. The regional disparities in employment and output rates have also narrowed in the United Kingdom, though comparisons with other countries are difficult to make.
2. Recent United Kingdom growth performance, while poor by international comparisons up to 1970, is fairly typical historically for Britain over a period as long as 80 years. The 1970s has shown a deterioration in growth performance, but this phenomenon has not been confined to Britain.[1]
3. A more influential argument is that conventional economic indicators neglect important aspects of the so-called 'quality of life'.[2] and since 1970 government has sponsored the publication of *Social Trends* containing 'quality of life indicators' alongside the long-established *Economic Trends*. While accepting this point, I do not consider that it is of particular relevance in this context. In any case, there is no scientific way by which one can choose which quality of life indicators are relevant and how movements in them should be traded off against one another. Consensus on the range of relevant indicators is simply a way of saying that

TABLE 2.1 Comparative data of economic indicators

Indicator	*UK*	*USA*	*Canada*	*Japan*	*West Germany*	*France*	*Italy*	*All OECD countries*	*Difference UK–OECD average*
1 GDP Growth (% annual rate)									
1960–64	3.8	3.8	4.9	11.7	5.7	6.2	5.8	5.0	−1.2
1965–69	2.3	4.4	5.6	10.4	3.5	5.2	5.6	4.9	−2.6
1970–74	2.7	2.5	5.0	7.2	3.6	5.3	4.0	3.7	−1.0
1976	3.1	6.0	4.9	6.0	5.6	5.2	5.7	5.3	−2.2
1977	0.0	4.9	2.6	5.1	2.5	2.9	1.7	3.7	−3.7
2 Unemployment (annual average %)									
1962–75	3.2	5.0	5.2	1.3	0.9	2.3	3.5	2.9	+0.3
1976	6.9	7.5	7.1	2.1	3.6	4.6	6.4	5.4	+1.5
1977	7.6	6.9	8.1	2.1	3.5	5.2	7.3	5.5	+2.1
3 Consumer prices (% annual rate)									
1965–75	8.8	5.5	5.6	8.4	4.3	6.5	7.0	6.4	+2.4
1976	16.5	5.8	7.5	9.3	4.5	9.6	16.8	8.6	+7.9
1977	15.9	6.5	8.0	8.1	3.9	9.8	18.4	8.9	+7.0

Source: Compiled from OECD *Economic Outlook* December 1978 Technical Annex.

commonly held value judgements require an extension of this range, but it would be difficult to argue that consensus extends to agreement on the ranking of this extended range of quality-of-life indicators. The fact remains that the main long-run policy concern of governments in the United Kingdom is the poor growth performance and for a very good reason.[3] So many of our social and political aims, particularly the relief of poverty, improvements in health, education and so on, clearly depend on this performance. In other words, favourable movements in several important social indicators, e.g. environmental improvement, morbidity and mortality rates and so on, are closely correlated with economic growth.

III Explanations of 'The British Disease'

If the efficiency of economic analysis were to be judged by the subtlety and elegance of economic models, then British economists would rank high in the order of scientific merit. However, in a hard world, models must be judged not solely by the esteem which an economist gains with his own profession but in terms of their explanatory power and their application to policy. Those who have attempted to satisfy the community at large as well as their fellow professionals in developing models of the causes of relative rates of growth have themselves recognised the magnitude of the task. One of our most prominent pundits in this area, Wilfrid Beckerman, has noted the extreme difficulty of separating cause and effect, 'since almost anything that might be expected to contribute to growth might equally well be caused by growth'.

There are three general explanations which have gained currency in the United Kingdom, all of which have had some influence on policy. The first associates growth with the behaviour of the business cycle. The larger and the more erratic the business cycle, the lower is the incentive to invest in fixed capital and therefore, it is held, the lower the rate of growth. (This is a highly telescoped exposition of a complicated theory, but will serve for our purposes.) The lower *relative* rate of growth in the United Kingdom can therefore be explained, so it has been argued, by the exacerbation of cyclical movements caused by 'stop-go' fiscal and monetary policies. Another way of putting this is to say that the 'political cycle' which calls for the linking of policy measures to the timing of elections puts a constraint on operating 'rational' fiscal and monetary policies which can take full account of the leads and lags in the economic system and so improve the 'fine-tuning' which is meant to reduce the amplitude of economic fluctuations.

This explanation has attracted a good deal of criticism latterly on both analytical and empirical grounds.[4] Analytically it rests on the strong assumption that the volume of investment is the main cause of growth and consequently that differences in that volume between countries will explain differential growth performance. However, the empirical evidence for 1955–73 shows that the percentage deviations from the trend rate of growth in the United Kingdom are lower than any other major OECD country, yet it is also the country with the lowest rate of growth. The cycles in the United Kingdom are very similar in length to those in Germany, but shorter than those in the United States and Japan. (Interestingly enough, the duration of the cycle cannot explain the pronounced difference between the very high growth rate in Japan over that period, 13.8 per cent per annum, and the low growth rate in the United States, 4.7 per cent per annum, in manufacturing industry. The cycle in both countries is almost the same length.)

Despite the strong doubts cast on the 'stop-go' thesis, we have to be careful in drawing inferences from these criticisms. There could be national differences in business reactions to cyclical movements and British businessmen could conceivably react more adversely to a given amount and timing of cyclical fluctuations than their overseas competitors. Nor do the criticisms dispose of the problem of the influence of governments on business confidence. There are several other important ways in which fiscal and monetary policy, as well as other policies, can affect such confidence, such as the degree of success in controlling the rate of inflation.

The first explanation is clearly based on a simple version of neo-Keynesian cycles and growth theory, but it is the second explanation which is more usually associated with neo-Keynesianism of the Cambridge variety, and particularly with the name of Nicholas (now Lord) Kaldor. It has gone through a process of mutation and I offer the 'up-to-date' version.[5] The growth in manufacturing output, it is held, is crucially dependent on the demand for our exports. This demand will depend on the income effect produced by the growth in world trade for manufacturing exports and the substitution effect represented by the ratio of the domestic price of exports to those of competitors. If it can be assumed that export sales are highly sensitive to competitiveness, i.e. to the substitution factor, then cost factors, and particularly unit labour costs, are the main determinant of exports and therefore of manufacturing growth. Kaldor 'completes the circle' in an interesting way. What determines the level of unit labour costs? Why, the average physical productivity of labour, of course! What determines the average physical productivity of labour? Why, the rate of manufacturing growth itself! This last proposition, known as 'Verdoorn's Law', is a supposedly empirical relationship closely akin to the proposition that it is the manufacturing sector rather than the services sector which is characterised by technical economies of scale. Thus the answer to the question – how do we explain the low rate of growth in the United Kingdom? – lies in the failure to improve the average productivity of labour by increasing the proportion of manufacturing value added devoted to investment. If this is done, growth would be self-sustaining. Average productivity of labour would improve, unit labour costs fall, exports improve and the associated increase in growth would improve productivity further, and so on until technical economies of scale are exhausted.

There are several puzzles in this analysis, though it may be logically unassailable.[6] These arise, as in the previous explanation, from some rather strong assumptions. To rely on the argument that average physical productivity of labour is the clue to 'export-propelled' growth means assuming that competitors are not in a similar position to reap productivity gains and that unit labour costs are not affected by conditions in the labour market. Indeed, in earlier versions of his thesis, Kaldor specifically argues that tight labour supply in the United Kingdom compared with the reservoirs of labour in France and Germany in agricultural employment was a major cause of the United Kingdom's relative poor rate of economic expansion in the post-war period. In ignoring his own argument, which is contradicted by the evidence of 'overmanning' in British industry compared with other countries, Kaldor's argument crucially depends on Verdoorn's Law – the dependence of labour productivity on the growth in manufacturing output. Yet the empirical evidence of the last decade offers little support for the existence of this Law. Furthermore, it is arguable whether the United Kingdom's comparative advantage in exports and import substitutes still lies exclusively in manufacture, and it may be that major service industries can also be the source of productivity gains associated with their expansion. The reason that service industries are overlooked may arise from the inadequate measures of productivity in service industries employed in national accounts statistics. Mention of the productivity of services offers a link to a complementary thesis by the Oxford economists, Bacon and Eltis,[7] which puts the blame for our low growth rate on the faster rate of growth in employment in the public sector, 'starving' the manufacturing sector particularly of skilled labour. Like Baumol's 'unbalanced growth' thesis, this relative shift of labour to the public, non-marketed, sector implies a shift to activities in which gains in productivity from technology may be limited. Clearly, this could have an adverse effect on the rate of growth. Personally, I am not convinced that this would arise from lack of opportunity to take advantage of improved technology, but rather from the lack of incentive among bureaucrats to introduce methods of production which reduce their employment opportunities! A rough-and-ready test of this proposition would be to examine the relation between the growth of government expenditure on goods and services and growth in GDP for a sample of countries. When this is done, there is no marked correlation between growth in GDP and growth in the government's share in GDP over the last decade.[8] This may be because, as in the United Kingdom, the growth in government's share has been relatively small in main OECD countries, with the notable exception of Sweden.

While the two previous explanations have been found wanting, they are based on more or less explicit models of the operation of the economy which are subject to statistical test. The third explanation rests much more on speculations which are difficult to combine into a conventional framework. Its point of departure is the lack of evidence of a firm correlation between the proportion of GDP in manufacturing output devoted to investment input and the rate of growth in manufacturing output. If we compare the United Kingdom and West Germany, for example, we find that the percentage of gross investment to net value added in manufacturing output is roughly the same over the last two decades, but the rate of growth in manufacturing output in West Germany is twice that of the United Kingdom. This seems a clear indication that it is not investment *per se* that is the important determinant of growth but the efficiency in its use.[9] In other words, quality of management and the constraints imposed on the exercise of managerial skills by trade union practices seem the all-too-obvious explanation. This commonsense explanation I find rather convincing, and I spent a lot of time in government service distilling the many individual pieces of evidence which support this position in order to influence officials and Ministers.

While there is a wealth of evidence from cross-country studies which support this explanation, it is another matter to account for the differences between the United Kingdom and other OECD countries. Economists fight shy of developing explanations of managerial inefficiency based on studies of education and training and the social attitudes which determine the choice of occupation. An exception has been Professor G. C. Allen[10] who has laid great emphasis on the influence of class conventions of the Victorian era which despised industrial activity and led to the neglect of applied sciences and engineering in schools and universities, and the low status thereby afforded to business studies. It is also difficult to devise tests to compare the constraints – government tax policies, availability of finance, trade union practices – which beset British managers and their overseas counterparts. However, the major difficulty is not with assembling and interpreting evidence, but with identifying the policy implications.

IV The Translation of Economic Thought into Policy

An economist can easily have his faith in human nature shattered or at least shaken by the obstacles encountered in 'selling' policies to politicians. However, he has largely himself to blame if this is the case. If an economist studied political behaviour as closely as he studies business or consumer behaviour, he would soon realise what he interprets as an irrational obstinacy on the part of politicians may in reality be intelligent and rational behaviour when viewed as an attempt to gain power and influence and not necessarily for the 'worst' of motives. Further, the economist's policy prescriptions, consistent as they may be with some highly sophisticated model which has been rigorously tested, assume that the governmental process operates like a car engine controlled by one driver. Members of a Cabinet of Ministers, even with a similar general political viewpoint, will have very different ideas about where the 'engine of state' should be heading – a reflection of their views on political survival both individually and collectively – and who should operate the controls. Even when it is agreed which controls should be used and who should operate them, account has to be taken of the delay in their operation, and the uncertainty of their results.[11]

British economic policies designed to cure the disease of slow growth offer ample illustration of these obvious prospositions. Within the space available I can only refer to recent policy developments. It may be said about the period from, say, 1955 to 1972 that it was characterised by the realisation that whatever the virtues of macro-economic policies as stabilisers, they did not appear to work when it came to promoting growth. In the latter part of this period it was hoped that reducing economic fluctuations, fiscal encouragement to investment and the use of a floating exchange rate to promote export competitiveness would form a sure foundation to promote 'the dash for growth'. (In late 1973 I was serving one Minister who was still talking about the prospect of growth at 8 per cent per annum as a feasible proposition.) In short, both the Kaldorian diagnosis and the suggested cures for sluggish growth, some of which were extensively applied, were becoming suspect among politicians, though this is not to say that policies were based solely on the Kaldor-type 'scenario'.

The landmark in British economic policy closely associated with the concern over growth is the White Paper, *An Approach to Industrial Strategy* (Cmnd. no. 6315, 1975) which, though hardly containing a full diagnosis of 'the English disease', clearly recognises that 'generalised inefficiency', as it has been called, is as important a cause as the alleged shortage of capital investment.[12] For this change of emphasis, government economists can take a good deal of the credit. When we come to possible cures, major divisions of opinion emerge of both a political and technical nature.

Consider the position, one with which I have some sympathy, which might be taken up in America by a supporter of a 'free market economy'. The removal of inefficiency would be closely bound up with the promoting of 'workable' competition. Engendering support for this position would require the electorate and political interest groupings to accept at least three propositions:

1. Wide support by both employers and workers for the present organisation of production broadly along capitalist lines.
2. Vigorous competition policy applied to both the product and the factor markets.
3. Rigorous control over government spending on goods and services coupled with avoidance of state deficit spending: 'keep the Budget small and keep it balanced'.

There may now be considerable scepticism about the validity of these propositions as a guide to long-term economic policy in America.

In the United Kingdom, both among influential politicians, particularly Labour politicians, and civil servants, these propositions are regarded as either irrelevant (because they command little political support) or ideologically suspect or, as in the eyes of prominent left-wingers, both. Though lip-service may be paid to competition policy, there is strong support for developing an industrial strategy which accepts *as constraints* the lack of commitment to capitalist organisation of production, monopoly power vested in trade unions, and the retention of a large public sector.

Given these constraints, we can see why the emphasis was shifted in British long-term economic policy towards the use of selective measures for the promotion of industrial efficiency. The general idea is to 'involve' industry itself in the planning process, so that recognition of the problem will in some mysterious fashion spur individual companies into action. Economic experts will identify sectoral prospects and industrial subsidy policy will be designed to back those sectors which are potentially, if not actually, efficient. If large companies who are major employers of labour do not conform with government objectives, for example by contracting their activities and shedding labour, they may be taken over by a National Enterprise Board which will put in its own directors. The whole exercise is under the surveillance of the National Economic Development Council.

I think that most economists, myself included, who have had experience with economic policy view these developments with considerable scepticism. The strategy might in a general kind of way improve business confidence, but simultaneously it diverts a good deal of time and energy of busy businessmen into negotiation with government and away from seeking markets and improving products. It is extremely doubtful if civil servants, even with business advice, can pick the winners, particularly as the success of the strategy rests on improving efficiency not at the industry but at the *company* level. It is difficult enough for those on the spot to pick profitable investment projects. I have expressed such heretical thoughts in government service and have received the stinging riposte: 'Well, what would you recommend in its place?' There is only one answer: reduce government tinkering with the private sector and accept that cures will only operate slowly.

This advice, you will appreciate, hardly appeals to politicians anxious to achieve quick results and therefore to support selective measures which dramatise their role in the process of government. To those politicians who discount the future at an even higher rate than that found in a profession noted for taking only a short view, one can well understand the attractions of what may be called the alternative scenario in economic policy. Thus if Mr Benn as Secretary of State for Industry had had his way in 1974, the fear of 'de-industrialisation' spurred on by growing import penetration would have led to an attempt to immunise the economy. This would have been done by massive reflation through both increases in consumption and investment expenditure, coupled with strict and widespread control over imports of finished manufactured goods in competition with domestically demanded British manufactures. There are more than echoes of Kaldor in this proposal, though it rests on the assumption that economies of scale associated with increased capacity utilisation would follow from reflation coupled with a massive investment programme. However, whereas unit costs might fall with economies of scale, there would be no incentive to promote efficiency in factor inputs, following the removal of the spur of foreign competition. In addition, the advocates of this view have tended to underplay the likelihood of retaliation against British exports of goods and services. A massive reflation programme would imply a considerable increase in imports of raw materials which have to be paid for by retaining efficiency in exports of goods and services and by keeping open export markets.

V 'Oil has got us into this mess, and oil will get us out of it'

The effect of the oil crisis on countries such as the United Kingdom is too well known to bear repeating. It is sufficient to point out that it has made it all the more difficult to decide on the scope and direction of policies designed to foster growth. In the first place, it has understandably led successive governments to concentrate on major short-term problems and therefore to promote schemes which preserve existing jobs rather than create new ones in sectors with long-term growth prospects. In the second place, it produced payments deficits which could not possibly be financed by exchange reserves and which forced the government to use a combination of 'floating downwards' of the exchange rate and borrowing abroad. The longer-run effects of the apparent lack of control of the foreign balance and of the rate of inflation has obviously done nothing to maintain the business confidence necessary to concentrate industry's attention on the long-run.

There is one outstanding exception to this pre-occupation with the short-term which is the development of plans for the period when the trickle of North Sea oil turns into a large flow; and these plans have much to do with the long-run prospects of the economy. There are many pitfalls encountered in estimating the economic effects of this rather sudden acquisition of a potentially very valuable natural resource and I do not propose to make an assessment of the alternative guesses currently under discussion. The present consensus of view among economists, for what it is worth, is that the early 1980s will see an end of our immediate balance of payments difficulties and to such an extent that within five years the United Kingdom should be able to generate a sufficient surplus to pay off the accumulation of indebtedness incurred on current account from 1973. Some allowance is made in these prognoses for a rise in the volume and value of foreign imports but a continuation of the present rate of increase of imported manufactures might jeopardise this result. In short, recovery of the balance of payments can occur thanks to oil.

The second result of the oil flow would be a very considerable addition to government revenue from the additional profits tax on oil companies. This affords the government a very important instrument for influencing the rest of the economy.

A most interesting debate is now in progress on this second result, reflecting the great divisions of opinion about the conduct of government policy for growth. It is coloured in part by ideological issues concerning the role of the state and by the relative priority of growth as compared with other objectives. The first view is that the additional revenue offers a splendid opportunity for reducing other taxes, particularly taxes on managerial and executive grades and on industry generally. This would help to improve the opportunities of business executives and skilled labour relative to alternative opportunities in other countries. It might also promote incentives to save both among corporations and individuals.

The second view regards the additional revenues as offering an opportunity for the government to restructure the economy rather than allow the private sector to adjust in its own way. Thus, a selective subsidy policy could be devised to implement the industrial strategy programme already described, in a manner complementary to social programmes which also require financing. Indeed, the social programmes, particularly those directed towards improved vocational training, restoration of scarred and unattractive industrial areas and improved leisure facilities may themselves be vastly extended and in a way which encourage greater confidence in Britain's future. This is a view which naturally appeals to bureaucrats whose power and prestige would be enhanced by such ambitious programmes.

I would not like to forecast who will win this debate when analysis is translated into policy. Perhaps both sides will be heeded, for whether Labour or Conservatives are in power, the realities of international mobility in business skills must force some attention to be paid to a more acceptable tax structure to retain the able and ambitious, while the existence of a 'pork barrel' of subsidies is too attractive a tool of government to be dispensed with immediately. My own position, is strongly in favour of the former policy, for my experience of the fashioning of a structural economic policy calling for an elaborate system of selective subsidisation leads me to be extremely sceptical of its effectiveness.

VI Conclusion

I have indicated earlier that the cure of 'the British disease' is a long-term process. It is also incapable of being expressed in terms of a fully articulated long-term model of the economy in which not only the appropriate instruments to promote growth can be identified but their effects quantified. The pursuit of growth, though not to the exclusion of other desirable goals, requires major changes in the attitudes and skills fostered in our educational system, a clear link between rewards and achievement and therefore the denial of special privileges to monopoly groups in both the private and the public sector. In a technological age it requires the recognition of the contribution of the trained professional as well as the traditional British intelligent amateur and the untutored genius. Above all it calls for a reversal of the trend towards centralised government and for diversity and experiment in industrial organisation rather than some blanket centralised plan. In this connection it means encouragement of the small firm as a source of innovation and enterprise, rather than promoting a government interface solely with large enterprises, simply because this is more congenial and convenient for those concerned. Giving specific content to this kind of programme is a difficult and challenging task, particularly in a country where both the intellectual elite and organised labour are suspicious of the free market economy.

I cannot be sure that this view of what needs to be done will obtain general approval and produce the necessary action, but I am encouraged by the fact that it is one which is getting a better hearing than I would have believed possible a few years ago. The severe shock of the oil crisis has produced much discontent, but as Dr Samuel Johnson would say, we might emerge from it 'our vigilance quickened, and our comprehension enlarged'.

NOTES

1. This commonly made point is re-emphasised in the *Report of the Committee on Policy Optimisation* (Chairman, Professor R. J. Ball), Cmnd. no. 7148 (1978), which, *inter alia*, reviews the British Treasury's economic forecasting performance.
2. The argument is an echo of John Stuart Mill's lack of concern at the prospect of reaching a stationary-state economy: 'I confess I am not charmed with the ideal of life held out by those who think that the normal state of human beings is that of struggling to get on . . . the best state of human nature is that in which, while no-one is poor, no-one desires to be richer, nor has any reason to fear being thrust back, by the efforts of others to push themselves forwards, *Principles of Political Economy* (1871) Book IV, ch. 6. I am glad to report that the final edition of his masterpiece removed this naughty passage on the USA: 'they have no poverty: and all that these advantages do for them is that the life of the whole of one sex is devoted to dollar-hunting, and of the other to breeding dollar hunters'!
3. Therefore, when the contemporary poet James Kirkup draws the moral in *A Visit to Brontëland*, 'the Brontës knew they had nothing but the moor and themselves. It is we, who want all, who are poor', it is doubtful if he encapsulates a general sentiment!
4. See Alan Whiting, 'An International Comparison of the Instability of Economic Growth', *Three Banks Review*, Mar 1976.
5. See particularly Lord Kaldor, 'Capitalism and Industrial Development: Lessons from British Experience', *Cambridge Journal of Economics*, June 1977. For criticism of this view, see F. T. Blackaby (ed.), *British Economic Policy 1960–1974*

(Cambridge: Cambridge University Press for National Institute of Economic and Social Research, 1978) ch. 14, and Alan Peacock, *Economic Analysis of Government and Related Themes* (London: Martin Robertson, 1979) ch. 16.

6. For a useful diagrammatic as well as algebraic presentation of Kaldor's model, see R. Dixon and A. P. Thirlwall, 'A Model of Regional Growth Differences on Kaldorian Lines', *Oxford Economic Papers*, July 1975.
7. See R. Bacon and W. Eltis, *Britain's Economic Problem: Too Few Producers*, 2nd ed. (London: Macmillan, 1978).
8. For evidence see Alan Peacock and Martin Ricketts, 'The Growth of the Public Sector and Inflation' in Fred Hirsch and John H. Goldthorpe (eds), *The Political Economy of Inflation* (London: Martin Robertson, 1978).
9. This is not to deny the influence of the composition of investment on growth. Michael Parkin in the discussion of this paper rightly pointed out my omission of the influence of the sharp decline in the 1960s and 1970s in the share of profits in manufacturing industry as compared with the share of wages and salaries. This factor together with the associated fall in the real rate of return on capital in manufacturing induced suppliers of capital to seek more profitable opportunities in property investment where the capital/output ratio would be expected to be higher. I am grateful to Professor Parkin for his observations which further emphasise the danger of seeking to simplify complicated economic issues such as the determinants of growth.
10. See G. C. Allen, *The British Disease*, Hobart Paper No. 57 (London: Institute of Economic Affairs, 1976).
11. It has been claimed that Keynesian economists, under the influence of its founder, deliberately ignore the complications of political decision-making, preferring to imagine that advisers on economic policy should proffer advice rather like an influential courtier to a benevolent despot. Though I believe this to be something of an exaggeration, there are elements of patricianism in the attitude of some Cambridge economists which suggest that they regard themselves as peculiarly suited to positions of power and influence! For further discussion of the political setting of Keynesianism, see J. M. Buchanan, John Burton and R. E. Wagner, *The Consequences of Mr. Keynes*, Hobart Paper No. 78 (London: Institute of Economic Affairs, 1978). For a criticism of the 'optimisation' models used by economists, see Alan Peacock, *Economic Analysis of Government and Related Themes* (London: Martin Robertson, 1979) ch. 1.
12. The formulation of the industrial strategy programme is authoritatively explained in Alan Lord, 'A Strategy for Industry', Ellis Hunter Memorial Lecture, University of York, 1977 and an apologia for the strategy itself is found in R. McIntosh, 'Future British Industrial Society', Mercantile Credit Lecture, University of Reading, 1976. At the time of writing Mr Alan Lord was Second Permanent Secretary at HM Treasury and Sir Ronald McIntosh, Director General, National Economic Development Office. For further elucidation of the 'nuts and bolts' of the strategy, see D. R. Stout, 'De-Industrialisation and Industrial Policy', in *De-Industrialisation* (London: Heinemann for National Institute of Economic and Social Research, 1979).

3 Welfare: Progress and Stagnation

Hugh Heclo

A lead editorial in *The Times* dated 1 July 1940, symbolised the temporary end of a very long debate (going back at least as far as the nineteenth century poor law) on British social policy. It declared:

> If we speak of democracy, we do not mean a democracy which maintains the right to vote but forgets the right to work and the right to live. If we speak of freedom, we do not mean a rugged individualism which excludes social organisation and economic planning. If we speak of equality, we do not mean a political equality nullified by social and economic privilege. If we speak of economic reconstruction, we think less of maximum production (though this too will be required) than of equitable distribution.

Within three months the Blitz was vividly demonstrating that extensive social services and other forms of collectivism were needed by all levels of British society and not, as originally planned, only by the working classes.

It was, and I believe is, an ennobling vision. One of the most important and distinctive things about modern Britain is that the welfare state acquired an ideological life of its own. More than a mere set of government programmes, Britain's welfare state became infused with a series of vague but deeply and widely held beliefs: as part of a common society, we *do* have shared needs; people – all people – *are* entitled to a decent life; privilege and greed *must not* be allowed to emasculate citizens' social rights; government *can* be a force for good in securing these ends. It was a dream shared not only by social thinkers such as Beveridge, T. H. Marshall and Titmuss but also by leading Conservative and Socialist politicians – Macmillan, Butler and Macleod no less than an Attlee, Bevan and Gaitskell. And most important of all, it was a dream shared by millions of ordinary people.

I count myself a friend of the British welfare state and its vision. But it would be foolish to ignore the fact that now, 40 years after the *Times* editorial, many people regard that dream as a blighted hope, however inspiring it may once have been. The litany of complaints – persisting inequality and privilege, new envies, discord and incivility – need not be repeated here. In fact, many observers of Britain are critical precisely because, as the editorial urged, the country has given so much priority to welfarism and so little to economic performance. This critique is shared by neo-conservatives (for whom Britain is a premier specimen of an economy crippled by social spending, high taxes and egalitarianism) as well as by some left-wing Socialists (who would shift priorities to various kinds of state capitalism to produce the economic growth that has eluded Britain's private sector). In both cases the answer to Britain's problems is seen to be giving the nation a new economic lease of life. The main difference is which social group is expected to own the leasehold.

The following pages suggest why both the neo-conservative and neo-socialist views represent a cramped, economistic view of welfare, of the state, and of the ideology that attempts the peculiarly difficult task of uniting welfare and the state. The theme of this chapter is that in nations, as in people, there is a third alternative to progress or decline, namely *stagnation*. This, above all, is what characterises the British welfare state. To be sure, social programmes have multiplied and spending has increased. This does not deny stagnation, at least if one believes there is more to the welfare state than a series of budgets and bureaucrats. At a deeper level, British social policy sought to create a vision of the good society expressed through government. It is as a public philosophy that Britain's welfare state has been constricted and unable to adapt to the larger world around it. Social scientists like to think that consensus produces continuity and order, and conflict produces discontinuity and change. But the stagnation that has characterised the post-war British welfare state suggests the opposite. Its consensus has laid the foundation for larger disorders; its conflicts have affirmed an unwillingness to contemplate change.

The following pages try to clarify the meaning of this stagnation by first considering what has been achieved in terms of material welfare and second, considering the role of the state that was circumscribed by the British vision of welfarism. It would be wrong to overlook the tremendous achievements made in Britons' physical well-being. But none of this has produced social solidarity as the welfare state founders had hoped. As a public philosophy the welfare state has stood mute and helpless in dealing with conflict among the new power blocs in British life. These blocs are not based on class, status, or party. They are based on the ability of different groups – some created by welfare administration itself – to exercise control over their means of consumption. Isolating welfare from industrial relations in the economy and unconcerned with problems of power in the state, British welfare state ideology has been an invitation to disruptive stagnation.

I Welfare: Inequality and Progress

Welfare in Britain is a story of material progress in a setting of persisting inequality. This is most obvious in terms of earnings and disposable income.

From the beginning of this century to 1976, the real income of male manual workers more than trebled. The bulk of this improvement occurred in the 25-year period after 1951, at the same time as government spending, taxation and bureaucracy were increasing rapidly. Between 1951 and 1976, the weekly earnings of a male manual worker about doubled in real terms (that is, from £37.8 to £71.5 per week at 1977 prices). After taking account of both inflation and taxes, real disposable income per person in Britain has also almost doubled in the same period.

Lower income groups have shared in this progress. From 1953 to 1973, the real income of those officially classified as poor (that is, below the income level for public assistance) increased 60 to 70 per cent, for welfare state benefits, such as basic retirement pension and public assistance rates, have largely kept up with the higher real earnings of those in the workforce.[1] Even during the terrible economic troubles of the mid-1970s, welfare benefits generally kept up with price increases, something that earnings in the labour force as a whole did *not* do. In other words, the costs of the 1970s economic dislocations were not allowed to be distributed haphazardly by market forces. Pensioners, those on public assistance and other economically vulnerable groups were sheltered by government's shifting costs elsewhere in society.

Despite the improvement in absolute material living standards, there has been scant progress in reducing inequalities of earnings and income. After reviewing the available evidence, two authors recently concluded, 'Rises in real standards of living over this century have been more dramatic than the reductions of inequality. While there has probably been some contraction at the top end of the distribution of earnings, the effects on the overall spread of net income have been quite small.'[2] Nor do all the taxes and transfer payments reshuffling income in the welfare state greatly reduce these inequalities. For example in 1974–5, the richest 10 per cent of Britons acquired 26.6 per cent of pre-tax income. After the government's tax/transfer reshuffle, this was only reduced to 23.2 per cent. The poorest 10 per cent of Britons received 2.8 per cent of all income before tax and 3.1 per cent after tax. The general picture of persisting inequality is even stronger when one analyses the distribution of wealth and productive capital as opposed simply to income and earnings.[3]

As it took form, the British welfare state was never particularly concerned with these larger issues of earnings and wealth distribution. From the 1940s to the 1960s it is difficult to find any programme or pronouncement that paid attention to the generation and distribution of earnings as an aspect of social policy. The welfare state vision stopped well short of crossing into the troublesome territory of industrial bargaining, wages and other union and management prerogatives. The same applies to questions of wealth. The set-piece debate on a wealth tax persisted. Nationalisation of certain weak industries occurred. But almost no one imagined that deliberate measures to spread participation in wealth-generating investment had anything to do with the welfare state and social policy. There were certain exceptions, but the results were meager. Writing at the outset of the Second World War, Keynes proposed to break the link between higher wartime earnings and inflation by creating a deliberate government policy affecting the distribution of financial assets. The workforce, which was rapidly becoming fully employed, would be rewarded not simply with higher take-home pay but also with pay in the form of capital, or as he put it, 'a share in the claims on the future which would otherwise belong to the entrepreneurs'.[4] Only a much scaled-down version of this idea was ever implemented. In the late 1950s, the original proposal by Richard Titmuss for earnings-related pensions featured investment of workers' accumulated state pension funds in productive capital in the stock market. This feature was vigorously attacked by Conservatives, private insurance and banking interests, and it was quickly dropped by the Labour party in all its subsequent pension proposals.

It is the Premium Bond system, more than anything else, that symbolises the British approach to widening ownership of financial assets. But the 'savings' are used to roll-over national debt, not to share in the growth of capital and the return it earns. Since Premium Bonds were introduced in 1956, the number of participants has grown to over 20 million bondholders. In effect, these bonds are government debt instruments sold only in small denominations so as to attract resources of those with modest means. The 'savings' that the Bonds attract earn no interest whatsoever; any return on the 'investment' consists of prizes awarded at a periodic drawing of lucky bond numbers. Even supposing that a saver eventually received his or her share of the prizes, the net long-term return is even lower than the 7 per cent interest on National Saving Certificates. Rather than being a wealth policy of the welfare state, the Premium Bond system is best thought of as a voluntary tax paid by government-organised gamblers.

It would be too simple and neat to suggest that Britain's welfare state has been interested in absolute poverty rather than relative inequality. One of the least productive set-piece debates in recent years has been that between the 'relativists', who argue that progress from subsistence standards is meaningless because it does not reduce relative distances among groups, and the 'absolutists', who contend that trying to eliminate relative inequality can only result in an even less desirable condition of uniformity. The British welfare state vision was really not directed at this theoretically tidy either/or choice between uniformity and inequality. Its founders recognised that well short of stultifying uniformity, a society could be organised so as to have a great many or very few people living below some minimum level of decency relative to the rest of the population. A society could remain diverse and still have a great many or very few citizens living, say, below a level equal to one-half the general population's median income level. The real point was not statistical; if all one cared about was the prevention of mass physical privation as it existed before the Second World War, then the welfare state could have soon declared victory and left the field. Its aim in eliminating 'want' had to do with a basic standard judged decent when compared with the rest of the population.[5] A comprehensive, integrated plan of social insurance was intended to prevent anyone, except in the most exceptional circumstances, from falling into any dependence on stigmatising, means-tested relief through public assistance. National insurance, co-ordinated through one central administrative system, would protect every citizen against each of the major threats to income security: accident, sickness, unemployment, old age and death of the breadwinner. Means-tested public assistance would be reduced to a small residual category of help for temporary or unusually severe hardship. As long as the citizen did his part – worked when he was able and paid his national insurance contributions – there would be the assurance of a respectable income base for him and his family. They would not depend on some modernised version of the dole. They would have paid their way. The focus of this welfare state vision was on how want would be prevented (i.e. through Beveridge's unified national insurance programme) rather than on the guarantee that in event of hardship government relief payments would be made.

Yet the hope for ending reliance on public assistance (with relief standards set relative to general economic levels) has been severely disappointed. This type of want has not been prevented. In 1976 there were no less than 2.8 million claimants for public assistance (now called supplementary benefits) whose households amounted to almost 5 million people. About one-half of the claimants were treated as 'exceptions', that is, receiving discretionary extra payments for exceptional circumstances beyond the standardised, means-tested benefits of the public assistance bureaucracy. As David Donnison, chairman of the Supplementary Benefits Commission and a strong believer in the British welfare state, put it in 1976, 'It is clear that our national system of means-tested benefits, with all the discretion and flexibility we have built into it, was never intended to support the massive numbers – now mounting to about 8 per cent of our population – which have come to rely on it.'[6]

National insurance has not prevented simultaneous and extensive use of the minimum safety-net provisions of public assistance. Since the late 1940s, two-thirds or more of assistance recipients have also had national insurance benefits. Since then, the proportion of all elderly state pensioners who have also had to rely on public assistance has changed little, rising from 22 per cent in 1951, to 28 to 29 per cent in the early 1970s, then falling back to 21 per cent in 1974. For unemployment insurance beneficiaries, the welfare component rose from 16 per cent in 1951 to 27 per cent by 1974. For those receiving sickness and invalidity benefits the proportions on the dole fell from 13 per cent in 1951 to 8 per cent in 1974; for widows below pension age with national insurance benefits the incidence of public assistance fell from 23 per cent to 10 per cent in the same years. The main point is that before and after the arrival of the British welfare state, a considerable and growing number of persons have had to rely on the nation's income maintenance programme of last resort. This need is a depressing sign of the kind of persisting inequality – an inequality in people's ability to support themselves above the basic social minimum – that post-war social policy was intended to eliminate.

The attack against want by comprehensive national insurance was central to the welfare state vision, but it was by no means the only concern. The Beveridge Report identified four other giants blocking the road to a peaceful, reconstructed Britain: squalor, ignorance, disease and idleness. If we briefly consider what has happened to several of these problems, the paradox of progress amid persisting inequality becomes even more obvious.

The squalor to which Beveridge referred could be found throughout immense sections of Britain, quite apart from the rubble produced by wartime bombing. What existed in 1945 was not so much urban decay, in our contemporary sense of deserted central cities, as run-down, over-crowded working class housing of the nineteenth century that was no longer suited to the second half of the twentieth century. By the 1970s the situation showed considerable improvement. Life for the average Briton had become more private, more spacious and more comfortable.

At the beginning of the 1950s a majority of Britons lived without the privacy of a bathroom; some 38 per cent of households lacked a fixed bath and 8 per cent a water closet; another 22 per cent shared their washing and/or toilet facilities with another household. By 1971, only 10 per cent were without such facilities and another 7 per cent had to share.

This improvement in physical amenities occurred at the same time that Britons were choosing to form more separate households of their own and enjoying a much larger and more modern stock of housing. While the total population increased by only 10 per cent between 1951 and 1971, the total number of households[7] rose 26 per cent and the available housing stock rose 43 per cent.

Despite impressions to the contrary, citizens of the British welfare state found increased possibilities to own their own homes. The much publicised public housing sector grew mainly at the expense of private rentals, in other words, at the expense of the sector which had traditionally accounted for the majority of unfit dwellings. But private home-ownership grew even faster, especially after the 1950s. Owner-occupation climbed from 29 per cent of all dwellings in 1950 to 52 per cent by 1974.

The result of all this was more elbow room. At the beginning of the 1950s two out of five households were sharing their dwellings with other households, a figure which was more like one in five by the late 1970s. In 1951 over 5 million Britons were crowded together in accomodation that had fewer rooms than people (i.e. housing with 1.5 persons or more per room), compared with 1.5 million persons living in such conditions by the 1970s. And contrary to popular impressions, the growth of the welfare state left fewer rather than more people in the institutionalised care so abhorrent to anti-collectivists.[8]

If squalor is taken to include the dirt Britons have to live with, then significant progress has been made here too. Smoke emissions into the atmosphere have dropped to one-fifth the level of the early 1950s, yielding, among other benefits, almost an extra hour of sunshine in London during the winter days. Although sulphur dioxide emission has not been tamed yet, the concentrates of this chemical in the atmosphere have dropped over the years. And while there is still much more to do, most rivers in the island have become somewhat cleaner than they were in the 1950s.

It is probably impossible to determine how much of this progress against squalor is due to welfare state programmes versus 'natural' processes in the economy and society. While some will wish to question whether the results justified the costs, the government's extensive housing programmes have undoubtedly helped produce these trends. House improvement grants were introduced in 1949 and by the 1960s were helping with the renovation of well over 100,000 dwellings each year.[9] Since 1951 public housing has added – given some year-to-year fluctuations – 180,000 units a year to the British housing stock. This has not, however, served to prevent growth of a quite considerable role for construction by the private sector which since the late 1950s has been producing as many or more housing completions each year as the public sector. Such private activity has itself been influenced by a variety of housing subsidy and mortgage tax relief schemes (in 1973–4 tax relief on mortgage payments was worth £500 million to mortgagors of mainly private housing, compared with central government housing subsidies to local public housing programmes of £323 million).

Yet despite these and other public efforts, considerable deprivation and inequality in basic housing standards remain.[10] While over-crowding has been reduced, it still varies directly with social class. Virtually every conurbation can be found to contain areas of extensive housing deprivation, with the problems multiplied in central cities and including not only private rental housing but some of the public sector's own council estates. It is about as unlikely that an unskilled manual worker will own his home as that someone in the professional or managerial class can be found renting (roughly 1-in-5 odds in each case). Access to home mortgages and thus to the major means of accumulating personal wealth is heavily concentrated among non-manual workers.

Roughly similar patterns can be found for the other social evils identified by Beveridge: significant improvement in basic standards amidst persisting inequalities.

Ignorance may not have been vanquished, but formal education has become a more prominent part of Britons' lives. Larger proportions of youth start earlier and stay longer in school than ever before. Since 1960 the proportion of 2- to 4-year-olds and 16- to 18-year-olds in school has approximately doubled. Yet strong differences in educational opportunity persist among regions and social classes. Compared with children from other socio-economic groupings, children of manual workers rarely attend preschool nurseries; by age 7 their reading, mathematical and oral abilities are well below average, and from that point on the social sorting by educational institutions helps ensure that the differences will persist.[11] In 1972 (before the school-leaving age had been raised from 15 to 16) approximately 6 of every 10 workers' children aged 15 to 19 had left school, compared with 1 in 10 of the children from professional families.

The health of the nation is clearly a complex subject where no simple set of indicators is likely to suffice.[12] For example, general life expectancy has increased fairly continuously before and after the National Health Service was created in Britain, and in countries with or without national health programmes during the twentieth century. However, the decline in infant and maternal mortality has been especially marked since the Second World War. If certified days of sickness (standardised by age and per person at risk) are any guide, Britons, especially men, have been feeling a little less well since the 1950s. But it should be noticed that the same statistic could mean not greater health problems but rather greater availability of services, greater expectation of assistance, greater (or lesser) efficacy of treatment, or a combination of these factors.

Taking a broad view of the post-1948 NHS era, what appears to have changed is not so much the amount as the type of sickness and disease. As a cause of illness or death, important declines have occurred among infectious diseases, especially tuberculosis, certain congenital anomalies and some respiratory diseases. To a great extent, these declines have been counterbalanced by an increased incidence of health problems that have more of the character of 'diseases of choice', in the sense of being fairly directly related to what we do to ourselves and our environment. Major increases have occurred in health problems due to arteriosclerotic heart disease, cancer, mental disorders, alcoholism and venereal disease (a declining cause of death but increasing cause of illness). We have become more able to control natural infections than man-made afflictions in the welfare state.

British health policy has managed to live up to its aspirations for universal coverage and comprehensive treatment free from the cash nexus at time of treatment. Almost all births now take place in hospitals or related facilities (33 per cent of births were at home in 1961 compared to 6 per cent in 1973). General medical practitioners (but not dentists) are now fairly evenly distributed around the country and the rapid growth of local health centres in recent years has helped to improve access further. The frequency of consultation with a GP differs only slightly among the various social classes, with semi- and unskilled male workers consulting their GP much more often than any other group.

The latter point, however, raises some warning signals about health policy. Despite the considerable spending effort devoted to Britain's NHS, major inequalities persist in the health of the people. More frequent visits to the doctor for manual workers are related to higher rates of reported disease and serious illness. Standardised for age differences, those in the families of unskilled manual workers are about twice as likely (somewhat less for females) than professional class workers to report acute or chronic sickness.

In a way it would almost be reassuring if one could simply account for these differences as instances of over-utilisation or working-class 'scrounging' on the NHS. But there are real class differences in the physical condition of the people, after a generation of collectivist health policies. Stillbirths are about twice as likely in semi- or unskilled workers' families as in professional or managerial class families.[13] New babies in the former families will average 100 g or more below the weight of new babies in the latter families. By age 14 boys and girls in working class families are 3 to 6 cm shorter than their professional and managerial class counterparts. And as Table 3.1 suggests, they will be more likely to see their fathers die at an early age, as had their fathers and their fathers before them. These class differences in mortality rates may even have increased since the 1920s. Whatever might be said about unnecessary visits to doctors' offices, presumably few in social class V are trying to scrounge death benefits.

TABLE 3.1 Standardised mortality rates for males in England and Wales

Social class	*Period*				
	*1921–3**	*1930–2**	*1949–53**	*1959–63†*	*1970–2†*
I	82	90	86	76	77
II	94	94	92	81	81
III	95	97	101	100	104
IV	101	102	104	103	113
V	125	111	118	143	137

* Males aged 20–64.
† Males aged 15–64; data for 1970–2 are provisional.
Source: Central Statistical Office, *Social Trends*, No. 6 (1975) Table 7.1.

II The State: Consensus and Decline

The preceding section suggested a paradoxical situation: post-war Britain's welfare state has witnessed considerable material progress amid persisting inequality. Fervent egalitarians can make a case that this is faint progress in terms of their social goals; so too can those who would rather compare post-war British economic performance with that of other nations rather than the nation's own long-term growth record. Still, if one stopped the story here, the verdict would probably have to be one of advancement rather than decline. Since the Second World War, Britons have not only created materially better lives for themselves, but they have done so while paying considerable attention to the less privileged members of their society.

Yet aspirations were high, and so is the current sense of disappointment. There was something more than material progress underlying the British version of the welfare state. At base, beneath all the reforms in health, housing, education, pensions and so on, was the idea of creating and sustaining an underlying social solidarity. This solidarity would be built around widespread human needs – once regarded as purely individual matters but now to be regarded as socially shared problems – and collective governmental provisions to meet them. This, it was hoped, would provide the underpinnings of a just social order above which the normal, healthy clash of interests would come and go.

What has become clear is that, far from achieving a sense of domestic solidarity, British social policy has been accompanied by more intense clashes of interests. Thus another and deeper paradox: the substance of welfare state consensus has remained intact amid a growing sense of social and political decline. Britons have tended to accept economic hardship, or more accurately slow growth, with equanimity; something of the spirit of the Blitz periodically reappears with each electricity blackout or transportation crisis. What undermines any sense of political community is the feeling that too many people are getting away with too much. There is no equality of sacrifice. Each group's single-minded pursuit of its own economic interest not only adds a new dimension to the traditional class conflict (now it is the middle class that increasingly sees itself as proletariat exploited by the working class). It also factionalises classes, dividing miners from engineers, railway engine drivers from ticket collectors and hospital maintenance workers from dust men. Far from becoming one nation, post-war Britain seems to have become a nation that is increasingly divided against itself. Contrast this with the original hopes for welfare state solidarity and the sense of decline becomes almost overwhelming.

In his recent Reith lectures, Professor A. H. Halsey has very sensitively portrayed this disappointment with the modern 'secular dream', which he describes in terms of equality, liberty and fraternity.[14] He goes on to argue that persisting inequalities have thwarted hopes of achieving the underlying goal of fraternity (or solidarity). This view leads to exhortations for more government intervention to increase equality and, unfortunately, to the likelihood of even greater social divisiveness. It also overstates the welfare state's egalitarian aims to the exclusion of its other ends.

It is difficult to see post-war British social policy as a struggle between values of equality and individual liberty, in which equality has lost so frequently as to undermine fraternity, to use Halsey's terms. A key feature of Britain's welfare state well into the 1960s was the lack of any vigorous debate between egalitarian and libertarian policy approaches. On the contrary, it was widely believed that both equality and liberty could be increased (or at least would not necessarily have to be traded off against each other) by adding a new factor – *security* – to the equation of British social politics. The new welfarism after 1945 denied the necessity for choice among these deeply held values and in doing so, laid the basis for an apparent decline of ideology. These general tendencies could be found in many countries after the Second World War, but in Britain the welfare state became an especially powerful political symbol with undertones of a higher morality. In other words, Britain's post-war reconstruction of social programmes tended to become a policy ideology.

The basis for the decline of Britain's welfare state as a public philosophy and its stagnation as a political force lay in this role as a policy ideology, a strong and persisting consensus as to where claims of welfare did and did not apply. It is therefore worthwhile examining this consensus in greater detail and observing how it was overtaken by events.

Common provisions to meet shared needs put government at the centre of British hopes to create a better, more just society. Some critics questioned the implications for bureaucratic control over people's lives but as the 1940s and 1950s progressed these people were in a distinct minority.[15] Few war-weary Britons doubted the capabilities or intentions of the national government to 'do good' – once there was the will to act.

This will to act and unhesitatingly use government was the first great element of consensus in the post-war British welfare state. It drew a sharp contrast between governmental mechanisms and private markets. Collective provision meant just that – government offices providing housing, health care, town plans, insurance payments and so on. In general it rejected market mechanisms to achieve social purposes. Alterations in party control of Whitehall did little to alter any presumption about this positive governmental role in the delivery of social welfare. Conservatives might promise in the 1950s to denationalise an industry here or there, but they would also continue to build public housing. They might pledge to lift certain economic controls, but they also swore loyalty to improving the NHS and raising pensions. Each post-war election reaffirmed the assumption that government was *the* instrument increasing welfare. Any serious political debate centred on who was best fitted to use this tool, rather than on whether or not it should be used.

How could a national government manage anything as huge as welfare on the societal level? By limiting the definition of welfare. Discussion in post-war Britain rapidly converged to define the appropriate arenas of the state's welfare responsibility. This may seem a strange statement in view of continued parliamentary dogfights. Yet more important than particular measures and controversies is what has been taken for granted on all sides concerning the boundaries of British social policy. The writ of the welfare state covered three areas: social services, particularly housing, health and education; income maintenance, mainly under the auspices of national insurance; and full employment for the workforce, generally through Keynesian economic management. This consensus on the appropriate frontiers of social policy was the second major element of consensus in Britain's welfare state. Almost no one advocated retreating from these frontiers, and few suggested using the claims of welfare and equity to push beyond them.

Unlike some of the other major policy decisions in British history – free trade, Ireland, the People's Budget – creating the post-Second World War welfare state was not the occasion of a great national debate. To a large extent the debate had already occurred during the domestic turmoil of the inter-war period and was completed by war. This determination – not to go back to those bad old days – was decisive in the effort to plan Britain's post-war future. The new commitment to common social services denied the old, invidious distinctions that paid more attention to income and class than to joint provisions for human needs, especially in terms of health care. Comprehensive national income maintenance programmes affirmed a right so often debated and seldom realised in the inter-war period – the right to a basic, dignified standard of living for all citizens. Post-war pledges to achieve full employment served to repudiate the terrible waste of workers' lives in the 1920s and 1930s.

What this consensus left aside was, simply expressed, any connection between social and economic policy beyond maintaining full employment. To be sure, there were periodic bouts of detailed economic controls. But government intervention was invariably justified, not from equity or other social policy considerations, but in terms of economic policy – to stabilise the pound, ease international payments deficits, increase productivity and investment, and so on. In fact, despite the rhetoric of 'free collective bargaining', there have been very few of the last 30 years in which British economic life has not operated under some formal or informal type of government economic controls. But these government interventions have been surface phenomena on the deeper processes of the labour market system. Conditions of employment, procedures for wage bargaining, managerial prerogatives – in short the whole array of industrial relations – has been an area in which British government has traditionally been loath to intervene, and then only for reasons of high economic policy. This government reluctance has been reciprocated by distrust from both employers and unions.

In other words, a well-defined, widely-supported welfare state collectivism has been combined in Britain with an almost classic *laissez-faire* liberalism in labour relations. This approach has affirmed that the common welfare is best discovered by the free play of collective bargaining and tests of strength between business and labour. The reasons for this situation range from a very powerful historical tradition of conflict in the workplace, to a party system that encourages an adversarial approach to dealing with industrial relations policy.[16] Segregating the welfare state consensus from economic policy and industrial relations was useful, in the short term, on a variety of fronts. For Conservatives doing so maintained contact with a central tenet of their free enterprise credo, something that was all the more important as other principles – opposition to state intervention in health, resistance to guaranteed income levels through government payments, and so on – were being quietly abandoned. It also made electoral sense to avoid antagonising trade union members, who needed no reminding of a Conservative history of 'union bashing'.

There were other less obvious interests served by keeping the welfare state in its place, that is, out of economic decisions and relations between the labour market parties. For the Labour party, which controlled the government during the crucial formative years of post-war social policy, any broad definition of welfare aims implied interfering with trade unions and their prerogative to bargain for inequalities in the workplace. Although speaking about the Attlee government's nationalisation plans, Schumpeter went to the heart of the matter when he wrote, 'A government that means to socialize to any great extent will have to socialize trade unions'.[17] Bringing trade unions and employers into full participation in defining the aims of social policy would have required exactly the same political boldness. Such leadership was not forthcoming in either government, trade union or employer circles and the complex system of occupational welfare went on to develop well outside the boundaries of the evolving welfare state consensus. The 1974–9 Labour government's desperate attempts to create a social contract – first urging unions to base calculations on a 'social wage' that included pay settlements and government social benefits, then trading tax cuts for pay restraint – showed how intimately connected were welfare policy and economic policy and how belated was the attempt to make the connection.

The hands-off approach to the social dimension of economic policy and industrial relations was also well suited to the norms of the British constitution, in the sense of government institutions preferring this way of doing business. It kept central government apart from and above any detailed involvement in the business and labour groups. Trying to use the 'small levers' of policy to affect the relations between these groups would undoubtedly have led the same groups to insist on similar access to the workings of government. Whitehall in general and the Treasury in particular did occupy itself from time to time in quite detailed regulation of consumer and producer behaviour in the post-war years. But as long as outsiders believed these actions were justified in terms of the government's larger responsibility for economic policy and the Treasury's expert, 'scientifically objective' knowledge the policy-making circle was protected from any serious participation by non-governmental groups. To admit openly that much murkier choices of a social policy nature were also at stake would have been an invitation to challenge the unity, authority and secrecy of the executive.[18]

As luck would have it, developments on the intellectual front simultaneously provided a powerful justification in Britain for circumscribing the welfare state consensus. Reacting to the inter-war years, post-war social policy placed extremely heavy emphasis on security; in employment problems, this could be readily and almost exclusively defined in terms of full-employment. Keynesian economics was addressed precisely to this problem, and by the end of the war its principles had taken firm hold within the relevant government circles. This approach focused attention on the 'big levers' – the huge aggregate variables of consumption, investment, interest rates. If these were sufficient to achieve the social policy goal of full employment, why become involved in the troublesome small change of labour markets, industrial relations and so on? Despite some early flirtations in the other direction, political leaders such as Cripps, Gaitskell and Butler ended up with essentially similar views concerning the sufficiency of macro-economics for social policy purposes. Nowhere was this more clearly expressed than in the transmigration of William Beveridge from a classic micro-economist to an advocate of social planning in labour markets, industrial and regional development; and then to a committed Keynesian at the time of Beveridge's greatest influence in outlining the post-war British welfare state.[19]

For a number of years, the welfare state consensus seemed to serve not only these various interests but also Britain well. Trouble developed when circumstances changed and one government after another discovered that the neat welfare state consensus, having been defined and circumscribed, could not be easily transferred. As a policy ideology, the British welfare state made clear the government's obligations for social services, income maintenance and full employment. It was largely silent about reciprocal duties, particularly those of powerful groups making claims on each other in the economy. The irrelevance of this consensus to some of the most pressing problems gradually became clear as it emerged that the government, far from being an impartial 'holder of the ring' was itself a powerful claimant. Nationalisation, industrial subsidies and the post-war growth of state social services produced a public and semi-public workforce that was eventually upwards of one-third of total employment.

What were the social underpinnings that could restrain any group's economic power in the name of a larger social welfare? How could a consensus mobilised around state welfarism exert pressure on economic issues? The British welfare state had little to say on questions of power and consent extending across the fabric of social organisation. In other words, the welfare state is not a policy. Its consensus has been partial and deceptive.

The first signs of the problems to come surfaced with the economic troubles of 1955 and the Conservative government's call for mutual sacrifice to restrain wages and prices.[20] Calls for mutual sacrifice in war-time and in the immediate post-war austerity period had been one thing; urging restraint in the general climate of economic growth emerging in the 1950s was quite another. Britain's welfare state ideology was compatible with the former but not the latter. It had grown out of a long social history in which the basic orienting question had been: 'Why, in the midst of so much industrial wealth, must so many be left vulnerable and suffering?' But as affluence tended to replace austerity in the 1950s, the underlying welfare issue tended to shift to another question: 'If others are getting ahead, why not me?'

Far from helping cope with this newer question, both elements of Britain's welfare state consensus only encouraged complacency. First, faith in government obscured the role of its own workforce as a sectional interest making claims that could impinge on the welfare of others. Working in a nationalised industry or a new welfare bureaucracy was supposed to be the corrective for diswelfares created by private interests and private markets; in fact these workers too were prone to put their own welfare above that of the community at large. Secondly, concentration on the national insurance – social services – full employment triad of the welfare state re-enforced tendencies to neglect the social dimensions of economic policy. Concentrating on the Keynesian levers of the macro-economy, government needed to make little investment in establishing the working relations, trust and sense of mutual obligation on which any future calls for economic restraint would depend. It was a new context in which welfare questions were raised not just in traditional terms of 'pulling up' the downtrodden but also of coping with every group's desire to be 'pulling ahead' economically. The established welfare state consensus was hard-pressed to cover both.

There is no need here to review the many attempts by successive governments to invent machinery that could produce mutual restraint and sacrifice. As Clegg points out, the experiments blossomed in bewildering confusion after 1960 and became frantic after 1969.[21] In essence, each of these attempts sought to make the industrial relations system safe for economic policy as defined by the government of the day. This generally translated into trying to control the economic effects of a largely uncontrolled system of industrial relations. And yet the idea of restraint and sacrifice – especially in an economic marketplace committed to a rhetoric of *laissez-faire* liberalism – implied a sense of priorities and fair shares that has more to do with social values than economic policy. Meanwhile, the welfare state as traditionally defined remained an article of faith irrelevant to the pressing issues of equity and social justice raised in this marketplace.

I do not mean to say that all would have come right if British policy-makers had simply expanded their definition of the welfare state to include the economic dilemmas the nation was facing. My point is that the major participants – socialists, conservatives, businessmen and trade unionists – have had a vested interest in keeping the troublesome issue of social policy in its place, that is, outside the play of forces in economic policy-making and industrial relations. As a result, the springs of social conscience and, in time, consensus that fed the Beveridge welfare state did little to guide or nourish difficult social choices posed by efforts to manage and revive the British economy. To create this healthier environment would have required each of the participants to spend political resources and lose some power of independent action. The political parties would have had to restrict the scope of adversary politics. Employers and unionists would have had to treat each other as equals rather than picture each other as the villain in the economic story. Whitehall would have had to reveal the tentative nature of its own economic analyses in order to gain meaningful consultation with the labour market parties.

As it is, the hoped-for solidarity of the welfare state has become enveloped in a politics of recrimination. Each election restates the question of who is to blame for economic failures and seemingly resolves it, only to run up against a reality that requires co-operative action rather than fixing blame. The result is that the dominant direction of Britain's political directors since 1960 has not been a trend to the right or the left but a series of u-turns. The labour government of 1964, citing 13 years of Conservative misrule, pledged itself to new social welfare initiatives and an economic rebirth while maintaining a hands-off attitude toward industrial relations. In fact little was done to push the welfare state out of its traditional groove. Events and not socialist plans led to a new sense of priorities after the 1967 devaluation, including the first Labour attempt to legislate a reformed system of industrial relations. The 1970s witnessed similarly desperate mid-course changes, first by the Heath government and then by the Wilson–Callaghan governments. There was a curious similarity in the execution of each u-turn. Experience suggested that Conservative rhetoric of private market competition and Labour rhetoric of free collective bargaining were no substitute for a larger commitment to social welfare. Eventually each government had to move beyond blame-fixing to make this larger appeal, but by then the politics of recrimination had done its work. Co-operation yielded to incentives for each powerful group to seek control over its own means of consumption.

The general election of 1979 carried on this tradition and, if anything, strengthened it. The customary consensus on the welfare state remained intact with the addendum that Conservatives found a popular response to the idea of selling council houses to tenants; given the heavy implicit subsidies that would be provided to such purchases the idea was hardly an abandonment of welfarism. Recrimination on economic policy was also upheld as a British tradition, with an added bite in the Conservative willingness to confront rather than construct working relationships with the trade unions.

If the analysis of this paper is accurate, there is little except office to be gained by maintaining the conventional policy ideology. To cope with persisting inequalities in the economy and society will be long, hard work that is made only more difficult in an atmosphere of economic and political confrontation. Such confrontation strengthens the will of each combatant to stand his ground, yielding conflict without change in social relations. Meanwhile the welfare state consensus remains comfortably above the battle of real interests. It thus indirectly facilitates a ruleless and ruthless economistic conflict on issues vital to social welfare.

Forty years after the *Times* leader in praise of the emerging welfare state, the dream seems to be dying, not from progressing too fast or too slowly but from stagnating as a policy ideology. Britain enters the 1980s facing more confrontation in the economy and irrelevance in the welfare state consensus. Perhaps the most apt characterisation for the debate about the welfare state today is that used regarding the returning nobility after the French Revolution: 'They had forgotten nothing and they had learned nothing'.

NOTES

1. Historical figures on earnings and related levels of welfare benefits are conveniently summarised in the issues of *Social Trends* (London: Central Statistical Office, annual).
2. Michael Rutter and Nicola Madge, *Cycles of Disadvantage* (London: Heinemann, 1976) p. 16.
3. See J. C. Kincaid, *Poverty and Equality in Britain* (Harmondsworth: Penguin, 1973); Royal Commission on the Distribution of Income and Wealth, *Report Number 1* (London: HMSO, 1975). For some arguments to the contrary, see G. Polanyi and J. B. Wood, *How Much Inequality?* Institute of Economic Affairs Monograph no. 31 (London, 1974).
4. John Maynard Keynes, *How to Pay for the War* (London: Macmillan, 1940).
5. As discussed in the Beveridge Report (para. 444), want referred to a minimum subsistence income 'sufficent to meet responsibilities'. Beveridge was not particularly concerned to clarify what in current terms would be called absolute versus relative definitions of poverty. But his references to and use of Rowntree's various poverty standards indicate that Beveridge accepted a view of minimum standards that changed in relation to the growth of the economy. In any event, it was the idea of a universal, national minimum standard above the means-tested poor law system that was the key goal.
6. David Donnison, Seth Memorial Lecture, University of Edinburgh, 23 Feb, 1976.
7. A household is defined as all those persons living together at the same address, preparing meals together and sharing housekeeping. In the post-war period more adults have chosen to form their own households; hence the larger rate of growth in households than in total population.
8. In 1971 the proportion of the population in hospitals and homes for the elderly was somewhat lower than in 1951 or 1931, despite the relatively greater number of aged persons. The proportion in prisons was about the same; it was higher in educational institutions and the proportion was lower in other miscellaneous institutions. The greatest change occurred in private institutional living – mainly hotels – where 2 per cent of the British population lived in 1931 compared with 0.5 per cent in 1971.
9. By 1974, such grants applied to approximately 300,000 dwellings, of which 40 per cent went each to owner-occupiers and local housing authorities, while the remaining 20 per cent went to private landlords and housing associations.
10. Sally Holtermann, 'Areas of Urban Deprivation in Great Britain: An Analysis of 1971 Census Data', *Social Trends*, VI (1975).
11. For a general discussion of findings on these and other trends, see Rutter and Madge, *Cycles of Disadvantage*.

12. See A. J. Culyer, R. J. Lavers and Alan Williams, 'Health Indicators' in Andrew Shonfield and Stella Shaw (eds), *Social Indicators and Social Policy* (London: Heinemann, 1972).
13. This and the following health data refer to Scotland for the year 1973 and are reported in the Central Statistical Office, 'Social Commentary: Social Class', *Social Trends*, VI (1975). These differences have persisted despite the fact that the height and weight of all Scottish children have increased during the twentieth century. See *Report of the Committee on Scottish Health Services*, Cmd no. 5204 (1936).
14. An edited version of the lectures appears in A. H. Halsey, *Change in British Society* (London: Oxford University Press, 1979).
15. See for example the series of publications by the Liberal Unservile State Group formed at Oxford in 1953. Yet even this group had to acknowledge that some members of the Liberal party had accepted 'collectivism' and retreated from pluralistic voluntarism. See especially Alan Peacock, 'The Welfare Society', *Unservile State Papers*, no. 2 (1961).
16. Among the notable examples of such work are, Rodger Charles, *The Development of Industrial Relations in Britain, 1911–1939* (London: Hutchinson, 1973); Hugh Clegg, *The System of Industrial Relations in Great Britain*, 3rd ed. (Oxford: Basil Blackwell, 1976); Michael Moran, *The Politics of Industrial Relations* (London: Macmillan, 1977); Gerald Dorfman, *Wage Politics in Britain* (Ames, Iowa: Iowa University Press, 1973); Leo Panitch, *Social Democracy and Industrial Militancy* (Cambridge: Cambridge University Press, 1976).
17. Joseph Schumpeter, *Capitalism, Socialism, and Democracy*, 3rd ed. (New York: Harper, 1949) p. 379.
18. It is worth recalling that the Attlee government, for example, published its major White Paper on incomes and prices with virtually no advance consultation with the TUC, a situation which the union movement willingly accepted.
19. Jose Harris, *William Beveridge: A Biography* (Oxford: Clarendon Press, 1977).
20. *Economic Implications of Full Employment* (London: HMSO, 1956).
21. Clegg, *The System of Industrial Relations*, p. 445. The story is well analysed in Douglas Ashford's new book, *Policy-making in Britain* (in press).

4 Westminster and Whitehall

Anthony H. Birch

I

In the twenty years following 1959 – the year the Conservatives made history by becoming the first party since 1832 to win three general elections in a row – informed opinion in Britain has moved from almost universal complacency regarding the British system of government to a condition of widespread disenchantment, cynicism and apathy. In the same period, a deep reluctance to tinker with traditional institutions has given way to the apparent belief that frequent institutional changes may help the country solve its problems. This change of mood was not predicted by political scientists. It is remarkable in view of the fact that the system of government of the 1950s was the culmination of a long period of political development, from the 1867 Reform Act. To understand what has happened, and where it is likely to lead, it is necessary to look first at the main features of the system as it was in the 1950s.

II The Status Quo Ante

The main operational characteristics of the political system of the 1950s can be summarised quite easily.

1. National government was completely dominated by the two main parties. Whereas MPs from other parties (or no party) had won 67 seats in the election of 1929 and 34 in 1945, they won only 12 seats (out of 625) in 1950, and 7 in 1959. The old arguments about the unfairness of the electoral system to small parties were still canvassed at Liberal party meetings, but elsewhere they faded into obscurity.
2. The Parliamentary parties were highly disciplined. Breaches of discipline were unusual, well-publicised, and sometimes had serious consequences: five Members (four Conservative and one Labour) who defied their parties at the time of the Suez crisis all had their political careers terminated in consequence. The government of the day had no difficulty in getting its legislation through Parliament and was in practice completely free from Parliamentary control of taxation and expenditure.

3. The civil service was in the hands of officials who were well-educated but unspecialised and largely untrained. They were recruited for life within four years of leaving school or university, without any regard for the subjects they had studied, and without any formal provision for postentry training. They were also politically neutral, with senior officials barred from all overt forms of political activity.
4. The entire administrative system was controlled by the Treasury, which also controlled the fiscal system, the Bank of England and the monetary measures that were used to guide (if not exactly to control) the economy. The Treasury's power over financial matters, especially the expenditure totals of all other Whitehall departments, gave it a crucial influence over the policies of central government. As Heclo and Wildavsky noted: 'There is considerable nonsense in the notion that the Treasury's concern can and/or should lie only in financial questions, not substantial policy.'[1]
5. In England and Wales the local government system was under effective central control in all important matters, together with many unimportant ones. A city council could not install a new set of traffic lights, for instance, without seeking the permission of the Ministry of Transport, who could even send an inspector down from London to observe the traffic and decide whether the lights were really necessary.

The overall effect of these features of the system was to give the government of the day greater powers than were enjoyed by the governments of most democratic states in that period. Unlike the American administration, the British Cabinet did not have to battle with the legislature for resources to implement its policies. Unlike the government of the Fourth Republic and other multi-party regimes, it did not have to worry about the likelihood of Parliamentary defeats. Unlike the governments of Switzerland and other plural societies, it did not have to accommodate the interests of varied ethnic and cultural groups. Unlike the governments of federal states, it did not suffer any constitutional limitations to its authority. Elections in the 1950s had the character of plebiscites to decide which of the two major parties would rule the country for the succeeding four years or so. It was understood that there would be few effective external checks on the power of the winner.

Of course, the governments of the period did not exhibit the strength and effectiveness that this sketch might suggest. They were strong on controlling traffic lights but not so good at building highways. They told each university how many square inches of library space could be provided for each student but they did nothing to prevent the wasteful duplication of small departments. They developed sophisticated techniques for tax collection but they were not very effective in stimulating investment in growth industries. As Dennis Kavanagh has pointed out, 'the strength and effectiveness of the British political system' in this period were 'not facts, but debatable assumptions'.[2]

However, comments of this kind are made with the benefit of hindsight. At the time the system was admired by politicians, journalists and scholars alike, in the United States as well as in Britain. An influential group of American political scientists took the view that some features of the Westminster model could be adopted with advantage in their own country.[3]

Looking back, it seems clear an important reason for complacency was the fact that the institutional and behavioural characteristics of the system were entirely compatible with the dominant ideological beliefs of the period. If there is a lack of coherence between ideology and institutions as, for example, there was in Britain in the 1830s or in the United States in the first decade of the twentieth century, there is likely to be discontent with the system and a campaign for institutional reforms. If ideology, institutions and behaviour all support one another, reformers are likely to be found only on the fringes.

The main components of the dominant ideology of the 1950s can be summarised as Keynesian economics, Fabian politics and high-minded liberal principles. Keynesian economic policies, first advocated by members of the Liberal party, had been embraced with equal enthusiasm by the Labour party, the Conservative party and the Treasury. From 1945 onwards all ruling groups were committed to financial measures of a Keynesian kind as the main technique of economic management. The object (in so far as it can be sketched in a few words) was to maintain a satisfactory level of employment and economic activity by controlling aggregate demand, so that an economic slowdown would be countered by a reduction in interest rates and/or a reduction in tax rates and/or an increase in government spending. Signs of 'overheating' in the economy would be met by the reverse of these measures, sometimes combined with restrictions on the availability of credit for consumers. The technique was known as 'monetary magic', until its magical properties became suspect in the 1970s.

The term Fabian politics is employed as a convenient label for two different but related commitments. The first was a commitment to centralised planning, a mixed economy and extensive social security. The second was a commitment to Parliamentary methods and to decisions made in London by an informed elite who were not greatly influenced by grass-roots pressures. The Fabian approach to politics emphasised incremental reforms and made sharp reversals of policy seem inappropriate. The Conservative government that took office in 1951 followed this approach in that it made no attempt to repeal more than about a fifth of the reforms introduced by the Labour government of 1945–51. It was not until 1974 that Britain acquired a government that made a systematic attempt to undo virtually all the changes made by its predecessor. Such a policy would have caused consternation in the 1950s.

The rather high-minded liberal principles of the prevailing ideology were reflected in the abhorrence with which virtually all British politicians and political commentators viewed American security policies during the McCarthy era. They were also reflected in the commitment to rapid decolonisation in Macmillan's speech in South Africa about the 'wind of change' that was sweeping across Africa, and in a touching faith (which evaporated during the 1960s) that Britain could bridge the gap between the advanced nations and the Third World by its leadership of the Commonwealth. The Suez expedition was clearly incompatible with these principles, and while Eden was supported by mass opinion in this venture he was heavily criticised by many sections of informed opinion. The moral outrage of Labour party leaders at this reversion to gunboat diplomacy stood in sharp contrast to the tough-minded attitude of French Socialist party leaders to the same crisis.

The most controversial and extraordinary example of the particular kind of liberalism which held sway in the 1950s, however, was the attitude of virtually the entire educated elite to the immigration of Indians, Pakistanis and West Indians which started in 1955. When the general public became aware of this development their attitude was one of unequivocal hostility to it, public opinion polls showing that between 80 and 85 per cent of the electorate believed immigration to be undesirable. This public hostility was accompanied by quiet but growing protests from local authorities who had to cope with the problem of housing and educating the immigrants, but the attitude of Home Office officials and the Conservative Home Secretary (supported by *The Times*, the *Guardian*, and the intellectual weeklies) was one of bland moral superiority. The immigrants were British subjects; it was a tradition that British subjects (all 700 million of them) should have unrestricted entry to Britain; public concern about the development was illiberal, if not racist; and the Home Office would not even publish figures showing the number of arrivals. This refusal was sometimes justified on the unconvincing ground that statistics were not kept in that form at the ports of entry, but Home Office spokesmen made little attempt to conceal their view that the public were best kept in ignorance of inconvenient facts of this kind.

III

The widespread complacency which surrounded this system of government in the 1950s disappeared between 1959 and 1966. Public pressure forced the government to change its policies towards Commonwealth immigration, but general disenchantment with the system arose not from dislike of particular policies or institutions but from the realisation that in the economic field Britain's European competitors were doing much better than Britain was. The post-war rate of economic growth, which was between 2.5 and 3 per cent per year, was not significantly different from Britain's growth rate in earlier decades or the American growth rate in the post-war years. What was different was that France, West Germany and other industrial countries were now growing much faster and offering severe competition in Britain's export markets.

The British public became concerned about this at the beginning of the 1960s. In 1960 various informed commentators drew attention to the superior economic performance of Britain's neighbours, and the extended credit restrictions that had to be imposed in the spring of 1961 made a severe dent in the complacency of the wider public. During this period, newspapers and journals published numerous league tables showing that Britain lagged behind her competitors in productivity, in rates of investment, in rates of economic growth, in the growth of exports, in the number of engineers and scientists being trained at universities and so on. The feeling became widespread that things were wrong and changes were needed. Harold Macmillan's government, moving with reasonable speed, made four significant innovations in the twelve months following June 1961: the establishment of the National Economic Development Council, the creation of the National Incomes Commission, the first application to join the European Economic Community, and the appointment of the Robbins Committee to make plans for the expansion of higher education. But the new mood of criticism was not satisfied by these moves, none of which brought about any immediate improvement in the economy, and the institutions of Whitehall came under widespread attack.

The first target, not surprisingly, was the Treasury, whose control of the economy was now widely criticised as unsuccessful. The Labour government elected in 1964 decided that drastic measures were needed to free the economy from the dead hand of Treasury control, and they set about this by creating a rival department, the Department of Economic Affairs, to take over many of the Treasury's functions and to prepare a National Plan for economic growth. This was an absurd experiment, doomed to failure. The division of functions between the departments gave the DEA control over long-term planning while leaving the Treasury with day-to-day control of financial matters. It was like a division of functions between husband and wife in which the wife did the shopping, paid the bills and managed the family bank account, while the husband compiled an elaborate dossier on the kind of mansion into which they might move if their financial situation ever permitted it. By the time the National Plan was published it was already outdated – 'had been overtaken by events' was the official euphemism – and in due course the DEA was quietly abolished.

A second target for the reformers was the civil service, or to be more precise the administrative class of the civil service. There was a long-standing tradition of criticism of this class by left-wing academics, on the grounds that its members were recruited in disproportionate numbers from the public schools and in wildly disproportionate numbers from Oxford and Cambridge. In the 1950s Oxford and Cambridge graduates took over 80 per cent of the places filled by open competition (as distinct from internal promotion). This criticism was now supplemented by a series of further complaints. It was said that not enough scientists and economists were recruited into the administrative class, that recruits were not given any systematic form of post-entry training, and that little attempt was made to develop (or reward) managerial skills. It became fashionable to link these criticisms loosely to the allegation that Whitehall was run by gentlemen amateurs.

Unfortunately, these criticisms were rarely developed in a penetrating or constructive way. Broadly speaking, there are three possible bases for criticism of an established institution like the civil service: in terms of observed failings that everyone recognises as failings; in terms of the values and ideologies of the critics; and in terms of an alternative model that can plausibly be portrayed as superior. Now, the most obvious of the agreed failings of Whitehall in the 1950s and 1960s involved an apparent inability to make accurate financial estimates for capital projects, combined with expensive failures to check the estimates and accounts of firms working on government contracts, such as Ferranti and Bristol-Siddeley. A criticism based on observed faults would therefore have led to the suggestion that the civil service needed more recruits trained in accountancy. However, none of the critics even mentioned this as a possibility.

With one notable exception, the criticisms were ideological in character: that is, they reflected the personal values of the critics. The attack on the dominance of Oxford and Cambridge graduates among the recruits was understandable, but it was not linked to an argument about efficiency. None of the critics maintained that Oxford and Cambridge gave a poorer education than other universities and none analysed the careers of higher civil servants to determine whether graduates of other universities were more successful, either in terms of promotion or in terms of a smaller propensity to be associated with administrative blunders or short-sighted policies.[4] Similarly, little attempt was made to explain why people with degrees in physics or chemistry would make better administrators than people with degrees in history or classics. The case for an education in economics was argued fairly often, but it did not square very well with the fact that the Treasury, so often singled out for criticism, contained a respectable number of economists among its senior staff. The argument about managerial skills seemed tangential to the main problem, since in Whitehall members of the administrative class had only a general and indirect responsibility for managerial activities, which were carried out, in a manner which was widely regarded as highly efficient, by members of the executive and departmental classes.

The one notable exception among the critics was Brian Chapman, whose criticisms of Whitehall were based on his belief in the superiority of an alternative model, namely the public services of France and several other continental democracies.[5] In Chapman's view, British higher civil servants compared poorly with their French and German equivalents not because their original university educations were poorer but because they lacked the subsequent training in the social sciences that French and German recruits received, and they also lacked the knowledge of their own countries, outside of the capital city, that the latter acquired in their early years of service. Chapman pointed out that 'the young German civil servant will spend time in local government, in a ministry, in some branch of the law courts: the young French civil servant will spend his first year serving as personal assistant to a prefect in the provinces, and at a later stage will spend a further period in a bank, a trade union, or an industrial or commercial concern'.[6] By comparison, British senior officials spent their entire careers in the relatively closed world of Whitehall, and lacked the worldly wisdom that they needed to provide effective leadership in economic and industrial planning.

The present author, who started his career in the administrative class of the British civil service, does not doubt that Chapman's view was broadly correct, and some confirmation of it can be found in the comments of other observers. Richard Chapman's portrait of higher civil servants yields a rather similar characterisation: highly intelligent people whose development is somewhat confined by their professional experience in Whitehall.[7] Hugh Heclo and Aaron Wildavsky refer to the senior civil service as having some of the characteristics of a private club.[8] Sir John Rothenstein, formerly Director of the Tate Gallery, has described the Treasury as 'a world of candour, of justice, of concern for the truth, above all perhaps of composure and tranquility'.[9] These are not the terms that would be used by an informed observer asked to describe the merits of the French Commissariat Général au Plan.

Early in 1966 the government appointed the Fulton Committee to propose reforms in the recruitment and organisation of the civil service. In its report the Committee endorsed virtually all the criticisms that were current, and declared that their intention was to remodel the service so as to fit it for the tasks of government in the last third of the twentieth century.[10] However, their recommendations were not as specific as they might have been, and some of them were couched in terms which gave a misleading impression of radicalism. Thus, the proposal that 'all classes should be abolished' did not mean that they really wanted a classless service (whatever that would be), merely that the distinction between the executive and the administrative classes should be blurred during the first few years after recruitment. The proposal to create a new Civil Service Department meant little more than that the officials working in the Civil Service Commission and the relevant sections of the Treasury should be put under one roof and given a new title. The considerable emphasis given to the development of management skills was misleading in so far as it gave the impression that management was a new concept in Whitehall. As one senior civil servant has pointed out, the mythology about management that developed in the late 1960s can best be compared with the pronouncements made in the same period which seemed 'to suggest that sex [was] a novelty or that fornication [had] just been discovered'.[11] In addition, one of the recommendations that might have made a considerable difference, namely that preference in recruitment should be given to graduates in 'relevant subjects' like the social sciences, was rejected by the government.

The effects of the Fulton Report were therefore less dramatic than might be supposed from a first reading of the document, but they were nevertheless considerable, and can be outlined briefly.

1. The blurring of the distinction between the executive and administrative classes has had a beneficial effect on the recruitment of university graduates. Before this change, there was a marked gap between the really brilliant graduates who managed to secure appointment to the administrative class (rarely more than 50 a year) and the usually mediocre graduates who were content to enter the executive class. This gap has now disappeared and the service has consequently been able to recruit numbers of gifted young people who would previously have failed to make the one and not been interested in the other. In 1977, for instance, 127 young recruits were appointed as administrative trainees in the home and diplomatic services.[12]
2. Each year a number of mature persons are recruited into senior positions, usually after about 8 or 10 years in some other occupation. This clearly widens the experience of the service and enables the government to seek persons with particular skills for particular vacancies. In the 5 years from 1973–7, 141 recruits from outside the service were appointed by direct entry as Principals, the main career grade in the higher civil service.[13]
3. The Civil Service College has been created to provide post-entry training for senior officials. The responsibility for increasing the expertise of civil servants rests almost entirely on this College, in view of the decision not to give any preference to social scientists at the time of general recruitment. As the majority of the most talented would-be administrators study subjects other than the social sciences while at university in Britain, this decision was almost certainly correct, but it made the work of the College even more crucial. Unfortunately, few informed observers regard the College as particularly successful. Its courses last only 4 or 5 months, which is simply not long enough to give a thorough training since the majority of students have no previous knowledge of economics, statistics, computation, or social and public administration. The staff of the College, through entirely competent, are not generally regarded as brilliant or outstandingly creative. The opportunity existed to appoint people from the business and academic worlds who were leaders in their own fields and could have presented the students with stimulating ideas, but this opportunity was not taken. Moreover, some of the academics who joined the College at its inception have now been replaced by civil servants. The latter may be excellent teachers, but the inevitable consequence is that the College courses socialise young recruits into the long-established Whitehall community and do relatively little to

widen their intellectual horizons or acquaint them with the realities of life in industry and commerce. The Civil Service College is simply not the equivalent of the French Ecole Nationale d'Administration, with its 3-year course, distinguished professors, and practice of seconding students for periods of practical work in large business firms or local public authorities.

4. Since the publication of the Fulton Report in 1968 successive governments have followed the recommendation that administrative organisations performing specialised services of various kinds should be 'hived off' to partially autonomous public agencies. The consequence has been a further proliferation of the bewildering variety of quasi-autonomous government boards, commissions, services, agencies and executives which confuse students of British public administration, to say nothing of the British public. This development blurs and weakens the lines of democratic control of the administrative authorities involved. It is quite impossible to give any general answer to the question of whether there has been any compensating improvement in administrative efficiency.
5. The Fulton Committee declared that the administrative process was too secret and recommended more openness and more public consultation before decisions are made. The consequence has been the emergence of official discussion documents, known as Green Papers, together with some modifications to the Official Secrets Act. However, the law about official secrets remains stringent and the Green Papers have only occasionally opened up an issue for effective public discussion. By North American or Scandinavian standards, the process of executive government in Britain remains extremely secretive.

Another widespread complaint of the 1960s was that the attachment of civil servants to established departmental policies made it difficult for incoming ministers to reshape policy. It is impossible to read R. H. S. Crossman's diaries or Joe Haines' revelations without feeling some sympathy for this point of view.[14] It must be extremely frustrating, for instance, for a minister wishing to do battle with another minister over a conflict between their departments to discover that his senior officials have already conceded defeat in a private meeting with senior officials of the rival department. Since 1964 a number of Labour ministers have attempted to strengthen their position by appointing personal assistants sympathetic to their own political viewpoint, a practice which has long been common in France, but is, as might be expected, somewhat unpopular with Whitehall officials. In 1978 there were about 40 such policy advisers.

Unfortunately, the general case for strengthening the arm of politicians in the Whitehall departments is somewhat weakened by the fact that the economic and industrial decisions that have proved most costly in recent years have nearly all been taken by ministers with the approval of the Cabinet. Since ministers are briefed by civil servants it is difficult to allocate responsibility precisely, but there can be little doubt that the following decisions, all very expensive in economic terms, were taken after lively discussion at the ministerial level, and that in many cases the reasons for the decision were essentially political. The decisions, in chronological order, are: the government-sponsored merger of Jaguar, Leyland and Triumph (all small but efficient automobile firms) with the gigantic but inefficient British Motor Corporation; the decision to devote most of the resources of the aircraft industry to the production of a certain loss-maker in Concorde; the subsidies given to obsolete and uncompetitive shipyards on the Clyde; the abortive plan to build a Channel tunnel; the decision to save British Leyland from the consequences of bankruptcy by massive government subsidies, inflated by the decision to keep all its plants open instead of concentrating production in those which were at least relatively productive; and the truly astonishing decision to put even more taxpayers' money into the maintenance of excess capacity in the automobile industry by subsidising Chrysler. The cumulative consequence of these decisions is that massive public investment, which could have equipped the country with one or more major new industries, has (in economic terms) been poured down the drain. And although in some of these cases ministers may have been given bad advice by bureaucrats, it would be quite wrong to suggest that more political advisers in Whitehall would have resulted in better decisions, since a major factor in all these cases was the desire of ministers to acquire political credit in the form of prestige, electoral popularity, or popularity with trade unions.

The general zeal for administrative reform that developed during the 1960s affected the titles and structure of government departments as well as the recruitment and training of public officials. The Ministry of Education became the Department of Education and Science. A Ministry of Technology was created, to disappear a few years later when people lost faith in technology. The Ministry of Labour became the Department of Employment and Productivity, though the second half of this title was quietly dropped when productivity failed to meet expectations. The Board of Trade was merged into a gigantic conglomerate known as the Department of Trade and Industry. After a few years this conglomerate gave way to four separate departments, known respectively as the Departments of Industry, Trade, Energy and Prices and Consumer Protection. The Ministry of Health was absorbed into the Department of Health and Social Security. When it became fashionable to worry about the environment, a Department of the Environment was created, this trendy title covered a variety of mundane responsibilities which included transport, municipal housing, public works and sewerage.

It would be hard to say that these and similar changes had any significant impact on the efficiency of central government. The experience of people who had regular dealings with these departments would seem to confirm the hypothesis that changes in institutions are apt to make little difference unless they are accompanied by changes in personnel. Local government officials noticed that, irrespective of the title of their department, Whitehall officials dealing with transport tended to wield all the powers available to them, for example by controlling speed limits and traffic lights, while Whitehall officials dealing with public health tended to adopt a more *laissez-faire* attitude, for instance by refusing to issue regulations about the fluoridation of water supplies. The real significance of these changes in administrative structure was not that they improved the system of government but that they signified growing discontent with it.

IV

The impact on public opinion of all these reforms, few of which resulted in changes that could clearly be recognised as improvements, was not positive. It was evident that Britain's economic situation was deteriorating and it did not seem that either of the main political parties had an answer to this problem. Moreover, many people lost faith in the principles that had underlain the governmental system of the 1950s. After 1973, the development of large-scale unemployment combined with rapid inflation undermined the confidence that people had had for the previous 30 years in the principles of Keynesian economics. In the vulgarised version of Keynesian theory that was popularly accepted, unemployment and inflation were seen to be alternatives, so that an increase in one would result in a reduction of the other. Faith flew out of the window when both grew simultaneously.

At the same time the Fabian approach to politics also fell out of favour. In the Labour party the leading Fabians lost influence, first because of Hugh Gaitskell's death and later because of their continued adherence to the view that Britain should join the EEC during Harold Wilson's temporary conversion to the opposite view. Debates in the Labour party were between pragmatists and radicals, with the old-style Fabians increasingly isolated. In the Conservative party, there was a perceptible movement to the right in philosophy and style, if not in actual policies. When Harold Macmillan came out of retirement in the mid-1970s to make a television appeal to leaders of all parties to unite to face the economic crisis, his appeal was ignored as irrelevant to the party battle.

Even the liberal principles of the 1950s came to lose their hold. The high-minded attitude that Home Office spokesmen had taken towards Commonwealth immigration gave way to a much harder attitude. The Labour party leadership became more tough-minded as Fabians were replaced by pragmatists. As one well-informed observer has noted: 'With Hugh Gaitskell's death . . . the main driving force of the Labour opposition to immigration control disappeared.'[15] In 1968 Parliament passed an Act to exclude East African Asians who were actually British citizens, not merely British subjects. The optimism which the mass media had expressed about black Commonwealth Africa was destroyed by the cumulative impact of the civil war in Nigeria, the success of military coups in several countries, the expulsion of Asians from Kenya and Uganda, the tendency of African leaders to side with Arab and Communist states over the conflict in the Middle East and the murderous regime of Idi Amin.

This erosion of belief in the governing principles that had supported national politics has led to a variety of reactions, which can be summarised briefly under four main headings.

First, there are still some academics and politicians who are 'pragmatists', in William Gwyn's use of the term: they believe that further reforms, e.g. of Parliament rather than the administration, might lead to major improvements. The main object of these critics is to develop more constructive debates in Parliament and to lower the volume of what Balfour called 'the never-ending din of political conflict'. It was hoped in the 1960s that the introduction of specialised committees of the House of Commons would serve this purpose, but the committees introduced since 1966 have not been as successful as their advocates had expected. They have given some backbench MPs the opportunity to become more specialised and more knowledgeable in particular fields, but there is no rush to serve on these committees, their reports attract little attention, and they have not extended the power of Parliament over the administration to a significant degree. The ambitious backbencher is far more likely to advance his career by lively contributions to abusive debates on the floor of the House than he is by patient work in specialised committees.[16]

A further development since 1974 has been the emergence of a group of critics, drawn from all parties, who believe that steps should be taken to reduce the adversarial aspect of British politics.[17] The institutional change which they think might have this effect is the introduction of proportional representation, and there is now a pressure group within the Conservative party which has this aim, known as Conservative Action for Electoral Reform. In the short term the prospects of success for this group are not at all good, and they have been harmed by the evidence that the present generation of Liberal MPs have more sympathy for the Labour party than for the Conservatives, so that electoral reform would probably lead to a series of Labour–Liberal coalition governments. But it is just possible that in the long run this movement of opinion may prove to be significant.

A second group of critics would probably have to be put in Gwyn's category of 'jeremiahs', for they believe that British government now suffers from a chronic condition of 'overload'. This is not the place to summarise the extensive literature on this topic,[18] but two contributions to it may usefully be mentioned. At a rather specific level of analysis, Richard Rose and Guy Peters have shown that there is now a built-in tendency for the costs of government services to grow more quickly than the national product, to such an extent that increased governmental expenditures may absorb the whole of the extra wealth produced by higher productivity. During the years 1971–7, the increase in governmental expenditures in Britain was almost one-third more than the growth in the GDP.[19] The consequence was that the working population experienced a net reduction in disposable real income in spite of the fact that the country became wealthier. The difficulty of urging wage restraint on trade unions in such a situation is obvious, and the growth of discontent with the system is not surprising.

In a much more general analysis, Anthony King has argued that Britain has become a more difficult country to govern in the past two decades because public expectations of what the government can do to promote the general welfare have increased markedly while the capacity of the government to achieve the desired ends has decreased.[20] This decrease in capacity is not, in King's view, something for which individual politicians or bureaucrats can reasonably be blamed: its main cause is that the increasing complexity of modern industrial society, combined with the increasing responsibilities of government, has made governments dependent on behaviour which they cannot control. As he puts it, 'The number of dependency relationships in which government is involved has increased substantially', while 'the incidence of acts of non-compliance by the other participants in these relationships has also increased substantially'.[21]

This is a depressing analysis because it is extremely difficult to envisage any reduction in the responsibilities of government. Moreover, the successive failures of government to live up to public expectations are almost certain to reduce confidence in the system and its leaders. As King remarks: 'Once upon a time . . . man looked to God to order the world. Then he looked to the market. Now he looks to government.' And when things go wrong the public blame 'not "Him" or "it" but "them".'[22] It is therefore reasonable to expect a gradual erosion of governmental authority and an increase in the incidence of acts of non-compliance. There may be a 'political multiplier effect in this situation.

If we turn from academic analyses to public behaviour, it is clear that the 1970s have indeed been marked by an increase in such acts. Though it is inherently difficult to produce statistical evidence, most informed observers agree that there has been an increase in individual acts of tax avoidance and tax evasion. More obviously, interest groups of all kinds have engaged in militant forms of 'direct action' that would have been thought out of bounds in the 1950s. In 1971 the Trades Union Congress instructed affiliated unions to refuse to comply with the requirements of the Industrial Relations Act. On several occasions unions deliberately put themselves into contempt of court by refusing to appear before the Industrial Relations Court or refusing to obey the Court's injunctions. In Clydebank, a bankrupt shipyard was occupied by workers to prevent the liquidator appointed by the government from carrying out his duties. During the 1972 miners' strike many thousands of workers took part in illegal and potentially violent picketing, at power stations and other places of work which were not directly involved in the dispute.

In the Derbyshire town of Clay Cross the Labour majority on the town council refused to apply the provisions of the Housing Finance Act, in open defiance of the law. In some areas hospital porters have refused to allow meals to be served to private patients, in an attempt to sabotage private medical practice. In other areas junior hospital doctors refused to work overtime because of a pay dispute, thus disrupting medical services and jeopardising the recovery of their patients. The tendency of people without houses to 'squat' in non-occupied premises, from which they then forcibly repelled the owner or his agents, grew to such an extent that at one stage there were said to be over 20,000 squatters in London alone. Housewives who wanted a ban on trucks in a residential suburb have sat down in the road with their babies to block the traffic. Groups opposed to road improvements or other public works projects discovered that they could hold these up indefinitely if they could first insist on a public enquiry and then create so much disturbance at the enquiry that the inspector was unable either to hear the witnesses or to be heard himself. One highly respectable charitable foundation, the Rountree Trust, actually decided to pay the salary of a pressure group organiser who specialises in the disruption of public enquiries. No observer in the 1970s could say that British political behaviour was characterised by deference, as some observers said in the 1950s.

A fourth reaction to the perceived failures of government has been a withdrawal of public support from the two main parties. Both Conservative and Labour parties have suffered a considerable loss of membership. Their youth movements have faded away and their constituency organisations are, in general, much weaker than they used to be. Neither party has accurate figures of membership, but both have expressed concern about the situation, very seriously in the case of the Labour party. At the polls in 1974 the electors turned away from the main parties in their millions. In England they turned to the Liberal party, in Scotland to the Scottish National Party, in Wales (though not so dramatically) to Plaid Cymru. Between the elections of 1970 and February 1974 the proportion of the vote cast for minor parties rose from 8.0 per cent to 22.1 per cent in England, from 17.3 per cent to 30.3 per cent in Scotland and from 18.7 per cent to 27.3 per cent in Wales. There was also an increasing tendency for people to abstain from voting in general elections. The combined consequence of all these factors is that the proportion of the registered electorate voting for the two main parties fell from 80 per cent in 1951 to 56 per cent in October 1974. The Labour government was supported by only 29 per cent of the electors in October 1974, a slender basis for the renewal of a popular mandate to govern. The proportion of the electorate voting for the two main parties rose in 1979, but still constituted only 61 per cent of the total registered electorate.

These changes in voting behaviour have had an effect on Parliament and Whitehall which may prove to be greater than all the institutional reforms outlined above. For most of the 1974–9 period the government of the day was in a minority in the House of Commons. The Liberals gained influence and were able to force the government to accept minor changes in the Budget. The Scottish and Welsh nationalists gained so much influence that the government devoted most of the 1977–8 session to bills to create Scottish and Welsh Assemblies. Government backbenchers secured the amendment of several pieces of legislation, to the great annoyance of their party leaders. The House of Lords gained influence and was able to defeat (in essence if not in form) the Dock Labour Bill which the Government had promised the Transport and General Workers' Union would be passed. It remains to be seen whether the Conservative Government elected with a solid parliamentary majority in 1979 can revert to the status quo ante formula of executive dominance of Parliament.

V

Is there any hope for an improvement in governmental performance in the foreseeable future? It would be a brave man who would offer a definite answer to this question, but certain possibilities can be identified. First, although the civil service reforms following the Fulton Report have not been dramatic, they constitute a clear improvement that may become significant as recent recruits reach senior positions. Second, ministers are now aware of the problems created by year-by-year increases in public expenditure and, with firm encouragement from the International Monetary Fund, steps have been taken to check this. Third, the economic expansion made possible by North Sea oil may create an increase in GDP greater than the increase in public expenditure, thus leaving room for a general increase in take-home pay and a possible relaxation of some of the tensions of the 1970s.

Beyond this, there is little hope of improvement from administrative reorganisation and no hope of the British creating an effective system of national economic planning on French lines. A Conservative government might cut out some of the wasteful subsidies given to inefficient industries and might reduce the excessive power now wielded by trade unions, but the cost of any radical changes on these lines would probably be a period of strikes and economic disruption. British membership of the EEC has resulted in the transfer of certain decision-making powers from London to Brussels, where they can be exercised within a wider frame of reference and with more freedom from political pressures. However, no British government is likely to support an extension of EEC powers while the greater part of the EEC budget is devoted to an agricultural policy inimical to British interests. While there are some grounds on which to hope for an improvement in governmental decision-making, there is no clear reason to expect dramatic improvement.

NOTES

1. Hugh Heclo and Aaron Wildavsky, *The Private Government of Public Money* (London: Macmillan, 1974) p. 348.
2. Dennis Kavanagh, 'The Deferential English: A Comparative Critique', in Richard Rose (ed.), *Studies in British Politics*, 3rd ed. (London: Macmillan, 1976) p. 70.
3. American Political Science Association, *Towards a More Responsible Two-Party System* (New York: Rinehart, 1950).
4. In 1976 a study was published showing that, among the recruits of 1946–50, Oxford graduates had been the most likely to get rapid promotion, with Cambridge graduates second and other graduates third. See Peta Sheriff, *Career Patterns in the Higher Civil Service* (London: HMSO, 1976) p. 65.
5. See Brian Chapman, *British Government Observed* (London: Allen & Unwin, 1963).
6. Ibid., p. 26.
7. See R. A. Chapman, *The Higher Civil Service in Britain* (London: Constable, 1970). (The two Chapmans are not related.)
8. Heclo and Wildavsky, *Private Government of Public Money*.
9. John Rothenstein, *Brave Day, Hideous Night* (London: Hamish Hamilton, 1966) p. 252.
10. *Report of the Committee on the Civil Service*, Cmnd no. 3638 (London: HMSO, 1968).
11. C. H. Sisson, 'The Civil Service After Fulton', in W. J. Stankiewicz (ed.), *British Government in an Era of Reform* (London: Collier Macmillan, 1976) p. 256.
12. *Civil Service Commission Annual Report, 1977* (Basingstoke: Civil Service Commission, 1978) pp. 16–17.
13. Information supplied by Civil Service Commission.
14. R. H. S. Crossman, *The Diaries of a Cabinet Minister* (London: Hamish Hamilton and Jonathan Cape, 1976); and Joe Haines, *The Politics of Power* (London: Jonathan Cape, 1977).
15. Nicholas Deakin, 'The Politics of the Commonwealth Immigrants Bill', *Political Quarterly*, XXXIX (1968) 42.
16. On the work and impact of specialised committees, see Frank Stacey, *British Government: 1966 to 1975* (London: Oxford University Press, 1975) ch. 3; and Alfred Morris (ed.), *The Growth of Parliamentary Scrutiny by Committee* (Oxford: Pergamon, 1970).
17. See S. E. Finer (ed.), *Adversary Politics and Electoral Reform* (London: Anthony Wigram, 1975).
18. For a useful survey of the literature up to the end of 1975, see James Douglas, 'The Overloaded Crown', *British Journal of Political Science*, VI (1976) 483–505.
19. Richard Rose and B. Guy Peters, *The Juggernaut of Incrementalism* (Glasgow: University of Strathclyde, 1978) p. 19. See also Rose and Peters, *Can Government Go Bankrupt?* (London: Macmillan, 1979).
20. See Anthony King, 'Overload: Problems of Governing in the 1970s', *Political Studies*, XXIII (1975) 284–96.
21. Ibid., p. 290.
22. Ibid., p. 288.

5 From Gentlemen to Players: Changes in Political Leadership

Dennis Kavanagh

> It is a very difficult country to move, Mr Hyndman, a very difficult country indeed, and one in which there is more disappointment to be looked for than success.
>
> Disraeli (1881)

I

Only a generation ago Britain's political institutions were the object of widespread admiration. Churchill's war-time leadership, the successful mobilisation of people and resources against Hitler and the Attlee government's achievements in social welfare and economic reconstruction all provided evidence of the ability of the institutions and leaders to cope with problems and maintain consent.

That admired political leadership emerged from the inter-play of a number of features. These included:

(1) the *political institutions*: the existence of disciplined, programmatic parties facilitated one-party majority government, and the concentration of formal political power in the Cabinet provided coherent, stable government;
(2) a *governing class*: this was drawn largely from the upper and upper middle classes, which had a long tradition of exercising political authority;
(3) the *political culture*: this included a consensus about political procedures, an incremental approach to bringing about change and trust in government and leaders.

Amidst growing criticism of the British political system there have been significant alterations in each of the three features mentioned above. First, the declining support for the two main parties and a fragmentation of the party system have already produced two periods of minority government since February 1974, and limited the Cabinet's ability to dominate the legislature. Membership of the EEC and referenda pose further challenges to established forms of political leadership. Second, there has been a trend towards the recruitment of *meritocrats*, or well-educated, self-made professional politicians, away from the *patricians*, who moved almost as a matter of course into public life, and the *proletarians*. The new generation of top political leaders is drawn from people whose social backgrounds are more modest than those of Attlee, Gaitskell, Churchill, Butler and Macmillan and yet more elevated than those of Morrison, Bevin or Bevan. Finally, there is sign of a less *deferential culture*. The authority of government is less secure. A Parliamentary majority securing the passage of legislation says little about a government's ability to gain compliance from society.

This paper focuses on two aspects of change among the post-war British political leaders. In *composition* there has been a marked *embourgeoisement* of the new generation of leaders. In *political style* there occurred a move in the 1960s to one which was oriented to change. Study of the composition is relatively straightforward and the subject is well-documented. The notion of political style, however, is more elusive and less easy to measure. By a style of leadership, I am referring to the leader's purpose or objects in politics and how he tries to achieve them. One broad distinction is between routine and crises styles of leadership, in which there is a conjunction of the leader's style and circumstances. For example, the political crises associated with the two great wars this century opened the way for Lloyd George in 1916 and Churchill in 1940.[1] The dynamism of both men had previously made them widely distrusted and, except for the war years, they spent long periods in the political wilderness. But a more useful distinction for our immediate purpose is between styles which are *mobilising* (emphasising decisions and task-performance, particularly a change in the status quo) and *expressive* (emphasising the maintenance of consensus and cohesion). The distinction is not dissimilar from David Apter's mobilising and conciliatory leader.[2] The former is mainly concerned to achieve his goals, and not overly concerned about opposition and the costs of disturbance; the latter is more concerned to represent and respond to diverse interests and arrive at compromises, if necessary sacrificing policy goals, as long as group unity is maintained.

Effective leaders have to take account of both role demands. It is possible, however, to classify most British Prime Ministers according to the relative importance they attached to being either mobilising or expressive leaders. For example, Stanley Baldwin and Ramsay MacDonald, both by temperament and political conviction belong in the latter category. They saw themselves as reconcilers, within and between parties, were weak partisans, and limited changes to those which would least disturb the social fabric. Churchill, as a peace-time Prime Minister, was concerned to live down the memories of his record in the 1920s and to promote social peace and placate organised labour. Joseph Chamberlain and Lloyd George are classic cases of mobilisers. Chamberlain campaigned for social reform and then tariff reform. Lloyd George, before 1914, was a powerful advocate of social reforms and then rearmament and, after 1928, measures to combat unemployment. Neither man was a respecter of party lines and both were widely distrusted among Parliamentary colleagues. Hugh Gaitskell's commitment to new goals provoked intense opposition, inside and outside of the Labour party. Attlee and Macmillan are difficult to cast in one or other group. Attlee's government took many important decisions but, as leader, he did not himself initiate a policy that would create divisions and was careful to align himself with the majority on divisive issues. Mr Macmillan straddles both groups. He was a skilled party manager, attentive to the needs of party unity, but who also managed to set in train a number of new policies.

The mobilising or instrumental style has a greater appeal when there is dissatisfaction with the status quo, a sense that new directions and policies are required. This has been cyclical in Britain. Such a mood developed in Britain in the early 1960s. The election of Harold Wilson as leader of the Labour party in 1963 and Edward Heath as leader of the Conservatives in 1965 introduced younger men who self-consciously distinguished themselves from their predecessors. Changes in political generations coincided with new types and styles of leadership from the era of Attlee and Churchill. It is tempting to perceive a relationship between the two themes of social background and styles, a transition from political leadership as a *status* (a position occupied by someone of high social status, and whose style is primarily expressive) to leadership as an *activity* (the leader as a person who is concerned with mobilising resources and doing things). However, I shall argue that there is little relationship between the two: in part the new men simply invoked new rhetoric and in part they accommodated themselves to a cyclical demand for change.

II Composition

Historically, political leadership in Britain has been exercised by men of high birth and breeding. The effects of universal suffrage, organised mass political parties, increasing professionalisation of political life, and decline of the landed interest have combined to erode the political influence of the aristocracy. But men from an upper class background have stubbornly retained a large hold in Parliament and Cabinet.[3] Of the members of Cabinets from 1884 to 1924 (the year of the first Labour government), 43 per cent were aristocrats (born or married into titled families); between 1933 and 1964 the figure was still an impressive 26 per cent. For the same two periods the proportion of ministers educated at expensive public schools actually increased from half to three-quarters. Yet there have been some interesting changes in recent years.

Labour

Before the war there were stark differences in the social backgrounds of Conservative and Labour MPs. Conservative MPs were drawn largely from the upper middle and middle classes and usually attended public school followed by Oxbridge. Many Labour MPs, on the other hand, came from the ranks of manual workers or trade union officials and, before 1922, few had attended a university. The party, indeed, had been formed in 1900 explicitly to increase representation of the working class in the House of Commons, when the Conservative and Liberal parties refused to adopt working class men as candidates. In terms of Parliamentary representation the party system at that time institutionalised class differences.

Since 1922 and, *a fortiori*, since 1945, embourgeoisement of the Labour party has produced a remarkable narrowing of this social 'gap'. Both parties now draw their MPs mainly from the ranks of the professions and the graduate middle class, though Labour still has a (shrinking) minority from the working class. Between 1906 and 1918, 89 per cent of Labour MPs were working class and between 1922 and 1935 the figure was still 71 per cent.[4] Since 1945, however, an average of 34 per cent have been former manual workers; the figure dropped to 29 per cent in the 1974 Parliament and the proportion is even smaller if we consider newly-recruited MPs. Even trade union sponsorship, originally a device for recruiting workers to Parliament, is increasingly offered to university graduates and people with no background in industry.[5]

The main 'switchboard' for entry to politics now is attendance at a university, usually by way of public school and then Oxbridge for a Conservative, or by grammar school and then non-Oxbridge for a Labour MP (though Oxbridge for Labour ministers). Emphasis on academic achievement for political recruitment and promotion has particularly affected the type of Labour MP. The 1944 Education Act enabled more children from the working and lower middle classes to enter grammar schools and universities and thereby achieve social mobility. Constituency selection committees increasingly see ability as requiring a university degree and professional qualifications.[6]

The shift to recruitment by educational merit is shown in Table 5.1, which presents figures on the education of MPs after the general elections of 1945, 1959 and 1979. This shows the proportion of MPs whose education has been purely prestigious (public school only), purely meritocratic (non-public school and university), prestigious and meritocratic (both public school and university) and lacking both prestige and merit.[7] The most striking change has occurred on the Labour side, with the median MP changing from one whose education lacks both merit and prestige in 1945 and 1959 to one who now has merit, i.e. a university degree. Between 1945 and 1979, while the proportion of graduates grew on the Conservative side from 59 per cent to 68 per cent, on the Labour side it grew from 33 per cent to 53 per cent.

TABLE 5.1 Prestige and merit in the education of politicians

Type of education	*1945* (%)	*1959* (%)	*1979* (%)
Conservative:			
Pure prestige	29	24	20
Pure merit	3	12	16
Prestige and merit	56	48	52
Neither	12	16	12
Numbers	213	365	339
Labour:			
Pure prestige	4	2	2
Pure merit	18	23	37
Prestige and merit	15	15	16
Neither	61	58	45
Numbers	400	258	269

Note: See text for details. Data for 1945 extracted from Colin Mellors, *The British MP* (Farnborough, Hants: Saxon House, 1978). For subsequent elections data drawn from Nuffield election studies.

There are, however, two distinct types of middle class members on the Labour and Conservative benches. First, although we lack authoritative data, many Labour MPs appear to be first generation middle class, having come from working or lower middle class homes, making their way *via* grammar schools and university into the professions and thereby acquiring skills useful for politics. Another contrast is that middle class Labour MPs are usually employed in the public sector, often in the service sphere, being teachers, lecturers, welfare and social workers. Conservative middle class MPs, on the other hand, usually come from comfortable middle class families, have been to public schools and are drawn from the private sector, being lawyers, accountants and business executives. As Johnson notes, in so far as the Labour MPs now send their own children to independent schools and universities, then they are a generation behind most Conservative MPs.[8]

If we turn to Cabinet appointments, the more interesting change is also on the Labour side. A feature of political recruitment in Britain, as in other societies, is that the higher one ascends the political hierarchy, the more socially and educationally exclusive it becomes. Cabinet ministers are usually of higher social and educational status than those ministers outside the Cabinet, who, in turn, stand above backbenchers.

In terms of social background, most Labour ministers have fallen into one of three broad groups. Labour has always found a place for the *patricians* (MPs who come from established upper middle class families, attended the prestigious public schools and Oxbridge and entered one of the professions).

Attlee, Dalton, Cripps and Gaitskell represented this *genre* and, more recently, Crossman, Gordon-Walker, Jay and Benn. In the inter-war years the party's willingness to find a place for men and women of high social standing, who often had previously been associated with other political parties, contrasted sharply with the practice of Socialist parties on the Continent.[9]

This group supplemented the *proletarians* (MPs from working-class families, who left school at an early age and then became manual workers, trade union organisers, or lowly clerical workers). Many of the pre-war leaders came from this second background. Herbert Morrison and Aneurin Bevan, who contested the 1955 leadership election with Hugh Gaitskell, and George Brown, who was runner-up to Wilson in 1963, were in this group. Table 5.2 shows that the Labour Cabinets of MacDonald, Attlee and Wilson in 1964 drew about half of their members from this group. During Mr Wilson's leadership, however, there was a steady exodus of proletarians from the Cabinet and they were replaced by the graduate middle-class ministers. By 1970 only three Cabinet ministers were drawn from this group. Although Mr Callaghan restored the social balance somewhat (the 1979 Cabinet contained Eric Varley and Roy Mason, both former miners,[10] Stan Orme, an ex-engineer and Albert Booth, an ex-draughtsman), the erosion of the working class element is clear.

TABLE 5.2 Social and educational composition of Labour Cabinets, 1924–76

Date	*Size*	*Aristo-cratic*	*Middle Class*	*Working Class*	*University (All*	*Oxbridge)*
1924	19	3	5	11	6	6
1929	20	2	4	12	6	3
1945	20	–	8	12	10	5
1964	23	1	14	8	13	11
1974 (Mar)	21	1	16	4	16	11
1976 (Apr)	22	1	13	7	15	10
Average	20	1.5	10	8.5	11.5	7.5

Source: D. E. Butler and Anne Sloman, *British Political Facts*, 5th ed. (London: Macmillan, 1979).

Notes: *Aristocrats* are those who had among their grandparents a holder of a hereditary title. *Working class* includes those whose fathers appear to have had a manual occupation when they were growing up. Schools are classified as public schools if members of the Headmasters' Conference.

The third group, now numerically and politically the most significant, are the *meritocrats*. These come from working or lower middle class backgrounds, attend state schools (usually winning scholarships to grammar schools) and go on to university. (In recent Labour Cabinets the group has been represented by such people as Wilson, Healey, Mrs Castle, Crosland, Dell, Hattersley, Shore, Rodgers, Rees and Jenkins.) These are scholarship boys and girls whose parents are from the working class or the lower ranks of the professions or white collar occupations. After university they usually enter the professions, becoming academics, journalists, consultants. In contrast to the proletarians their social mobility has been achieved prior to a political career by dint of going to university. The contrast is seen in the reflections of Clynes, waiting to be sworn in by the monarch as Labour's first Lord Privy Seal in 1924:

> I could not help marvelling at the strange turn of Fortune's wheel, which had brought MacDonald, the starveling clerk, Thomas the engine-driver, Henderson the foundry labourer and Clynes the mill-hand, to this pinnacle . . . .[11]

Any discussion of the changing social backgrounds of Labour MPs and ministers invites the question 'so what?'. It also has to take account of subtle differences in the political socialisation of members of the same objective social class. The gradual decline of working class members on the Labour benches is clear. The main source of supply of workers now is the trade unions and these are usually former officials, with desk-bound jobs. It is extremely difficult for a working class activist, a self-starter like MacDonald, Snowden or Morrison, to enter politics unless it is through a trade union. 'The political class' is now probably more homogeneous in occupational and educational terms than at any time since 1922 when Labour MPs were first returned in large numbers. It is already possible to discern the emergence of a Labour 'establishment', based on dynastic and kinship ties. In the 1974 Parliament children of former Labour MPs included Jenkins, Marquand, Foot, Benn, Janner, the Silkins, Mrs Summerskill and Mrs Dunwoody. They followed in the steps of Noel-Baker, Henderson, Cripps and others. And if we also took account of MPs who were the sons and daughters of trade union officials (e.g. Barbara Castle) or local Labour politicians (e.g. Roy Hattersley) then membership of a 'political family' would emerge as an important factor cutting across social class.[12]

Conservatives

On the Conservative side the change has been more modest. Compared to the inter-war years, the party has shed the aristocrats, landowners, big businessmen and idle rich. Hence, following the Maxwell-Fyffe reform (1949), which prohibited constituencies from accepting large donations from candidates and members – thereby helping the less affluent candidates – the type of Conservative MP has within limits broadened. Since the war only two Conservative MPs have been from the working class; the party stubbornly remains the preserve of upper middle class professional and business occupations. The proportion of MPs coming from public schools has remained steady at around 75 per cent and, though more MPs have a university education, the Oxbridge dominance is unchallenged. The middle class MPs who have gradually replaced the aristocrats on the Conservative benches tend to share the same educational background. The continuity in the educational and occupational background of Conservatives is illustrated in Table 5.3, which compares Conservative MPs in 1923 and October 1974. The former year is chosen because it comes nearest to matching the 277 Conservative MPs of 1974.

TABLE 5.3 Conservative MPs 1923 and 1974

Date	*No.*	*Etonian* (%)	*Public school* (%)	*Oxbridge* (%)	*All university* (%)	*Professional* (%)	*Manual* (%)	*Women* (%)
1923	258	25	79	40	50	52	4	1
1974 (Oct)	277	17	75	56	69	46	1	3

Source: David Butler and Michael Pinto-Duschinsky, 'The Conservative Elite, 1918–78: Does Unrepresentativeness Matter?', in Z. Layton-Henry, *Conservative Party Politics* (London: Macmillan, 1980).

The Conservative party has sometimes been led by men who, though wealthy, lacked blue blood and estates; Disraeli, Bonar Law, Baldwin and Neville Chamberlain, are examples. But throughout the twentieth century the party has been suffused with upper class values, an 'establishment' of wealth, exclusive London clubs and major public schools. Until 1964 more than half of Conservative Cabinet ministers in this century had been old Etonians, and a large minority belonged to or were related to the aristocracy. Churchill, for example, was the grandson of a Duke, Eden owned vast estates and was related to Lord Grey of the 1832 Reform Act, and Sir Alec Douglas-Home was related by marriage to the same Lord Grey and was the first hereditary peer to become Prime Minister since Lord Salisbury. Macmillan, though himself a wealthy publisher, the product of Eton, Balliol and the Guards, and married into the Cavendishes, one of England's oldest political families, counts as a *parvenu* in this gallery. Reading the biographies and memoirs of Churchill, Eden, Macmillan, Sir Alec Douglas-Home and others, one is reminded of the life-style of the eighteenth and nineteenth century aristocracy. There is the same friendship and kinship with other 'notables', the same early entry to politics, and the same anticipation of political success that so impressed W. L. Guttsman in his study of the nineteenth century political elite. He commented:

> One is struck again and again by the extent and intimacy of their personal contacts. They are inevitably related to the greater freedom and ease of intercourse which stems from a considerable degree of independence.[13]

Not surprisingly, ministers from different backgrounds felt uneasy. Even Bonar Law regretted 'his wanting of birth . . . afraid that the Party might follow unwillingly because he had no blue blood in his veins'.[14] In the 1960s outwardly confident ministers like Reginald Bevins and Charles Hill felt isolated among colleagues whose privileged family background and education seemed to give them an assured social status and cohesion.[15]

In little more than a decade, that apparently secure Establishment which confidently managed the emergence of 'the leader' has almost disappeared. The watershed was the election of Edward Heath as Conservative leader in 1965. Before the war Heath and Mrs Thatcher would have been unlikely choices as Conservative MPs, let alone as leaders.[16] Heath's mother was a housemaid and his father had started his working life as a carpenter, and Mrs Thatcher's father was a grocer. Winning scholarships to local grammar schools and Oxford established their claims for advancement.

Many of Heath's close Cabinet colleagues in 1970 were also from non-upper class backgrounds and were soon dubbed 'Heathmen' by the mass media. The number of old Etonians in Heath's Cabinet dropped sharply to 4 from 11 under Sir Alec Douglas-Home. The '*products of opportunity*' (Mr Heath's phrase), self-made professional politicians from the city and suburbs, took over from the products of political families and possessors of landed estates.[17] They were the equivalent of Labour's 'meritocrats'. However, we need to repeat the limited nature of the social revolution. Mr Heath and Mrs Thatcher were not typical of their front bench or even back bench colleagues. Both were and are surrounded by public school, Oxbridge MPs. The 1979 Conservative Cabinet, for example, includes, in addition to Mrs Thatcher, only John Biffen who did not attend a select Headmasters' Conference school, and only four non-Oxbridge ministers.

We have noted that knowledge of the social origins of politicians does not on its own permit one to make confident predictions about their behaviour or attitudes. But the general shift from *patricians* and *proletarians* to *meritocrats* does provide a link with other changes in the context of British politics. There is, for example, the decline of social deference among the working class as a basis for voting Conservative in the 1950s and 1960s, though one may doubt whether it was ever so important. According to McKenzie and Silver the deferential voter believes that these patricians are 'uniquely qualified to govern by birth, experience and outlook';[18] as Bagehot noted, high social status was an outward sign of political talent.[19] This view commanded acceptance outside Britain. Schumpter, for example, in stressing the importance of well-born politicians, suggested, 'experience seems to suggest that the only effective guarantee (of quality) is in the existence of a social stratum, itself a product of a severely selective process, that takes to politics as a matter of course'.[20] He regarded Britain as the only country which possessed a political society, endowing its members with traditions, experience and a professional code.

That social and cultural context has almost vanished. The increasing demands on politicians and governments mean that both are expected to justify themselves by performance. The shift has been to a more instrumental evaluation by voters. In the rural areas, the influence and participation of local aristocrats and land owners in Conservative politics has declined. In urban areas the leadership of substantial businessmen has also largely disappeared.[21] Contemporary local leaders are more 'ordinary' professional and business men – solicitors, executives and accountants. There is now less agreement about the bases of deference to leaders, and probably less social and cultural distance between leaders and voters.

There is now less hierarchy in the Conservative party. Traditionally, a Conservative leader's self-confidence rested both on his high social status and ideas about the independent authority of government; government was, in L. S. Amery's words, an 'independent body' which derived its authority from the Crown. The sense of hierarchy was also reflected in the way the leader 'emerged' prior to 1965. There was little pretence of democratic selection. Senior party figures, after sounding out opinions, designated one man and the appointee was then universally acclaimed by the party. But neither Mr Heath nor Mrs Thatcher was able to exploit a superior social status. The adoption of formal election procedures for the leadership in 1965 meant that they owed their elevation (and, since 1975, possible dismissal) to competitive election by back benchers, further weakening the sense of hierarchy.

The changes in the social background of the two front benches have also affected the image of the parties. The diminution in ostensible class difference, particularly with regard to university education, between the two front benches in the 1960s coincided with a decline in the number of voters perceiving 'a good deal' of difference between the parties and with a weakening of the class voting. Obviously, the convergence in policies in the 1960s was important here, as was the growth of television as a source of political information. But the idea that one party represented the poor and the other the privileged hardly fitted the homogeneous middle class graduate character of the two front benches that viewers could see for themselves on the television.

More speculatively, we might expect a different attitude to political activity. Patricians, after all, learned a tradition of politics that arose from practice and relied on hunch and instinct; they usually had a sceptical view of what could or even should be achieved by government. Many Conservatives enjoyed private incomes, saw politics as a part-time activity and came into politics to enjoy the amenities and companionship of a fine club. Aristocrats in high office have usually been easy-going (though the judgement is equally applicable to non-aristocratic Prime Ministers like Campbell-Bannerman, Asquith, Bonar Law and Baldwin), attracted to public affairs by family traditions and '*noblesse oblige*'.[22] Politics was not a 'vocation' which excluded other activities, for 'The man who puts politics first is not fit to be called a civilised being, let alone a Christian.'[23] In contrast the socially mobile meritocrats, lacking this background, might be expected to be more motivated to bring about change and to see their task as 'making' instead of 'attending to' the arrangements of society.[24]

III Style

Change is a convenient rallying cry of the political 'outs' of the day. British politicians are ambiguous about change *per se*, however. Historians usually emphasise the gradual nature of change in British politics and the preference for an adaptation of existing forms, combining the values of tradition and modernity. At times, however, dissatisfaction with the *status quo* and demand for change has decisively affected the political agenda, in terms of what politicians propose as policy, how they justify their preferences on the issues of the day, and the image they present to voters. At the beginning of the twentieth century, for example, it was the demand for National Efficiency, and in the 1960s it was Modernisation or Remodernisation.[25] The thematic similarities between demands made by opinion formers in these two cases is remarkable and in both cases transcended party lines. For example, the main complaints of both were addressed to Britain's economic weakness, international decline, and the amateurism and lack of expertise among administrative and economic elites.

Many of the prescribed remedies were also similar; new men who would be 'experts', possessing scientific or technical skills; reforms in government institutions which would permit more 'rational' policies; and the integration of Britain within a larger unit (the Empire in 1900, the EEC later). In 1900 the target was the set of assumptions represented by Gladstonian Liberalism, in the 1960s it was tradition and rule by an 'old boy' network. Both would agree with Sidney Low's claim in 1904 that 'Government in England is government by amateurs' and that the complexity of government required new skills beyond those of 'good intentions and a respectable character'.[26] Finally, in the 1960s, as at the beginning of the twentieth century, there was optimism that the importation of new men and new techniques would arrest the British decline.

During the first half of the post-war period the two main parties had been largely satisfied with the state of Britain. There was room for improvement, but in the 1945 Parliament Labour had achieved much of its long-standing programme, consolidating the welfare state and bringing the basic industries under public ownership. The succeeding Conservative governments accepted most of these changes. There was some common ground between the parties on maintaining fully employment, the mixed economy, the welfare state and granting independence to the colonies. Winston Churchill observed to his doctor, Lord Moran, 'I have come to know the nation and what needs to be done to stay in power.' The Conservative's third successive election victory in 1959 showed that the party was adjusting successfully to the prosperous electorate. The government's use of Keynesian techniques of economic management banished the twin evils of unemployment and economic stagnation.

The satisfaction of the 1950s, however, was soon followed by a sense of failure – political, economic and international – that led to the 'great reappraisal' of policy in 1961. In that year the Macmillan government made the first approaches for membership of the Common Market and turned to economic planning to find a way out of the stop-go cycles of the economy. The sense of decline was fuelled by a number of events; the Suez failure in 1956, the abandonment of the Blue Streak and with it any credible claims to possess an independent nuclear deterrent, sterling crises and growing awareness of the low rate of economic growth compared to other countries.

Both parties responded to the sense of decline by looking for new policies, a process accentuated by the election of new and younger leaders. Both the new leaders were grammar school boys, had entered Parliament after the war and spoke of the challenge of change. Mr Wilson became leader of the Labour party in February 1963. Making an issue out of Britain's low rate of industrial growth he emphasised the importance of science and technology and held out the prospect of a new Britain 'that is going to be forged in the white heat of this revolution'.[27] His promise was that Labour's plans would get the economy moving and society modernised. In retrospect it is remarkable that so many communicators (having led the cry for change and modernisation) saw Wilson as the British version of Kennedy's 'New Frontier'; here was a youthful technocratic leader promising modernisation and transcending the old divisions in the Labour party. According to Anthony Sampson, Harold Wilson was 'a man of determined isolation and professionalism, different from any previous incumbent in Downing St'. In his company, 'pretensions and passion dissolve in the dry atmosphere of technical discussion'.[28]

Mr Heath became the Conservative leader in 1965 after the party's first open, competitive election. He was chosen for qualities which were thought to match those of Mr Wilson and which Sir Alec Douglas-Home lacked – toughness, industry and expertise on the economy. Though a 'new man' in terms of his social background, he had established his credentials by rising through the ministerial hierarchy. Mr Heath's determination had already been demonstrated as Chief Whip at the time of Suez, in his handling of the EEC negotiations, and the abolition of resale price maintenance in 1964 in face of bitter opposition within his own party.

Mr Heath expressed impatience with the flabby consensus of the post-war era, years of British decline. He was committed to more personal responsibility, incentives, taking decisions which would adjust to an increasingly competitive world, and avoiding 'the easy way of subsidy, and still more subsidy, of Government intervention, and still more Government intervention'. The party had to find new ground from that occupied in the

1950s. The new policies, foreshadowed in *Putting Britain Right Ahead* (1965) and the Conservative manifesto in 1970, aimed at changing the structure within which government and the economy worked. It was anticipated that cutting direct taxation, reducing government intervention in industry and wage bargaining, reorganising central government, relating welfare benefits to need, requiring trade unions to operate within a tighter legal framework, and gaining entry to the EEC would create the climate for greater enterprise, competition, efficiency and economic growth. This package was accompanied by a more abrasive style. The new, middle class Conservatives were less guilty about the 1930s than their Conservative predecessors and adopted a tougher approach to the trade unions.

If one tries to capture the central themes which the leaders projected in the 1960s the *leitmotif* is competence and efficiency, with little reference to the traditions or ideologies of the parties. In common with President Kennedy's call, 'Let's get America moving again', the parties moved from a stationary to a dynamic view of society. At the same time voters appeared to be more interested in the performance of the parties, judging them instrumentally, according to the benefits they were likely to deliver.

An important theme was 'the scientific revolution' (first referred to in Labour's policy document, *Signposts for the Sixties*) and its implications for modernisation and economic planning and growth. There were demands for more economists to be taken into government and more physicists and chemists recruited to the civil service. There was a shift from the patrician's Parliamentary skills to the technocrat's expertise; the amateur, the dilettante were out, the professional, the specialist were in. Witness Mr Wilson addressing the Labour Conference in 1963: 'in the Cabinet room and the boardroom alike those charged with the central direction of our affairs must be ready to think and to speak in the language of our scientific age'.

A good illustration of the change in mood was seen in 1964 in the resigned acceptance by many Conservatives that Sir Alec Douglas-Home was an electoral liability and in his replacement by Mr Heath. Sir Alec's aristocratic background and grouse-moor image (though not dissimilar from his immediate predecessor's), and his lack of authority on questions of industry and the economy were thought to disqualify him from the top job.

There was, appropriately enough, a belief that problems would be solved by a new technique, a reorganisation of institutions and the managerial approach. In 1964 Labour established the Department of Economic Affairs to formulate a national plan for the economy, and a Ministry of Technology to explore advanced technology. There were also new techniques of central resource allocation (e.g. PESC, for public expenditure, and PAR, the Programme Analysis Review); the creation of new ministries and then the amalgamation of ministries into super-departments in 1970; aids for policy analysis (e.g. the Central Policy Review Staff in 1970 to look at the broader strategic aspects of policy, the importation of business consultants in 1970, and then the Prime Minister's Policy Unit in 1974). The motive was a 'managerialist' search for a greater central capability and more coherent policy-making at the centre.[29]

It was also a period of institutional reform. The decade saw an orgy of Royal Commissions and committees of inquiry into Parliament, the civil service, the Constitution, local government and trade unions. The chief reforms affected the civil service and local and central government. The emphasis again was on greater efficiency. The Report of the Fulton Committee on the Civil Service indicted the tradition of the arts graduate, 'generalist' administrator. The report called for the recruitment of civil servants with more relevant specialist knowledge of the work of government departments, though, as critics observed, it failed to present criteria of relevance.

Finally, government became larger and more interventionist, though this was contrary to Heath's original intentions. Government tried to reform the trade unions, and took sweeping powers to control prices and incomes and intervene in industry. The growth in the size of departments, proliferation of new ministries and and responsibilities (e.g. Arts, Sport, Disabled, Prices and Consumer Protection, Energy), and the increasing share of the national income passing through the government's hands are measurable if crude indicators. Mr Wilson frequently complained that during his last spell as Prime Minister the burdens had greatly increased since 1964 in the shape of papers to read, people to see and international gatherings to attend. The need for more co-ordination was a measure of the growing complexity of government. Party manifestos and policy-making by the parties became more wide-ranging and detailed. For example, R. A. Butler's policy exercise after 1945 relied on three broad committees and sketched themes; in contrast Mr Heath had 30 committees, many of which went into detail on specific points.

The fashion for economic growth, modernisation and efficiency said little about the direction of change or the nature of the desired society. The party slogans 'Let's go with Labour' (1964), 'You Know Labour Government Works' (1970) and the Conservative 'Action Not Words' (1966) and the habit of Wilson and Heath to claim they were 'getting on with the job', suggested a restless concern with activity or movement for its own sake. In common with trends in Western Europe and the United States, there was a convergence of policies and a sense that many major social problems had been or could be solved, producing the depoliticisation of the 1960s. The politicians' technocratic approach involved a preference for

> minimising the apparent relevance of rival ideologies, while maximising that of non-ideological, pragmatic, techno-administrative solutions (and the reduction of politics) . . . haggling over the respective merits of those 'solutions' which the experts deemed to be possible.[30]

In 1964 Mr Wilson defined Socialism as 'applying a sense of purpose to our national life' and 'purpose means technical skill'. He went on to praise skill in various occupations and complained that in government and business people too often considered social qualifications rather than technical ability as desirable. In introducing the policy doucment *Putting Britain Right Ahead* in 1965, Heath defended its concentration on details and neglect of philosophy by claiming that people were more interested in '*how* we do things rather than in what needs to be done'. And the 1966 manifesto stated, 'Our first aim is this: to run this country's affairs efficiently and realistically, so that we achieve steadier prices in the shops, high wages, and a really decent standard of social security.'

IV Assessment: Progress and Decline

We now know that the Wilson–Heath era coincided with a continued relative decline in Britain's position in the world. The country's relative economic performance, however measured, declined even more sharply in the decade 1965–75 and this when the parties had based their appeals explicitly on an ability to 'get Britain moving'.

With Mr Wilson the breakthrough was to come about through 'purposive' intervention and economic planning. This ambition was finally abandoned with the forced devaluation of the pound in 1967. Mr Heath was committed in 1970 to a smaller scale of government and allowing the market a greater influence in the economy. Within two years his government was armed with a full-blooded set of controls over prices and incomes and far-reaching powers to intervene in industry. The sense of failure and the diminishing correspondence between what the parties said they would do and what they actually accomplished contributed to the general lack of confidence in the party leaders and the political institutions. The governments of Mr Wilson and Mr Heath inherited many common problems and often turned to similar policies. But there was one important difference between the two men, when it came to inducing change and modernisation.

For Mr Wilson, modernisation was effective rhetoric; to be for change was fashionable in the early 1960s, just as the rhetoric of conciliation became fashionable a decade later. Ministerial colleagues suggested that Mr Wilson was more interested in the image than in the substance of government. Crossman's diaries reinforce claims that the government lacked a coherent policy or firm direction, frequently treating major issues in a perfunctory manner. As early as 1965, Crossman reports Wilson saying: 'my strategy (!) is to put the Tories on the defensive and always give them awkward choices'.[31]

Talk of the scientific revolution enabled the Labour party to paper over its cracks on public ownership and defence. By temperament, Wilson proved a conciliator, in marked contrast to his predecessor, Hugh Gaitskell. Gaitskell was impatient of equivocations and formulae which compromised fundamental policy differences. His habit, as a self-confessed rationalist, was to bring differences into the open, articulate disagreements, take a vote on an issue and then declare the majority view as party policy. He was not sympathetic to traditional symbols and myths, such as Clause 4, when they interfered with his task of reforming the party's policies and image.[32] For much of his leadership, the party was bitterly divided and Gaitskell himself was regarded as a factional leader.

Wilson thought that this directive style was no way to lead the Labour Party; the party was 'a broad church', its different factions had to be coaxed to a common course of action. His primary objective was to keep the Labour party together. This is the not dishonourable explanation of the way he held himself apart from factions, his refusal to take an early firm stand on several issues (the outstanding exceptions were on devaluation and trade union reform), his apparent changes of mind, in line with majority party opinion, and his careful balancing of different factions in the Cabinet. The critics inveighed at the fudging, the soothing formulae, the trimming, and the unheroic style. But it kept the party together and Mr Wilson safely in the saddle.

Mr Heath was a more determined character, and radical rhetoric was backed by appropriate actions. Many of the party's specific policies were enacted after 1970, often in face of bitter opposition in and out of Parliament. In speaking of 'the challenge of change' he told the 1970 party conference that 'If we are to achieve this task we will have to embark on a change so radical, a revolution so quiet and yet so total, that it will go far beyond the programme . . . far beyond this decade and into the 1980s.' Perhaps a mark of the radical nature of the Heath government's legislation is that much of it was withdrawn from the statute book soon after it left office and its policies reversed by the succeeding Labour government. The Housing Finance Act was scrapped, the statutory controls on incomes and the Industrial Relations Act were repealed, and the terms of membership of the EEC were renegotiated. By tradition major reforms in Britain usually undergo a gestation period, in which they germinate, gather support and gradually come to be regarded as inevitable.[33] Mr Heath felt that vested interests had been accommodated for too long and that action was necessary if the country's decline was to be arrested. But his forthright appeal to the electorate in 1974 for support was rebuffed.

It is worth noting how the two 'disturbers' of the mid-1960s were chastened by experience. By 1970, Harold Wilson was already being compared with Baldwin as a safe, easy-going leader. In the 1974 elections he presented himself as a healing, unifying figure. In a revealing interview he compared himself with a family doctor helping people 'to achieve . . . peace and quiet', rather than wanting to 'sit on people's doorsteps'.[34] By October 1974, Mr Heath had also lost his cutting edge; he then espoused the cause of conciliation and national unity, arguing that the problems facing the country and the necessary mobilisation of consent required a coalition. Bold leadership in the style of a British Gaullist had been frustrated.

Two interesting questions arise; first, why the failure and second, what might be done to improve the performance of leadership? If we ask why things did not turn out better, only a small part of the answer lies in the shortcomings of the parties and the leaders. The optimist may point to a few crucial decisions which, from hindsight, might be judged poor – e.g. not entering the Common Market in the 1950s, not devaluing the pound before 1967, trying to play a world role with inadequate resources, maintaining the pound as a reserve currency and so on. The difficulty with this type of analysis is not only the simple assumption of causality – if *x*-policy were followed then *y* and *z* would happen – but also that any system has to allow for errors. Moreover, if there are several poor policy decisions, then one has to look deeper. The monolithic and adversary style of party politics is at present a favoured candidate for blame. But the problem with this as a comprehensive explanation is that excessive partisanship and abrupt discontinuities of policy between the parties is only apparent in the years 1970–4, whereas the shortcomings pre-date this short period.

It may be that Britain has become a more difficult country to govern during the post-war years. Governments are beset by more intractable problems.[35] The effectiveness of public policies is now more dependent on the co-operation of other groups and the actions of other governments, interests are better organised to refuse compliance, and resource constraints limit the possibility of increasing both take-home pay and public benefits. Complexity and resource constraints are universals of the policy process, yet we have to acknowledge that they affect other countries too.

This is not to deny that formal power is still concentrated in the Whitehall machine, that a determined minister can get his way, or that Cabinet domination of Parliament speeds the passage of legislation. It is still the case that, in spite of a more populist tone, demands for more open and accountable government, the broadcasting of Parliament, and the light shed by the Crossman diaries, British government remains closed. Ministers are still comparatively free from scrutiny and the public detached from politics. In this sense one may agree with Lord Hailsham that political power in Britain is concentrated in the executive and that the Cabinet resembles an 'elective dictatorship'.

But today this formal power matters less in its impact on society. Here is the major paradox about British politics, which a latter-day Bagehot would surely spot. While the political institutions are strong or *mobilising*, the political culture is constraining or *conciliatory*. The surface strength and stability of British government appear to help the mobiliser. Government derives its authority from the ancient prerogative of the Crown, a Cabinet with a majority in the Commons exercises full sovereignty. The attitude is exemplified in L. S. Amery's statement that British democracy is 'government of the people, for the people, with, but not by the people',[36] or, more prosaically, that 'the government's job is to govern'.

But at the same time, the policies of other centres – producer groups, international corporations, trading partners – have crowded the role of Parliament and Cabinet in the last 30 years. The need to take these groups into account seems to produce immobilism. The cultural factors are also important in depressing the scope for the mobilising style. British government has traditionally been exercised within certain parameters; it is limited in its remit, leadership is parliamentary and liberty is negative, i.e. the people are left alone. The other side of this relationship is that only in war-time have the British been responsive to energetic or mobilising leaders. British Prime Ministers are hardly popular figures; they are regarded as partisan leaders. Since 1945, only Macmillan and Wilson have maintained the support of more than half of the electorate for two years or more, according to Gallup polls.

Political skill is shown within the Parliamentary arena. Approval among this Parliamentary elite is more decisive than a popular following in reaching the top in British politics. Thirteen of the eighteen Prime Ministers of the twentieth century first assumed office without the sanction of a general election. The average times spent in the House of Commons for an MP prior to becoming a party leader and Prime Minister have been 24 and 26 years, respectively. This lengthy apprenticeship provides ample opportunity for learning the skills appropriate to managing the party and Parliament and usually ensures that leaders have those qualities.[37] Acceptability to colleagues at the levels of party, Parliament and Cabinet have attracted and rewarded a personality and style in which qualities of reliability, self-restraint, and trustworthiness have figured prominently. Managing the party and Cabinet, or advancing in the civil service all place a premium on the avoidance of conflict. Foreign observers are struck by the emphasis on *community* over performance among the Whitehall elite.[38] Objections to dynamic personalities who posed threats to the consensus system have usually been decisive. It also suggests why – apart from exceptional circumstances like wars – those leaders who enter as mobilisers like Wilson in 1964 and Heath in 1970, gradually find it necessary to conciliate.

Assertions of a national destiny by Joseph Chamberlain or Oswald Mosley, a national identity by Enoch Powell, and the Dunkirk spirit by Wilson in 1967 or Heath in 1974 all fall on deaf ears in peace time. The 'State of England' literature, with its call for directive leadership implicitly, though mistakenly, suggests that things were different in the past. In view of this disjunction between the institutions and the culture it is more understandable why the diaries and autobiographies of recent ministers convey a sense of governments being hemmed in, of trying to cope, rather than adhering to an overall strategy. Harold Macmillan thought that over the years authority had increasingly been concentrated in the hands of Prime Ministers. But he also felt that power seemed 'like a dead sea fruit, when you achieve it, there's nothing there'. Another Cabinet Minister entitled the first chapter of a book on British politics, 'Where Has All the Power Gone?'.[39]

There have been two broad reactions to awareness of interdependence, diffusion of power and sense of decline. One is to call for 'strong' leadership, a strengthening of the authority of political leaders and government institutions in Western states. The purpose of such a leadership is to roll back demands by groups and lower expectations of what government can do. Both Mr Wilson and Mr Heath tried to tame the trade unions by legislation and appeals to public opinion. The former retreated when he found he could not carry his Cabinet or party, and Mr Heath's Gaullist use of a general election in 1974 failed. In 1979 Margaret Thatcher has come to office acting much as Mr Heath did in 1970. It remains to be seen how she will cope with the great interests of the realm.

An alternative is that maintaining consent and coping with complexity require more power-sharing. The greater the number of decision-points and decision-makers the greater the need for agreement. Effective leadership may now depend on a modern version of John Calhoun's doctrine of concurrent majorities among big groups, giving 'to each division or interest . . . either a concurrent voice in making and executing the laws, or a veto on their execution'. The two emphases fall respectively on the mobiliser and the conciliator.

To be more effective the conciliator requires different institutions. It is here that the adversary nature of the two-party system, combined with the effects of the winner-take-all Parliamentary battle and electoral system, and more interventionist government which does require consent if it is to be effective, is important. Electoral reform (and its probable offshoot, coalition), corporatism, devolution, membership of the Common Market, and resort to referenda have been canvassed as devices for promoting more consensual or cooperative policies. There have been moves in all directions in recent years, and each represents a turning away from the one-party centralised, hierarchical form of government we have known since 1945.

This article has discussed the post-war changes in composition and style of British leaders. While the move away from the patricians and the proletarians is probably irreversible, the consequences of trends to the meritocratic leaders are complex. There seems to be little relationship between social background and the adoption of mobilising or conciliatory styles. Wilson and Callaghan are examples of conciliator, Lloyd George, Heath and Mrs Thatcher are examples of the mobiliser; but all are self-made. Mobilisation is not a function of being in or out of government nor is it the exclusive property of a party. If anything, movement between the two styles of leadership appears to be cyclical, with one eventually breeding a reaction in favour of the other. The leaderships of both Wilson and Heath show how one may end with a style radically different from that assumed at the outset. The task of British leaders is, as ever, to speak the two languages, conciliatory and mobilising. The one seeks consensus as a necessary basis of policy effectiveness. The other is 'hard', concerned with earning Britain's place in a competitive world, rooting out economic inefficiencies at home and winning markets abroad. There seems little doubt that, borne down by the inertia of institutions and values, leaders have failed to achieve a happy combination of the two voices.

NOTES

1. The distinction is often applied to France and the United States. For Britain, see Dennis Kavanagh, *Crisis, Charisma and British Political Leadership* (London: Sage, 1974).
2. David Apter, *The Politics of Modernization* (Chicago: Chicago University Press, 1945).
3. W. L. Guttsman, *The British Political Elite* (London: MacGibbon & Kee, 1963).
4. R. Rose, 'Class and Party Divisions: Britain as a Test Case', *Sociology*, II (1968) 129–62.
5. W. D. Muller, *The Kept Men?* (London: Harvester Press, 1977).
6. On this trend, see Michael Young, *The Rise of The Meritocracy* (Harmondsworth: Penguin, 1961).
7. See R. Rose, *Politics in England Today* (London: Faber, 1974) p. 159.
8. R. W. Johnson, 'The British Political Elite, 1955–1972', *European Journal of Sociology*, XIV (1973) 35–77.
9. Egon Wertheimer, *Portrait of the Labour Party* (London: Putnam, 1929).
10. Both of these former ministers had received further education. However, two other Labour ministers, Roy Jenkins and Merlyn Rees, were sons of miners.
11. Quoted in C. L. Mowat, *Britain Between the Wars* (London: Methuen, 1955) p. 173.
12. Johnson, in *European Journal of Sociology*, XIV, p. 51.
13. Ibid. p. 181.
14. Quoted in Eric Nordlinger, *The Working Class Tories* (London: MacGibbon & Kee, 1967) p. 42.
15. Reginald Bevins, *The Greasy Pole* (London: Hodder & Stoughton, 1965); Sir Charles Hill, *Both Sides of the Hill* (London: Heinemann, 1964).
16. Niger Fisher, *The Tory Leaders* (London: Weidenfeld & Nicolson, 1977).
17. On the decline of landed estates among Conservative MPs, see Andrew Roth, *The Business Backgrounds of MPs* (London: Parliamentary Profiles, 1972) p. 94.
18. R. T. McKenzie and A. Silver, *Angels in Marble* (London: Heinemann, 1968) p. 242.
19. W. Bagehot, *The English Constitution* (London: World's Classics, 1955).
20. J. Schumpeter, *Capitalism, Socialism and Democracy* (London: Allen & Unwin, 1943) p. 291.
21. D. Butler and M. Pinto-Duschinsky, 'The Conservative Elite 1918–78: Does Unrepresentativeness Matter', in Zig Layton-Henry, *Conservative Party Politics* (London: Macmillan, 1980).
22. Guttsman, *The British Political Elite*.
23. Lord Hailsham, *The Case for Conservatism* (Harmondsworth: Penguin, 1959) p. 13.

24. Cf. Guttsman, *The British Political Elite*, p. 310.
25. B. Semmel, *Imperialism and Social Reform: Social and Imperialist Thought 1895–1914* (London: Allen & Unwin, 1960); G. R. Searle, *The Quest for National Efficiency* (London: Blackwell, 1971).
26. Sidney Low, *The Governance of England* (London: Ernest Benn, 1914) pp. 197 and 304.
27. Harold Wilson, Speech to Labour Party Conference, Scarborough, 1963.
28. Anthony Sampson, *Anatomy of Britain Today* (London: Hodder & Stoughton, 1965) pp. 172–3.
29. See Peter Self, 'Are We Worse Governed?', *New Society*, 19 May 1977.
30. John Goldthorpe, 'Theories of Industrial Society', *European Journal of Sociology*, 12 (1971) 284.
31. R. H. S. Crossman, *The Diaries of a Cabinet Minister*, vol. 1 (London: Hamish Hamilton and Jonathan Cape, 1976) p. 50.
32. Wilson compared Gaitskell's reform to 'Taking Genesis out of the Bible'.
33. Anthony King, 'The Election that Everyone Lost', in Howard Penniman (ed.), *Britain at the Polls* (Washington: American Enterprise Institute, 1974) p. 7.
34. See D. Butler and D. Kavanagh, *The British General Election of October 1974* (London: Macmillan, 1975) pp. 256–7.
35. Anthony King, 'Overload: Problems of Governing in the 1970s', *Political Studies*, XXIII (1975) 483–505.
36. L. S. Amery, *Thoughts on the Constitution* (London: Oxford University Press, 1947) p. 22.
37. For a further development of this argument, see Kavanagh, *Crisis, Charisma and British Political Leadership*.
38. On this feature, see Robert Putnam, *The Beliefs of Politicians* (New Haven: Yale University Press, 1975) and Hugh Heclo and Aaron Wildavsky, *The Private Government of Public Money* (London: Macmillan, 1974).
39. Ian Gilmour, *The Body Politic* (London: Hutchinson, 1969).

6 The Impact of Organised Interests

Graham Wootton

For two decades the dominant perception of Britain has been of a nation in decline, a 'fact' of perception not necessarily mirrored by reality. This chapter focuses upon evidence of decline for which organised interests might plausibly be held responsible. There appear to be two: economic decline, and erosion of the authority of government. To what extent, if at all, can such decline be attributed to the organised interests, in aggregate or especially the trade unions? The reason for singling out the unions is not simply that the general public and the mass media impute to them much of the blame. Seasoned scholars tend to do the same.

First of all one needs to find out just what might be laid at the door of the organised interests. That naturally entails some broad judgment of economic performance, which for at least two-thirds of the period under review was marked as much by progress as decline. Secondly, in the residual area where condemnation is deserved, it will be suggested that such other interests as 'the overseas lobby' should also be called to account, if indeed succesive governments are to be exonerated.

Some successful challenges to the authority of government have certainly been mounted in the last decade by the trade unions. But has that authority been permanently weakened? The record will disclose that, in the 1930s (to go no further back), several successful challenges to authority were mounted, and, as it happens, not by unions but by employers. From that chastening experience, authority must be presumed to have recovered, unless the thesis is changed to assert that *this* decline started in the 1930s and is now accentuated by the unions. But in that case the cast of characters would have to be changed too. A still longer perspective will reveal that 'pressure from without' has been characteristic of the British polity for at least a century and a half, even if British political scientists and historians chose not to write about it.[1] The phrase implies encroachment on or invasion of authorty in ways clearly perceived as unconstitutional. Perceptions of the unconstitutional do change, however, if very slowly; perhaps the British polity can sustain more shocks, from any quarter, than it is nowadays given credit for. This discussion will end with a proposal for concept refinement, distinguishing (as in French) between immobilism (*immobilisme*) and immobility (*immobilité*).

I Economic 'Decline'

Organisational theory casts doubt on the attribution of goals even to the simpler varieties of the species, much less entities as differentiated and complex as governments and bureaucracies, not to mention a total society such as Britain. Even so, some statement of national economic objective is obviously essential if economic performance is to be assessed. Here one follows in the footsteps of those Olympians – American and Canadian economists of distinction – who, from the heights of the Brookings Institution in Washington, looked down on British mortals in 1967 and produced a celebrated analysis of performance and prospects. They identified four fundamental economic objectives: full employment, economic growth, reasonably stable prices and adequate balance of payments surpluses.[2] A fifth goal listed in one of the chapters of that report will not be followed. Professors Richard and Peggy Musgrave, discussing fiscal policy, propose a fifth objective – 'a satisfactory distribution of income'.[3] With that – suitably elucidated – one is in sympathy, but historically it can hardly be taken as an actual national objective, whereas parties and governments reached a substantial working agreement about the other four objectives.

In what follows the post-war period will be divided into two parts, (a) the 1950s and 1960s, and (b) the 1970s. Although such a cutting of the 'seamless web' of history is always challengeable, strategic variables changed significantly between the end of the 1960s and the early years of the 1970s.

Full Employment

In 1944 the Churchill Coalition Government in its landmark White Paper committed the nation to securing and maintaining a high and stable level of employment. For the first two decades of the general period under review, that promise was kept. Unemployment from 1950 to the mid-1960s had risen above 2 per cent of the labour force in only three years, so that the British record was 'substantially superior' to the American even allowing for differences in the measures (which would have made the percentage about 3 per cent).[4] By contrast, the American rate in the period 1950–65 had been below 4 per cent in only three years.

Reasonably Stable Prices

From 1950 to the mid-1960s the annual average price increase was 3.4 per cent, and in only five years did prices rise less than 2 per cent.[5] For 1959–74 the annual rate, compounded, was 5.5 per cent.[6] The figures mask some very sharp fluctuations, notably following the world-wide commodity boom associated with the Korean War, when the annual rates of inflation in 1950–

2 reached a painful 9 per cent. Even lower rates tend, of course, to be arbitrary and unjust in their consequences. On the other hand, as David Worswick recalled in 1977:

> as little as ten years ago it was still possible to argue cogently that the kind of inflation which Britain had experienced since the war probably did more good than harm by acting as a safety valve for the relief of the pressure from different sectors of society for ultimately irreconcilable claims on real income.[7]

Those on fixed incomes (including the unemployed) and in weak bargaining positions would no doubt have dissented, but the great majority does not seem to have been seriously incommoded by what is accounted 'creeping' inflation.

Economic Growth

The post-war decades have been decades of economic growth. Certainly, some economists kept on saying that the country should have been doing much better. Four per cent growth was exceeded in only four of the years from 1950 to 1966.[8] In fact, that rate was the highest attained since 1870–1913 (see Table 6.1).[9] Magnificent it may not have been, but growth it certainly was. And it was translated into rising mass consumption; between 1950 and 1964 there was an average increase in consumption per head, man, woman and child, of about 34 per cent. By 1964 there were 8.2 million cars in private hands which increased to 13.4 million in 1973. By 1967 some 7 million UK residents, presumably forsaking Scarborough and even the Isle of Wight, were taking trips abroad – Spain, France and points west as well as east – and by 1973 the number rose to 11.5 million. It is worth recalling here the sober judgment of the leader of the Brookings team, Professor Richard Caves, writing of the period since the Second World War:

TABLE 6.1 Annual rate of growth of total output: UK

	1870–1913	*1913–50*	*1950–60*	*1956–61*
GDP total (%)	2.2	1.7	2.6	2.1
GDP per capita (%)	1.3	1.3	2.2	–

> Her rate of growth, her attainment of full employment are, in the perspective of history, fit objects of pride, and more impressive because they were achieved despite the immense problems of postwar reconstruction, dwindling overseas earnings, and increased competition in export markets.[10]

Balance of Payments

On this score, there were grounds for groans and lamentations. Almost as soon as the war in Europe was over, a balance of payments crisis loomed. Once again, the government looked westward to where the land was bright, in 1946 getting a Canadian loan of $1250 million and an American loan of $3750 million. Three years later, however, the government let loose its thunderbolt, a massive devaluation of over 30 per cent precipitated by a flight from the pound due to the belief that devaluation was in prospect.[11] Whether or not as cause and effect, the balance of payments on current account then developed a surplus throughout the 1950s with the exception of the two years, 1951 and 1955.

This was erratic progress, but progress, granted the values underlying the accepted goals of economic policy. In fact, behind the several ups and downs, lay some genuine triumphs, imperfectly understood even by specialists. Professor Albert Imlah has shown that the balance of trade (or visible, or commodity, or merchandise trade) had alsomost invariably been in deficit, possibly from as far back as 1688, certainly from 1822. These adverse trade deficits, however, had been more than offset by the earnings of invisible trade in services (banking, insurance, brokerage and above all, shipping), and by interest and dividends from overseas investments. Just before the First World War, interest and dividends had come to exceed invisible income from services. Together, they produced a handsome balance of payments surplus on current account averaging over £200 million a year in that period.

By the 1930s, however, that structure was clearly sagging. Only two years (1930 and 1935) produced such a surplus. Invisible earnings were no longer playing their historic role. The Second World War naturally entailed an intensification of that damaging trend. After 1945, with the lend – lease tap turned abruptly off, the task of paying one's way was truly herculean. A strategy imposed itself. Hold down imports (hence physical controls and rationing) making an already drab and partly devastated Britain still drabber and more forlorn. By pushing up exports, create a favourable balance of visible trade, last achieved in 1822. Increase the visibles balance, against the trend of the 1930s. But where was the merchant shipping? Moreover the geese that laid those golden eggs of interest and dividends (twice as profitable as shipping services, 1935 – 9) had been slimmed down drastically. Keynes estimated a dis-investment of £1100 million to keep the ship of state afloat in wartime. That meant, he calculated, a loss of invisible income of about £100 million a year.[12]

Thus a fundamental problem for Britain was how to escape from a balance of payments deficit? Sustained initially by loans and then by Marshall Aid in 1948 and by continuing dis-investment (an annual average of over £400 million in the five-year period, 1946 – 50),[13] Britain did begin to break out of its own prison. Between 1947 and 1950 imports were damped down, and exports were expanded 60 per cent by volume, short of the 75 per cent objective but still a remarkable achievement. By 1960 the volume doubled what it had been in 1947 or 1938.[14]

That export achievement, evidence of structural adaptation, does not speak directly to the balance of trade, much less the balance of payments. In 1952–4, the trade deficit averaged about £250 million a year, but after that there was improvement through 1958.[15] In fact, both 1956 and 1958 produced trade surpluses, the first since 1822, and the year in between narrowly missed doing so. Even in 1957 exports paid for 99 per cent of imports: taken together those three years constitute a great landmark. Thereafter, it was downhill throughout the 1960s, passing two other historic landmarks, trade deficits of more than £500 million (1964) and of £643 million (1968). Then to everyone's surprise, aided perhaps by inadequate record-keeping in the past, the 1969 deficit of £141 million turned into a surplus of £3 million the following year. That was only the seventh such surplus since 1797.[16]

As to the balance of payments, since Britain had faltered in the 1930s, it was hardly to be expected that in the post-war circumstances the trend would be easily reversed. In 1950 a large surplus was in fact registered, but then a quite extraneous factor – the outbreak of war in Korea – precipitated a runaway rise in import prices in 1951, and a deficit greater than the surplus of the year before.[17] Thereafter, however, throughout the 1950s, with the exception of one year (1955), the nation gained the relief it would seem to have earned, paying its way on current account.

The 1960s showed an uneven but generally worsening balance of payments pattern. In 1967, the government was forced to devalue the pound by 14 per cent. It obtained a standby credit from the IMF and loans of £1300 million from it and foreign bankers. The nation experienced a go–stop economy with a vengeance – curbs, cutbacks, deflation – with its attendant discouragement and possible psychological damage. In fact, 1969 brought glad tidings; physical exports covered 98 per cent of the cost of imports and, with an invisible balance of £500 million or more, yielded a surplus on current account of over £400 million. In 1970, there was a current account surplus of some £630 million. A total currency inflow of some £12,000 million enabled the short- and medium-term debt to be reduced and the reserves augmented.

Getting Our Bearings

Within the context of these events what is it that organised groups have to answer for? Full employment and economic growth were achieved – that leaves the issues of inflation and the balance of payments. How *creeping inflation* should be (and should have been) regarded is debatable,[18] but one can see why the *balance of payments* phenomenon – that 'biennially recurrent oscillation between exchange panic and fool's paradise' (as D. H. Robertson put it) – was perceived to be *the* crucial issue.

So now the question has been narrowed down to: *if* successive governments are to be exonerated for balance of payments problems, which interests are to be indicted? The answer is a hypothesis: the overseas lobby, a term coined by the Oxford economist Roger Opie to denote the forces which worked furiously in early 1966 to prevent the Temporary Import Charge from being extended or replaced by other forms of direct controls on imports.[19]

Several other authorities, seemingly of different political persuasions, have acknowledged the reality underlying the concept. Soon after Mr Opie wrote, economic journalist Samuel Brittan cited 'the "entry at any price" approach to the EEC' as an example of the overseas lobby at work. In the mid-1970s David Lomax, editor of a bank quarterly review, deplored that lobby's strength 'within Whitehall, where virtually no departments were putting national economic self-interest first among their objectives'.[20] The different vantage points occupied by these writers and their range of political opinions encourage one to ask what impact the overseas lobby had on what was perceived as the balance of payments failures.

Certainly *some* group has to be held to account. For the little known truth is that, taking one year with another, Britain in this period was actually paying its way on international account. For 1949–58, as was long ago pointed out by the Radcliffe Committee, Britain had earned cumulatively a balance of payments surplus of well over £1000 million. There had been, they found, 'no fundamental lack of balance in the United Kingdom's trading position. . . . The repeated exchange crises have not been due to any failure on the part of the United Kingdom to pay its way'.[21] But surely, it may be said, that changed in the 1960s? In fact, the basic position did not change: Britain continued to pay its way internationally so far as its own international transactions were concerned. As A. R. Conan (former Assistant Secretary of the Commonwealth Economic Committee) pointed out in 1969, the position appeared to be otherwise because various large debits were set off against Britain's own earnings. These debits reflected economic aid in several forms, including grants; defence expenditure *for other countries*, such as £200 million a year in the Far East (chiefly Singapore and Malaysia), and about £100 million a year in the Middle East and Mediterranean; and other very substantial items.[22] Similarly, Meyer, Corner and Parker asked if the annual average surplus on current account in 1953–9 had been rather more than £150 million, why had 1960–6 produced annual average deficits of about £80 million? Their answer was

> The difference was largely due to an increase of, on average, £230 million a year of net government expenditure overseas. . . . Had it not been for the increased cost of the British Government's overseas commitments, the

annual average balance of payments of 1960–66 would have shown a surplus of around £150 million, as in 1953–59.[23]

Military expenditure overseas was up from £100 million in 1950 to £273 million in 1966.[24] That a British military presence overseas was desirable, one would not contest. But could the nation really afford to have 372,000 military overseas 10 years after the war had ended and 200,000 in the year of the 1967 devalution? By then the balance of payments cost per man was of the order of £1200, as against some £400 per man in 1955.[25] For British costs incurred in Germany, there was meant to be an offset of German and American purchases of goods in Britain but this incorporated 'a certain amount of window dressing', i.e. goods that would have been purchased in any case.[26]

Whatever the truth about the general commitment, the East of Suez policy was surely misconceived from the start. It seems not to have been grasped in 1947 (or if understood, it was covered over), that the granting of independence to India (much as that represented progress), would undermine the British defence system east of Suez. For India really was the dazzling jewel in the Crown. It was not just trade, or even that Indian export earnings had been conveniently 'incorporated' to serve the UK balance of payments.

The essential point is that it was the Indian Army that, militarily, had made Britain a great power.[27] This large standing army, distinct from Britain's own small professional army, had formed a great strategic reserve for the defence of British interests throughout the East, their safe transport guaranteed by British mastery of sea lanes to China, Persia, Ethiopia, Singapore, Hong Kong, Egypt, Nyasaland, Uganda and the Sudan (not to mention those territories, such as Burma and Afghanistan, within easier reach). Between 1838 and 1920 the Indian Army was deployed outside India on nineteen occasions.[28] In the First World War, about 1.2 million served overseas; during the Second World War, representatives of a still greater force were to be seen in the Middle East, North Africa and Italy. Between the wars the Indian Army had been dispatched to several points, notably Iraq (which as Mesopotamia was opened up for British interests by men who had learned their trade in the Indian Political Service). What could have been neater – this combination of the world's greatest Navy with some of the world's greatest fighting men, especially as they cost the British taxpayer not one shilling, the Indian Army being a charge on the Indian Exchequer?

Thus, progress (Indian independence) entailed grave difficulties for Britain. Apart from the direct and indirect impact on the balance of payments, a really effective military presence in the East could no longer be sustained in either men or treasure. Not, at least, in conjunction with full employment; a high level of public expenditure; the maintenance of sterling as an international and reserve currency and of the City of London as a short-term lender, all within the framework of very small reserves,[29] and fixed exchange rates.

The decision to abandon the East of Suez policy was not announced to Parliament until January 1968. One wonders whether an overseas lobby was at work, helping to keep the issue off the Cabinet agenda for a decade? It must be conceded that the concept is almost as elusive as the identity of its members. According to time, place and issue, it would seem to have embraced some combination of the then Finance Group within the Treasury, responsible for sterling, the balance of payments, economic aid, and relations with the Bank of England; the Bank of England itself and the City of London as a whole, especially in the sense of the 'new moneyed interest' (new in the late seventeenth century);[30] the Foreign and Commonwealth Offices, and the Ministry of Overseas Development. Access to the Cabinet would have been through the overseas Policy and Defence Committee, a standing committee normally chaired by the Prime Minister. If so, the overseas lobby is neither an organised interest, nor a purely institutional one but a hybrid, a Whitehall – City of London complex on the analogy of the military – industrial complex in the United States to which President Eisenhower once drew unexpected attention.

Whether such a combination of governing and non-governing elites (rather than organised interests in the usual sense) was behind the policies that bore down heavily upon the balance of payments account will have to be left to a distant day when the records are available.[31] But if those interests are acquitted, then government itself must be summoned back to take the blame. Since it was the author of the Independence Act of 1947, Labour in particular has to face charges. Even if the decision was not wrong he who calls the tune must be ready to pay the piper. One thing is certain: for one of the most fundamental policy miscalculations of the period, the unions as such bear no responsibility whatsoever.

The 1970s

We need little reminding that this period has revealed an uglier face. By the first quarter of 1972 unemployment was 4 per cent or close to 900,000, but the spectre of a million unemployed was apparently driven off by an expansionist budget,[32] so that at the end of 1973 the total was less than half a million, a bit more than 2 per cent. Fools' paradise again: in the third quarter of 1975 unemployment rose again, although it was officially perceived as 'a temporary problem flowing from the oil crisis'.[33] In late 1977 the total unemployed was about 1.4 million, a rate of 6 per cent. Since then unemployment has fluctuated while remaining well over a million. Unemployment can be described as 'the blackest stain on the Government's economic record'.[34] For once the hackneyed phrase seems justified – it looks like the end of an era of full employment that opened in 1944.

Economic growth had also faltered even before the oil price increase of late 1973 staggered the industrialised world. In 1974–5 the GDP fell significantly for the first time since 1929–31, and the following two years brought only slight relief.[35] In the first half of 1978 GDP may have been up 2.5 per cent over the corresponding period of 1977.[36] An annual growth rate of 3.5 per cent was what the IMF thought Britain capable of sustaining in 1979–80 – if correct policies were followed. The setback to hopes of economic growth meant that two of the policies earlier marked by substantial success were scarred by failure in the 1970s.

In the early 1970s *inflation* ceased to creep and began to race. In the summer and autumn of 1975 the rate exceeded 25 per cent. After that, the improvement was drastic, in relation to the immediately preceding horrors, but inflation rates of just below 10 per cent were not good in themselves.

Always erratic in the period surveyed, the *balance of payments* returned a very comfortable (and comforting) surplus in 1970 on both current and capital account. It was even handsomer the following year. But then with no warning, the hurricane struck: a deficit on current account in 1973 of over a thousand million and an almost unthinkable £3.8 billion in 1974. Two more years of deficits followed until 1977, when, against expectations, a surplus of £250 million was achieved.[37] But the trail of devastation could still be clearly seen.

Thus, the first question to be posed answers itself: the nation suffered a disastrous setback, uncomplicated by traces of progress. What is complicated in the extreme is the extent to which the organised interests could be held responsible for it, even when 'it' narrows down to one basic issue, inflation.

The trade unions have often been cast as the villains of inflation. In the earlier post-war period the unions come on the scene in the demand-pull interpretation of inflation in periods of full employment: 'A permanent sellers' market for labour means a permanent upward pressure, or more accurately an upward pull, on wages, a correspondingly upward movement in costs . . . .'[38]

In principle, the cost-push explanation differs fundamentally from demand-pull in that its proponents claim that the *push* can occur even when the *pull* is weak or non-existent, i.e. when demand is not excessive. This assumes market imperfections for products, and especially for labour. The principal cause is deemed to be the exercise of 'monopoly power by the trade unions'.[39] Support for that view as applied to the period starting 1969–70 is to be found in the work of several distinguished authorities in the United States as well as Britain.[40]

There is no doubt about the facts, taken in isolation. In December 1969, the Labour government itself declared that annual increases in most wage and salary settlements needed to fall within the range of 2.5–4.5 per cent. Early the following year (an election year incidentally) it was endorsing settlements tantamount to an annual rate of 12 per cent.[41] The third quarter of 1970 saw an average wage settlement (for manual workers) 'of about 11 per cent', way above any current increase in productivity.[42] In the year ending October 1970 average hourly wage earnings rose by 16 per cent, double that of the previous 12 months.[43]

What do those facts mean? Simply (according to some) that manual workers had fallen behind during the latter part of the 1960s. Although the nation as a whole had done well then, as shown in the previous section, manual workers had either barely increased their *real* disposable income, or had actually lost ground.[44] Hence, the explosion of 1969–70 simply represented their efforts to catch up with the mainstream.

The effect of such arguments is to transfer the debate to an earlier point in time. More fundamental attacks on cost-push theories have come from other quarters, of which two will be mentioned here. Mr Panić has drawn attention to the accelerating rates of inflation observed almost everywhere in the (more or less) market economies in the period 1969–74, essentially before the OPEC price increase had fully worked through. His own thesis – an aspirations gap – cannot be discussed here, but his question from the evidence is apt: could organised labour really have been the main cause of inflation in all these different settings?[45]

A more thorough-going attack on cost-push theories, and indeed all interpretations other than the monetarist, has come from Michael Parkin. From his empirical tests of the various theories, Parkin concluded that the evidence was 'not consistent with the wage-push view'. Although monetarists disagreed substantially among themselves about the role of trade unions, they agree that these 'do not and cannot cause inflation'. In fact, the inflation take-off in the late 1960s and 1970s was generated by the build-up of money supply growth from 1967.[46] However, some heavyweights of the economics profession are 'highly critical' of this conclusion.[47]

Seeing economic experts in such disarray, the generalist tends to flounder. The only safe ground is agnosticism, yet some judgment, however tentative, is called for. It may be reached by asking oneself: which theory of inflation is congruent with what one already knows or believes? I am predisposed towards some sort of cost-push theory, the sort that attempts to explain why, as David Cobham puts it, 'the "pushers" push'.[48] The changes in attitudes towards authority and the growing self-confidence on the part of the stewards and union leaders that one then discerned are consistent with what Professor Phelps Brown has called their new capacity for self-assertion from the late 1960s onwards. As he himself shows, 'revived' could replace 'new', for something like this occurred in those very militant years before the First World War. But what, then, accounts for the revival of these attitudes? Two decades of near-full employment.[49] Since full employment had originally prompted the demand-pull theory, that line of thought might facilitate its assimilation to cost-push.

Challenges to authority – the defeat of the Industrial Relations Bill in 1969, the emasculation of the 1971 Act, the miners' strikes, especially in 1974, and so forth – may well have formed part of a new pattern. If so, the actions of the unions in the political as well as the economic spheres would have a certain unity. Accepting that unity would encourage acceptance of the cost-push theory. Where would that leave the monetarist view? Change in the money supply would come to be regarded not as causal but rather derivative from deep-seated conflicts within the industrial system, an intervening not an independent variable.

One final consideration may be adduced. Up to a point,[50] the accelerating rates of inflation in many of the market economies may well reflect this new capacity for trade union self-assertion. Governors in the pre-First World War period feared the rise of the lower classes because it was common to all countries and based on the principle of the equality of all men. If they were not accommodated by the comfortable classes, they would form a whirlwind threatening the fatherland.

Was this prognosis wrong? It might be argued, with Professor Phelps Brown, that the whirlwind was simply deflected by two World Wars, the Depression and other forces of 'displacement', and that it gathered momentum again in the late 1960s. For it was not only in Britain that militancy erupted at that time. The events of May 1968 in France included unofficial strikes and the illegal occupation of factories. In Italy, too, strikes and demonstrations were often launched within the plants but without official union backing, reaching a climax in *l'autunno caldo* (hot autumn) of October 1969. Even in West Germany, workers in the public services as well as in the heavy industries walked out by the hundred thousand; other 'wildcats' followed in 1973–4, even including foreign workers. All that and much more undoubtedly got results: greater job control and very large, inflationary, wage settlements.[51]

It should be acknowledged at this point that the unions are also partly to blame for the low productivity of British manufacturing industry, in which 'one Dutch man-hour = two British man-hours'.[52] This means that the growth rate could (in principle) have been higher even in the historically satisfactory first sub-period, when 'the British weakness in productivity was partly hidden by the continuing world boom'.[53] Here the ambiguity of decline and progress comes to the surface. By applying one form of the comparative method (same country, different points in time), Britain experienced progress; by the other form (different countries, same point in time), Britain suffered what could be called, if confusingly, decline.

No doubt, low productivity has many sources, but one of the main ones must be restrictive practices and over-manning. It is true, as Lord Askwith, a successful arbitrator in labour disputes, long ago remarked, that, for example, restriction of output 'appears to be applied more by the men than by the unions'.[54] But that does not really absolve the unions, because they vigorously support their members when management tries to get rid of such practices.[55]

This of course is an old story, told by such independents as economist Alfred Marshall in 1897 and Brookings expert Edward F. Denison in

1967.[56] As an extension of Mancur Olson's views, it could be argued that it is not in the interest of the unions to work for efficiency, because such an effort entails a cost, and the benefits would accrue to them even if they had not lifted a finger. Here an approach through political sociology might be profitable, seeing restrictive practices and over-manning as embodiments of what John Stuart Mill called 'the standing feud between Capital and Labour'. While the unions do bear responsibility for restrictive practices, they do so within an industrial context that, fundamentally, is not of their making.

II The Erosion of Authority

The other side of the coin from the increased militancy and inflationary surge of the late 1960s was the unions' successful opposition to the Industrial Relations Bill of 1969 and their emasculation of the Industrial Relations Act of 1971. In 1969 the Labour government (or at least Prime Minister Wilson and Barbara Castle) declared the Industrial Relations Bill essential to the national interest. But then, in one of the most blinding revelations since Saul of Tarsus fell to the earth on the road to Damascus, they discovered that the nation did not really need that bill after all. Of course, the voice they heard was the voice of the Trades Union Congress. Soon after that the government went to the country and lost, following which the Conservatives tried to intensify legislative pressure on the unions. The 1971 Industrial Relations Act was by-passed, initially by a boycott of the institutions, and then by a policy of non-co-operation that had never been anticipated by the drafters of the Bill and that constituted a quasi-boycott, i.e. of the legislation itself.[57]

Other degrees of boycott and non-co-operation were displayed by unions in the same period. Members of the National Association of Schoolmasters adopted non-co-operation (1969) as a means of getting Labour back-benchers to press the Minister for an inquiry into the workings of the Burnham system. Surrey members of the National Union of Teachers, keen on the comprehensive schools policy, threatened to boycott selection procedures for the country's grammar schools (1970). That summer saw three out of four family doctors refusing to sign medical certificates because the government had refused to refer a question of their pay to the Prices and Incomes Board.

Further along the continuum of non-co-operation is the political strike. In an unprecedented threat in 1974, 100,000 nurses were ready to withdraw from the National Health Service unless salaries were increased. Among political strikes actually mounted were those by farmers and miners. In 1970 members of the National Farmers' Union – made up of course of employers – kept back supplies from slaughterhouses and livestock markets in order to influence the annual price review negotiations. Dissatisfied with the settlement, the NFU later struck 31 livestock markets in England and

Wales, which the president of the Federation of Meat Traders characterised as 'sabotage'.[58]

The political strikes with greatest impact were those launched by the miners in 1972 and 1974. The ground for these national stoppages, the first of the kind since the General Strike of 1926, had been laid in 1969, with unofficial strikes in Yorkshire and South Wales. Undoubtedly, the miners in the 1960s had lost ground relatively as the industry declined, though productivity increased. But in 1971, behind the Coal Board, which had conceded a 12 per cent wage increase the previous year, stood the government trying to hold the line on inflation. Early in 1972 out went the miners, self-consciously doing 'battle against Government policy', as their president said.[59] Six weeks later they succeeded in breaking that policy: after a late night session, the Cabinet – no less – conceded something like 21 per cent. Just two years later the miners did it again, only this time they broke the government, Edward Heath having taken the issue to the country and lost in the only way that matters – seats; he kept an edge in votes over the other governing party, Labour. The 1974 miners' challenge was the more serious constitutionally because it attacked and breached what had been turned into a statutory incomes policy.

Does all this amount to decline, or an erosion of authority? It is seldom that a government loses a Bill, least of all to the organised interests. But it does happen. In 1936 another attempt to re-organise the industry was embodied in the Coal Mines Bill. As in 1930, the coal-owners attacked vigorously. Even before the second reading, the Cabinet was in retreat, and the promise at that stage of three important amendments in Committee did not suffice. So the Prime Minister agreed to another day for second reading, which however was never taken up; in effect the Bill was withdrawn. And this was 'one of the strongest Governments of recent history', as Ivor Jennings remarked.[60] In 1937 the proposed National Defence Contribution precipitated 'vociferous' opposition from the outside interests. It was taken out of the Finance Bill before the division on the second reading, and replaced later by a more acceptable formulation.[61]

No doubt the unions did prevent the worthwhile implementation of the 1971 Industrial Relations Act. Some of the methods used did challenge authority, e.g. strike action against the new National Industrial Relations Court which had jailed five dockers for refusing to obey its order to stop 'blacking' a company in Hackney. The TUC called for a one-day general strike, the first such call since 1926. It was not launched because the authorities got the dockers out of Pentonville in double quick time. This (and much more) was truly the 'politics of defiance'.[62]

The emasculation of an important Act of Parliament by the organised interests is new only to those who do not read history. In 1930, for example, as in 1971, the consultation-of-interests system had not worked, i.e. the government had not won the agreement of the interests, notably the Mining Association, before legislating. It forged ahead, anyway, with its Coal Mines

Bill (empowering compulsory amalgamations but with price fixing and the regulation of output); a great cry was heard in the land from a great array of interests; the government got its Bill (heavily amended in the Lords) – but the work of the Commission established under the Act was 'so bitterly opposed by the mining employers' interests' that it achieved 'very little'.[63] Similarly the British Medical Association held up the implementation of the 1946 National Health Service Act until it got what it wanted, which was tantamount to an amendment of the Act. Examples of non-co-operation by agriculture and business could also be cited.[64]

That does not rule out the possibility of a deterioration in the 1970s. As the union movement was undermining the 1971 Act, the National Union of Mineworkers was exacting from the Cabinet its 21 per cent wage increase. But the NUM's 1972 strike was political insofar as enlarging the public sector enlarges the area of political strife. The NUM's 1974 strike was political in the other sense: a deliberate attempt, based on its new market power derived from the energy shortage, to breach the statutory incomes policy. It succeeded in doing this.

Looking back at the sub-period as a whole, however, one would agree with the Conservative MP, Timothy Raison, that 'generally the record of the unions has not been bad in this respect'.[65] Nor does it appear that those challenges that were successful seriously eroded the authority of government more in the 1970s than in the 1930s.

It follows that if governments now find it more difficult to govern,[66] it is for reasons other than the impact of organised interests. If there is stagnation, it is not pluralist(ic) stagnation so far as the substance of policy is concerned.[67] The government gets most of its Bills, sustains most of its initiatives: there are whole areas of policy untouched, or unsullied, by the hands of the interests. Here, at least in discussing the interests, it would make for clarity if we distinguished, as in French, between immobilism and immobility. The latter (*immobilité*) is descriptive: things do not move. The former (*immobilisme*) implies causation: things do not move because the interests are obstructive or destructive.[68] Looking back over the whole post-war period, Britain does not seem to have suffered immobilism. Nor is Britain immobile. In the difficult post-war era, Britain has changed continually without ever breaking up – that in itself represents a kind of progress.[69]

NOTES

1. For a sketch, see Graham Wootton, *Pressure Groups in Britain, 1720–1970* (Hamden, Conn.: Archon Books, 1975).
2. Richard E. Caves (ed.), *Britain's Economic Prospects* (Washington, DC: Brookings Institution, 1968), Introduction and pp. 21–2.
3. Ibid., p. 21.
4. Ibid., pp. 21–2n.1.

5. A. J. Youngson, 'Great Britain, 1920–1970', in Carlo M. Cipolla (ed.), *Contemporary Economies*, vol. VI (Hassocks: Harvester Press, 1977) p. 153.
6. M. Panić, 'The Inevitable Inflation', *Lloyds Bank Review*, July 1976, Table 1.
7. G. D. N. Worswick, 'The End of Demand Management', ibid., Jan 1977, p. 9.
8. R. E. Caves, *Britain's Economic Prospects*, p. 22.
9. Angus Maddison, *Economic Growth in the West* (New York: Twentieth Century Fund, 1964) p. 28 and Appendix A, p. 194.
10. Caves, *Britain's Economic Prospects*, p. 3.
11. Joan Robinson, *Economics: An Awkward Corner* (London: Allen & Unwin, 1966) p. 65.
12. Richard Cooper, 'The Balance of Payments', in Caves, *Britain's Economic Prospects*, pp. 153–4.
13. Phyllis Deane and W. A. Cole, *British Economic Growth, 1688–1959*, 2nd ed. (Cambridge.: Cambridge University Press, 1967) p. 37.
14. A. J. Youngson, 'Great Britain, 1920–1970', in Cipolla, *Contemporary Economies*, vol. VI, p. 156.
15. Caves, *Britain's Economic Prospects*, p. 199.
16. Albert H. Imlah, *Economic Aspects of the Pax Britannica* (Cambridge, Mass.: Harvard University Press, 1958) Table 2.
17. P. H. Ady, in G. D. N. Worswick and P. H. Ady (eds), *The British Economy in the 1950s* (Oxford: Clarendon Press, 1962) p. 149.
18. See for a start Lawrence Krause, 'British Trade Performance', Caves, *Britain's Economic Prospects*, pp. 202 and 212; J. Black, 'The Volumes and Prices of British Exports', in Worswick and Ady, *The British Economy in the 1950s*, p. 120.
19. Samuel Brittan, *Steering the Economy* (New York: Library Press, 1970) p. 470.
20. D. Lomax, 'Our Fragmentary Political Economy', *National Westminster Bank Quarterly Review*, Aug 1975, p. 4.
21. Quoted by A. R. Conan, 'Does Britain Pay Its Way?', *National Westminster Bank Quarterly Review*, Feb 1969, pp. 4–5.
22. Ibid. For a full and lucid exposition, see W. A. P. Manser, *Britain in Balance* (London: Longman, 1971).
23. F. V. Meyer, D. C. Corner and J. E. S. Parker, *Problems of a Mature Economy* (London: Macmillan, 1970) p. 499.
24. Cooper in Caves, *Britain's Economic Prospects*, p. 168.
25. Ibid., p. 169.
26. Ibid., p. 171.
27. Ronald Hyam, *Britain's Imperial Century, 1815–1914* (New York: Harper & Row, 1976) p. 207.
28. Ibid.
29. From 1951 to 1967, plus or minus $3000 million. During the same period the reserves of some European countries increased several-fold. See Brittan, *Steering the Economy*, pp. 422–3.
30. Wootton, *Pressure Groups in Britain*, p. 14.
31. But Cabinet conclusions are parsimoniously recorded and other papers will probably turn out to be sparse. Much in any case would not have been committed to paper.
32. F. W. Paish, 'Inflation, Personal Incomes and Taxation', *Lloyds Bank Review*, Apr 1975, p. 2.
33. David Blake, *The Times*, 25 Sep 1978.
34. Ibid.

35. Information Division of the Treasury, *Economic Progress Report* (London: HMSO, July 1978) p. 3.
36. British Information Service, *Latest Developments in the British Economy* (New York, Sep 1978).
37. Chancellor of the Exchequer (Dennis Healey), *The Times*, 27 Sep 1978.
38. Honor Croome, 'Liberty, Equality and Full Employment', *Lloyds Bank Review*, July 1949.
39. Paish, in *Lloyds Bank Review*, Apr 1975.
40. Lord Kahn, 'Thoughts on the Behaviour of Wages and Monetarism', *Lloyds Bank Review*, Jan 1976, p. 8, also quoting the late Professor Harry Johnson. See also Professor Sidney Weintraub of the Wharton School, 'An Incomes Policy to Stop Inflation', *Lloyds Bank Review*, Jan 1971, pp. 1–12.
41. E. H. Phelps Brown, 'Labour Policies: Productivity, Industrial Relations, Cost Inflation', in Sir Alec Cairncross (ed.), *Britain's Economic Prospects Reconsidered* (Albany, NY: State University of New York Press, 1970) p. 138.
42. Weintraub, in *Lloyds Bank Review*, Jan 1971.
43. Kahn, ibid., Jan 1976.
44. See D. Jackson, H. A. Burner and F. Wilkinson, *Do Trade Unions Cause Inflation?* 2nd ed. (Cambridge: Cambridge University Press, 1975); Leo Panitch, *Social Democracy and Industrial Militancy* (Cambridge: Cambridge University Press, 1976).
45. Panić, in *Lloyds Bank Review*, July 1976, p. 9.
46. Michael Parkin, 'Where is Britain's Inflation Going', ibid., July 1975, p. 9.
47. Kahn, ibid., Jan 1976, citing Sir John Hicks.
48. David Cobham, 'The Politics of the Economics of Inflation', ibid., Apr 1978, p. 22.
49. E. H. Phelps Brown, 'A Non-monetarist View of the Pay Explosion', *Three Banks Review*, Mar 1975. See also his chapter in Cairncross, *Britain's Economic Prospects Reconsidered.*
50. Panić, in *Lloyds Bank Review*, July 1976; Phelps Brown, in *Three Banks Review*, Mar 1975; also Kahn, in *Lloyds Bank Review*, Jan 1976. Lord Kahn traces the movement back to the breakdown of the Dutch statutory prices and incomes policy in 1959.
51. See *Industrial and Labour Relations Review*, XXVIII (Oct 1974 and Jan 1975).
52. *The Times*, 28 Sep 1977.
53. Ibid.
54. Writing in 1920, cited by A. L. Levine, *Industrial Retardation in Britain 1880–1914* (New York: Basic Books, 1967) p. 84.
55. In agreement with Professor Ben Roberts, *Lloyds Bank Review*, Oct 1968, p. 31, as against the Donovan Commission's 'Most restrictive practices are not enforced by the unions as such.'
56. Marshall, quoted in Everett J. Burtt Jr, *Social Perspectives in the History of Economic Theory* (New York: St Martin's Press, 1972) p. 209; Edward Denison, 'Economic Growth', in Caves, *Britain's Economic Prospects.*
57. Michael Moran, *The Politics of Industrial Relations* (London: Macmillan, 1977); Colin Crouch, *Class Conflict and the Industrial Relations Crisis* (London: Heinemann, 1977).
58. Graham Wootton, *Pressure Politics in Contemporary Britain* (Lexington, Mass.: Lexington Books, 1978) p. 168.
59. Paul Ferris, *The New Militants: Crisis in the Trade Unions* (Harmondsworth: Penguin, 1972) p. 40.

60. W. Ivor Jennings, *Parliament* (Cambridge: Cambridge University Press, 1940) pp. 8, 130.
61. Ibid., pp. 8, 130, 231.
62. Moran, *Politics of Industrial Relations.*
63. J. W. Grove, *Government and Industry in Britain* (London: Longman, Green, 1962) p. 299.
64. G. Wootton, *Pressure Politics*, ch. 9.
65. *Sunday Telegraph*, 7 Jan 1979.
66. Cf. 1934–7, when governments lost not only the Coal Mines Bill and the National Defence Contribution in its original form, but had to withdraw the Unemployment Assistance Regulations (1934) and fundamentally modify the Incitement to Disaffection Bill (1934) and the Population (Statistics) Bill, 1937. The Hoare–Laval Pact was also repudiated, as was Sir Samuel Hoare. Was Britain ungovernable then?
67. For possible pluralist stagnation through procedural delays entailed by the consultation of interests, see Wootton, *Pressure Politics*, ch. 10.
68. *Pluri dictionnaire Larousse* (Paris: Librairie Larousse, 1975).
69. Cf. Gaetano Mosca, *Elementi di Scienza Politica* (Turin: Fratelli Bocca Editore, 1923) p. 471, n. 1.

7 Immigration and Racial Change

Donley T. Studlar

Privately, such (immigration) figures are regarded by ministers as having a political importance outweighed only by the regular economic indicators.

Peter Evans, *The Times*, 21 Feb 1978

Race and immigration have become a profoundly important issue in British politics, both quantitatively and qualitatively. Although the numbers of non-white immigrants entering the United Kingdom are often the focus of debate, this is only the most easily grasped symbol of the underlying question of what political action should be taken about the ethnic composition of British society. Despite anti-immigrant public opinion and government action to limit immigration, the non-white population of the United Kingdom has risen from approximately 1 per cent in the late 1950s, when the issue first was raised politically, to 3.5 per cent currently. The most authoritative estimates of the non-white population in the year 2000 are that it will be in the 6 or 7 per cent range. More importantly, non-whites will be concentrated in urban areas to such an extent that possibly one-third of the population of inner London and other urban areas will be non-white.

From the first, British governmental policy toward race and immigration has been reactive. The social and political changes wrought in the United Kingdom by the non-white immigrants were completely unforeseen at the time of the first post-war migration in 1948. The possibility of a large influx of immigrants was ignored, and no forethought was given to the consequences of appreciable numbers of non-whites settling in Britain. Later, as problems arose, the British government attempted to handle them in its usual empirical, 'muddling through' manner. At no time, has the government thought through and carried out a systematic policy on race or immigration, even though many of the changes brought about in Britain by non-white immigration are irreversible.

In so far as elite analysts gave race or immigration anything more than passing thought in the 1950s, almost all saw incorporation of the migrants from the Commonwealth as a sign of continued British influence and responsibilities in the larger world. It took considerable time and effort for mass opinion, first in the West Midlands and then elsewhere, to convince the elite that a colourblind policy could not continue without serious social and political repercussions. After recognising that large numbers of white British saw coloured immigrants as a sign of domestic deterioration, the elite has become reconciled to this interpretation. While few elite members enthusiastically voice popular prejudices, arguments for the benefits of a multiracial Britain almost inevitably have the qualifying phrase – 'within limits' – attached.

I The Issue Defined

Immigration as an issue concerns the entry of non-white British subjects from 'New Commonwealth' states, principally the West Indies, India and Pakistan (including Bangladesh). 'Immigration' is used interchangeably with 'coloured immigration'. Some observers contend that immigration and race relations should be separated as issues; the former concerns who should be admitted to the state and the latter concerns how people of different ethnic heritages are treated within it. Moreover, identifying immigration and skin colour makes anomalous the position of coloured people born in the United Kingdom. Immigration and race, however, are commonly understood in Britain to be intimately connected. The internal racial composition of society and the attendant political problems are a direct result of recent immigration. Here, the term 'race-immigration' designates the general political issue.[1]

In the immediate aftermath of the Second World War, the government, and indeed, practically all political leaders, considered it unthinkable to make invidious distinctions among British subjects anywhere in the Commonwealth. This attitude was reflected in the British Nationality Act of 1948, which reaffirmed the traditional Imperial practice of admission into the United Kingdom of any British subject, including the citizens of newly independent Commonwealth states.[2] Ten years later, however, immigration control was no longer unmentionable, at least among the public at large and within the backbenches of the House of Commons. In the interim, West Indian and later Asian workers had come to the United Kingdom in pursuit of readily available employment. Nevertheless, the immigrants constituted less than 1 per cent of the British population in 1958. The racial disturbances of that summer discredited the idea, widely accepted in educated circles, that the British were incapable of colour prejudice. Moreover, extensive decolonisation and the failure of many Commonwealth states to respond to British attempts at leadership made it less imperative, in the eyes of some politicians, for Britain to maintain free entry of British subjects in order to sustain the unity of the Commonwealth. The continued immigration of coloured Commonwealth citizens became viewed more as a domestic issue primarily involving colonial, Commonwealth, or foreign relations. It was the Home Office which introduced and administered policies for immigration control.

Changes of attitude occurred because a permanent coloured immigrant population with full citizenship rights had become visibly concentrated in the industrial areas of London and the West Midlands. The first significant parliamentary debates on controlling Commonwealth immigration took place in 1958. The Conservative government, wishing to maintain the notion that Britons were colourblind, refused to give any indication that control of immigration was being contemplated. Advocacy of such control was the province of local political leaders and extremist MPs within the Conservative party. Somewhat more respectable, however, were the resolutions for immigration control passed by the Conservative Party Conferences of 1958 and 1961. When the Conservative government finally responded to this mass initiative by introducing and eventually passing the Commonwealth Immigrants Act of 1962, the Labour Party under Hugh Gaitskell's leadership furiously opposed the bill as undermining the conception of a multi-racial Commonwealth.[3] The Commonwealth connection, however, quickly lost its importance once Labour gained office.

Labour came to power after the general election of 1964 and the counter-cyclical victory of a racist Conservative candidate in Smethwick. In the minds of many political observers, the Smethwick result, coupled with the subsequent Leyton by-election defeat of the same Labour stalwart, Patrick Gordon Walker, convinced the Labour party that mass anti-immigration feelings were electorally too explosive to oppose.[4] Instead, Labour adopted a policy of accommodation. After a futile attempt at consultation with the states sending immigrants, Labour sponsored even more restrictive 1965 immigration measures. The almost simultaneous passage of the first Race Relations Act was further indication that racial differences stemming from immigration were increasingly viewed as an internal problem. The official doctrine of limits on further entrance of immigrants to allow for the absorption and adjustment of those already in Britain has not changed since then.

These first limits on immigration occurred before the economic downturn of the late 1960s. The market demand for immigrant labour was still strong in the United Kingdom in the early 1960s, as it was in other West European states. Despite the economic need for this labour, social and political reasons led Britain to become the first West European state to limit its flow of immigrant labour. Richard Crossman commented at the time of the 1965 act that 'this has been one of the most difficult and unpleasant jobs the government has had to do. We have become illiberal and lowered the quotas at a time when we have an acute shortage of labour'.[5] Despite pangs of conscience in the Labour party, this policy was considered highly successful, especially when race was not an issue in the general election of 1966.

The Kenyan Asian crisis of 1968, however, demonstrated that the race-immigration problem had not been permanently solved. Asians with British passports were being evicted from Kenya as undesirable foreigners under a policy of Africanisation. Labour, the party which claimed to uphold the idea of the multi-racial Commonwealth against the Conservatives' 'Little (white) England' policy, now extended immigration restrictions to people claiming citizenship of the United Kingdom and Colonies. This willingness to act in defiance of previously understood British commitments to admit freely any subject holding a British passport, especially in time of duress, prompted Crossman's comment that this measure 'would have been declared unconstitutional in any country with a written constitution and a Supreme Court'.[6] Feeling betrayed, racial liberals in the Labour party spoke of 'the race relations catastrophe'. Soon after this episode, during discussion of the second Race Relations Bill, Enoch Powell made the speech, popularly known as 'the Rivers of Blood' speech, which resulted in both his eviction from the Conservative parliamentary leadership and his singular role as the spokesman for anti-coloured opinion in the country. Commonwealth commitments of both major parties, as well as economic considerations, had been over-ridden by restrictionist public opinion and backbench parliamentary pressure, now led by a renegade Opposition MP.

Since 1968, race-immigration has essentially remained on a plateau with potential repercussions which most politicians prefer to avoid. Attention to the issue has been sporadic. Despite considerable evidence that immigration was a critical voting issue in the general election of 1970,[7] it was of little moment in the two 1974 general elections.[8] Further immigration restriction in 1971 was breached by the 1972 emergency entrance of Ugandan Asians driven out of Africa by General Amin. The Conservative government admitted the Asians only reluctantly in the face of public opposition to their entry.[9] By the late 1970s, however, race-immigration was of increasing concern in British politics. Racial clashes in the summers of 1976 and 1977 and the emergence of a National Front party campaigning almost solely on opposition to immigrants made it evident that the issue was persistent. The advocacy of further immigration control by Mrs Thatcher, in tones reminiscent of Enoch Powell a decade previously, shows that the Conservative party may make this an openly partisan issue, in contrast to official major party positions since 1965.

Some observers have contended that the fundamental debate about race-immigration has already occurred. Katznelson has argued that it took place in 1958–65.[10] This, however, was only a partial debate at best. After the passage of the 1962 Commonwealth Immigrants Act, Labour did not oppose the idea of immigration control in principle. Aside from Smethwick and a few other constituencies, race-immigration was not debated in the election campaign of 1964.[11] More recently, former Prime Minister Edward Heath criticised Mrs Thatcher for creating an 'unnecessary national row' about immigration, and dismissed as 'nonsense' the idea that politicians have discussed immigration insufficiently. Yet the issue has only infrequently occupied the centre stage of British politics; most of the time it has been off in the wings. Even when race-immigration has been the focus of attention, political leaders have felt uncomfortable in dealing with it and have been eager to dispense with it as soon as possible. Whatever their own opinions about immigration, most British politicians have looked upon Enoch Powell as a distasteful rabblerouser rather than as a politician who has raised a serious issue for political debate. Many people before and after Powell have voiced accusations of a political conspiracy among major party leaders to avoid discussion of the issue. While 'conspiracy' is perhaps too Machiavellian a term, attempts have been made to keep race-immigration off the political agenda through an elite consensus.[12] Indeed, Mr Callaghan's first comments after Mrs Thatcher's 1978 remarks about further immigration control included a call, later reiterated, for an all-party approach to immigration. The two major parties have been able to maintain a political consensus about immigration most of the time since 1965. Not speaking about the issue remains the preferred norm for major party politicans. Race-immigration has continued to be a major political issue in Britain, notwithstanding the absence of a fundamental partisan political debate.

II The Empire Comes Home

Traditionally Britain has been a country of emigration, not immigration. Large numbers of Britons have gone abroad, especially in the service of the Empire, but very few foreigners have arrived on the shores of the United Kingdom. Temporary visitors have stimulated little controversy, but nativist sentiment has frequently had political impact when the migrants seemed to be permanent.[13] The greater the immigrants' similarity to the British in colour, religion and culture, the less the resistance to their entrance in fact, if not in form.

Elite and mass attitudes toward non-whites, both at home and abroad, have been very different. The idea of racial equality has had only a limited impact upon British popular attitudes. The history of the Empire suggests that racial equality in a multi-racial society is not an idea that British peoples accept when the consequences are close at hand.[14]

However, British elite attitudes toward racial differences have traditionally been liberal and tolerant.[15] They have also been paternalistic. The elite knew what was best for the masses, both white and non-white. While differences among ethnic groups were often recognised in practice, the educated elite ignored or minimised such differences in public discussion, especially in the declining years of the Empire. The Empire, however, was really a racial hierarchy with the native British on top, followed by white settlers and non-whites on the bottom, within the latter category there were substantial differences in treatment. Even though the Mother Country was open to all British subjects, the process of migration (and power) extended from the United Kingdom outward. Non-white people were not expected to advance politically as fast as white settlers.[16] The older dominions ruled by white settlers – Canada, Australia, New Zealand and South Africa – achieved independence first.

The post-Second World War Commonwealth seemed to effect a change in the racial hierarchy. The Commonwealth symbolised the formal equality of states formed out of the Empire. In the mid-1950s, multi-racial equality of peoples within states was proclaimed as a Commonwealth goal. The realisation of this ideal, of course, has left a great deal to be desired in several states, not only those dominated by white settlers. As part of the multi-racial ideal, unlimited immigration of Commonwealth residents into the United Kingdom continued throughout the 1950s. Once substantial numbers of whites and non-whites began to rub shoulders within the United Kingdom itself, however, racial friction and public demands forced a change in elite behaviour.

The British public has never really accepted the idea of multi-racialism, especially at home. To the public, coloured people are dependent people over whom Britain has ruled. Now the formerly subordinate inhabitants of the colonies are settling in the Mother Country; furthermore, they are bringing their own religions and cultures with them. Is it any wonder that the average Briton has consistently opposed further coloured immigration?[17] The natural order of things, with the United Kingdom dominating its colonies and white men dominating coloured people, has been upset.[18] This change was considered regrettable but acceptable as long as the implications were not too close at hand.

A growing and highly visible coloured population in the United Kingdom, however, has stimulated a restrictionist response from the British public, an attitude that was not limited to residents of immigrant-populated areas.[19] Analyses of anti-immigrant sentiments in Britain have been able to find only minimal differences among different social groups.[20] The source of the widespread opposition to immigrants lies in the political culture.[21] The British sense of political community, of who belongs to their group, is exceptionally strong. Whatever their legal claims to British citizenship, coloured people are perceived as being outside the political community. In the eyes of the general public, the sophisticated arguments for multi-racialism are not convincing. In Richard Rose's phrase, they view immigrants as 'British blacks' rather than 'black Britons'.[22]

Legally, of course, there is no question about admitting immigrants having full citizenship rights, either upon entrance or, since 1971, after a period of probation. 'Felt citizenship', however, is another question, on both sides. Up until the present time immigrants have been relatively unassertive in British politics. In many ways they are still objects of the British political process,[23] a typical situation for first generation newcomers to a society, especially when they are as diverse in social background as British immigrants. Often they are more attentive to politics in their former political system than to politics in the United Kingdom.[24] This situation may change somewhat, however, as second and third-generation coloured people become politically conscious.[25]

British identity is very difficult to specify.[26] The worldwide commitments and complex arrangements for rule that were maintained under the British Empire have led to several different statuses beyond the fundamental one of British subject. Being a British citizen, however, is not the same as being a British subject, as the 1962 Commonwealth Immigrants Act made clear. Distinctions have even been made among citizens of the United Kingdom and Colonies on the basis of who issued the British passport. It is still a topic of debate as to 'who belongs to Britain', or, perhaps more appropriately, 'to what degree do certain people belong to Britain?'. Unlike most states, even those with extensive colonial holdings, the United Kingdom has never clearly defined who is entitled to British citizenship. As long as British subjects did not come to the United Kingdom in large numbers for permanent settlement, this was no pressing problem. Now it is.

British nationality and citizenship law is, as one commentator puts it, 'a jungle'.[27] Britain's former colonies have clear definitions of citizenship; only the Mother Country does not. Nobody, has been able to identify how many overseas subjects are entitled to come to Britain under current law. If the governing parties are uncertain as to what constitutes a British citizen and what commitments they have to overseas residents, it is hardly surprising that the white British public has arrived at its own informal notion of 'who belongs here', a conception which is hostile to further immigration and is at best uncomfortable with the multi-racial composition of Britain.[28]

How can the conundrum of formal British citizenship be resolved? There is widespread agreement that the British Nationality Act of 1948 should be revised. How to do this, however, is not so obvious. The Labour government brought forward a Green Paper on citizenship in 1977 which suggested a two-tier plan, with 'British Overseas Citizenship' ineligible for entrance into the United Kingdom. Publication of this idea immediately evoked criticisms that it renèged on previous British commitments, might leave some people stateless, and still left British citizenship rights ambiguous. The extent of Britain's overseas commitments, past and present, makes it difficult to avoid such pitfalls in revising nationality law. The alternative, however, is to limp along with the present very muddled law and to hope that no more crises arise like the Kenyan and Ugandan Asians. To continue tempting fate with the current statute or to produce a new one which will eliminate the rights of some groups to enter the United Kingdom is not an easy choice. In coping with their legacy of Empire, British governments have always been reluctant to act.

III The Limits of Class Politics

Intense mass feeling has impelled British governments to limit immigration at particular points in time. The pressure of public opinion and backbench parliamentary opinion stimulated the Immigration Control Acts of 1962 and 1968. The 1965 and 1971 measures were the products of the general election campaigns of 1964 and 1970, respectively. The Race Relations Acts of 1965, 1968 and 1976, on the other hand, did not arouse mass interest nearly as much, although that does not mean that politicians ignored public opinion.[29] The Bills presented to Parliament, however long they may have been planned, often seemed hasty and ill-considered when debated.[30] At the time each of these Acts was passed, some politicians expressed the hope that the adoption of the legislation would mark the end of the race-immigration debate. In each instance, this has been a vain hope.

But why should race-immigration be treated as a marginal issue? Katznelson has perceived the essence of the matter:[31]

> However managed and defused, class is still at the core of the British political dialogue. As a result, for the mid-twentieth century British politician, class issues have presented few unknowns. In discussing issues of class, he knows, broadly, what is expected of him; his rhetoric and behavior conform on the whole to relatively clearcut norms. For the typical politician, on the other hand, domestic racial issues, when first raised, were worrying, confusing, incoherent, anomic. Consequently, most British politicians have been anxious to depoliticize race, to make the politics of race coherent by creating policies and institutions *outside* of the usual political arenas that are capable of eliminating race once and for all as a public political issue, thus permitting them to deal with the more congenial, well-defined issues of class.

In short, race-related issues are not considered to be 'normal' issues in the British political process. There are three related reasons for this:

(1) race is a relatively new and unfamiliar issue in Britain;
(2) it is a type of issue which is inherently difficult to settle;
(3) British political institutions, which emphasise pragmatic, incremental methods to deal with problems largely stemming from differing economic circumstances have special difficulty in handling ethnic issues.[32]

Even after 20 years of experience, party politicians are uncomfortable with race-immigration and would rather avoid the topic. Most politicians have not found that they can cope satisfactorily with the issue. The comment of a Labour MP is instructive: 'One just cannot win on this issue'.[33] Racial conflict bears seeds of disruption for British society. Once it is aroused, who can predict how it will affect established political alliances? The cross-party support that Enoch Powell attracted is one indication of the potential of race issues for realigning the British party system.[34] Better to avoid confronting such nasty and unpredictable issues. If immigration is kept to a minimum and anti-discrimination legislation is passed, perhaps in time the issue will solve itself.

Several factors, however, have made this strategy less successful than it might have been. External political events, such as the eviction of Asians from Kenya and Uganda, the persistence of anti-immigrant public opinion, and individual politicians willing to break the code of reticence such as Powell have hampered this approach. The Kenyan Asians episode is a good example of this. Despite the fact that the Labour government knew of the potential for a forced exodus of the Asians in 1965, it took no action until early 1968, by which time the exodus had begun, the public was aroused, and Powell and Duncan Sandys were criticising the government for inaction.[35]

In terms remarkably similar to Katznelson, a Conservative MP has offered an analysis of why immigration is a secondary issue in the thinking of most British politicians:[36]

> It is a subject in which no one takes any pleasure. It's regarded as a non-respectable political subject, worthy of tub-thumping at party conferences rather than a serious subject. I can count the number of people in the country who think seriously about race relations on the fingers of one hand – no, two hands – which I think is a pity. Politicians like to think about broader, sweeping concerns – foreign policy. economics, trade, industrial relations – rather than specific social issues.

The idea that race-immigration is a 'social issue' in which most politicians are not interested is supported by Ronald Butt, who suggests that race is an issue of conscience for many MPs, similar to abortion or capital punishment.[37] Unlike the other examples of issues of conscience, race-immigration is debated on an ostensibly partisan basis. On the other hand, legislative action on race-immigration does bear some similarity to these issues. The major parties sometimes do not oppose each other on third reading and abstentions and/or cross-party voting occur relatively frequently. On one occasion, the government has even suffered a defeat on an immigration measure.[38] Under these circumstances, most politicians would prefer to let sleeping dogs lie.

When political leaders do think about race, they often attempt to place it in a more familiar category, that of class. If one can classify racial discrimination as just another form of class disadvantage, then the issue becomes more readily comprehensible within the boundaries of conventional thinking about politics. One can argue that hostility toward immigrants is a surrogate for the problems of unemployment, inadequate incomes, and poor housing, i.e. race only reveals the already-present economic problems of society. According to the Labour critique, if the coloured immigrants and the white working class can unite, a concerted attack on the economic roots of these problems could be made. Such analyses are inadequate because they fail to treat race as an issue on its own merits. Several studies, both of conventional anti-immigrant attitudes and of the more virulent anti-immigrant hostility of National Front supporters, have shown that anti-coloured attitudes are *not* strongly related to either individual or group economic deprivation.[39] Furthermore, it is highly unlikely that immigrant groups will achieve sufficient working-class consciousness or that trade unions will be sufficiently able to overcome the racial hostility of their membership to sustain an effective alliance.[40] However much some political leaders would like to believe that racial politics is only a manifestation of class politics, in fact the two are distinct policy areas.

This treatment of race-immigration issue is more understandable if one places it in a broader perspective. Several analysts have argued that conflicts between ethnically distinct groups are difficult for political systems to handle because such conflicts are essentially non-bargainable.[41] The conflicts originate in communal differences among groups. In contrast to economic issues, it is hard to make incremental adjustments in ascriptive distinctions such as language, religion and skin colour. Furthermore, economic issues are often capable of positive-sum settlements, in which both sides ultimately gain; communal conflicts, including race, rarely are. Hence the latter are potentially more destabilising for a political system, particularly one such as Britain where class conflict is considered the norm.[42] Rose and Urwin provide a summary view of this position:[43]

> The key determinant of the degree of strain is whether or not the demands are bargainable. Nonbargainable demands tend to take the form of ultimatums, or to involve zero-sum conflicts in which victory for one group involves deprivations for others, as, for example, in the political doctrine of white supremacy in the American South. . . . The chief characteristic of economic controversies is that they are typically expressed in terms of money. Money is a continuous variable capable of indefinite subdivision for purposes of providing incremental adjustments in the distribution of economic benefits. In short, it is something that is very easy to bargain about. . . . Communal issues are nonbargainable. For example, children must be taught either in French or in Flemish as their first language of instruction. Symbols of ethnic identity are similarly indivisible. For example, a flag cannot be British on one side and Irish on the other.

By constantly attempting to avoid political decisions on racial issues, and by dealing with such questions only on an *ad hoc* basis when forced to face them, British politicians have not had to cope with the 'trench warfare' of institutionalised communal divisions.[44] Advocating class politics, however, does not make racial issues disappear.

T. Alexander Smith has suggested that the non-bargainability of communal issues, including race, is part of a larger pattern of government action which sets these issues apart from economic ones, including those of class.[45] His analysis of these issues comports well with how the race-immigration question has been handled in Britain. The characteristics of communal issues are as follows:[46]

(1) a wide scope and intensity of conflict over deeply held non-economic values;
(2) the major role in the policy process being played by backbench legislators, supported by moralistic pressure groups;
(3) low levels of party discipline, and
(4) legislative rather than executive resolution of the issue.

The broad pattern put forward by Smith appears to be upheld in England.[47] Government leadership on race-immigration is weak because politicians are leery of the political and social consequences of exacerbating group tensions. Since communal issues are 'dysfunctional for parties and their leaders',[48] most politicians de-emphasise these issues and follow public opinion rather than leading it.

IV The Eternal Issue?

In attempting to deal with the race-immigration issue in the United Kingdom, three inter-related problems are central:

1. to develop a clear definition of United Kingdom citizenship in order that the exact extent of commitments to British citizens abroad can be known;
2. to provide black British citizens already in the political system with sufficient security and hope about their situation that they will not feel themselves to be second-class citizens;
3. to reconcile white Britons to the multi-racial nature of British society by assuring them that multi-racialism will be limited.

Opinions differ about the priorities among these problems. Non-whites and white liberals are most concerned about finding an answer to the second problem. British politicians have spent the most effort in coping with the third problem, as white fears have led to a continuous Dutch auction on the number of allowable immigrants. The least political attention has been devoted to the first problem, since it seemed to demand less immediate attention. Yet finding a satisfactory answer to the nationality and citizenship question, would provide a framework within which the other two problems would be potentially more manageable.

Suggestions about how to deal with these problems abound. Most depend upon how one evaluates the government's past performance on race-immigration. Racial liberals see the sequence of government actions since the initial introduction of the Commonwealth Immigrants Bill in 1961 as a chain of disasters, mitigated only by the passage of anti-discrimination acts. Although the argument for unhampered free entry of all British subjects is rarely heard today, liberals often voice concern about overly stringent and discriminatory immigration laws. On the other side of the political spectrum, Powellites also see the performance of government as poor, but for different reasons. By allowing the non-white population in Britain to grow, government control of immigration has shown itself to be too little and too late. More stringent measures are necessary.

While critical of specific measures, moderates generally view the record more favourably. Britain has coped with an inherently difficult political problem. Violence and other violations of human rights have been avoided without permanent alienation of either whites or non-whites from the political system. Preoccupation with race-immigration as an issue on the political agenda would only lead to heightened tensions and further difficulties. Non-white immigrants, especially Asians, still find the United Kingdom attractive enough to want to settle. Perhaps in time, public recognition that Britain is *de facto* a multi-racial society will lead to an acceptance of social pluralism, although assimilation is hardly likely. In this regard, the greater tolerance of the young is a hopeful sign. Such a mutual accommodation of ethnic groups might be called 'antagonistic acceptance'. Even this most favourable evaluation of political performance on race-immigration does not argue that progress has occurred. The system has simply coped well enough to avoid precipitous decline.

In dealing with nationality law, the rights of non-whites, and white attitudes British empiricism has had its difficulties. Nationality law, the fundamental problem, remains unreformed. There are also increasing signs that the much feared 'second generation problem' of the United Kingdom-born children of immigrants is close at hand. High levels of unemployment, especially among young West Indian youths in London, has led to tension with the police and occasional outbreaks of violence. This problem has been partly defused by the recent net exodus of West Indians from the United Kingdom. Moreover, the children of Asian immigrants have not yet manifested such hostility toward the political system.[49] Nevertheless, as larger numbers of coloured people are born in the United Kingdom, their resentment at being treated as less than equal citizens can be expected to increase. On the other hand, there is a disaffected group of whites as well. Disappointed by the failure of the two major parties to stop immigration completely, they either abstain from voting or support a minor party or leader.[50] In recent years the National Front has become the preferred vehicle of protest for many of these people. Surveys of National Front supporters show them to have a high degree of political cynicism.[51] A more popular long-term repository for whites disappointed with race-immigration policy has been support for Enoch Powell, which has continued at substantial levels within the ranks of all parties.[52] The political system is thus faced with a disaffected white element as well as the prospect of a largely alienated coloured populations.

If the United Kingdom is to improve its political performance on race-immigration, a more direct approach to the problem may be necessary. Undoubtedly this would be difficult to introduce in Britain, but confronting the problem of race-immigration directly could result in substantial improvement of the situation, as seems to have been the case in the United States. Although more people in Britain seem willing to face the issue today, the prevalent response is still avoidance of a 'nasty subject'. The most basic data lie uncollected, either through official or private colourblindness. For years there has been resistance to enumerations, based on race or ethnic background either of school children or of the general population. Even those who have been most vocal in their condemnations of past policy argue that collecting statistics by racial categories will only lead to invidious distinctions being made between groups. A suggestion that a question on ethnic background be incorporated in the 1981 census was greeted by a prominent British academic specialist in race relations as 'extraordinarily dangerous. It goes into the area of racism by saying there is some basic difference between white and West Indian, which there is not'.[53] School teachers and prestige media writers also prefer to ignore racial distinctions as unpleasant.[54]

This deliberate inattention to racial distinctions is a reflection of British political culture. In the United States, statistics on race have invariably been viewed as aids in attacking discrimination, even to the extent of enforcing controversial affirmative action programmes requiring a quota of non-whites in many institutions. Within the United Kingdom, traditional notions of individualism have had more impact, especially as they apply to private acts.[55] The British are reluctant to have the government interfere with the liberty of the individual subject to do as he pleases.[56] Furthermore, the idea of official recognition and enforcement of non-economic 'group rights' is not readily accepted in British political culture. Despite the multi-racial and multi-cultural reality, officially Britain operates on an assumption of assimilation. Even liberals who want to change current British racial practices often do not want to call attention to race as a 'problem'.[57] But how is anything constructive to be done about racial animosities unless race is recognised as a 'problem' on its own merits? The assimilationist assumption that coloured people will merge into the working class is erroneous. Race is a problem in Britain *per se*.

Since 1961 British politicians have been attempting, with mixed success, to reconcile the white British public to multi-racialism by promising that coloured minorities will be limited in number.[58] The government has also attempted to alleviate discrimination against coloured residents of the

United Kingdom by providing some legal protection of civil rights. The three race relations acts that have been passed, however, have not proven to be very effective.[59] The ineffectiveness of these acts has led to demands for a general Bill of Rights to protect the rights of all British citizens.[60]

Measures that non-whites and their supporters see as progress, however, are viewed by many native whites as decline and vice versa. Meanwhile, politicians are likely to see any successful short-term holding action as beneficial in that the situation has not deteriorated into something worse. In this way, short-term policies of increased immigration control and race relations acts have become a cumulative long-term policy.

Race-immigration has resulted in major changes in British society and politics. With a growing non-white population, the issue is not likely to diminish in the forseeable future, whether politicians are comfortable with it or not. Despite 20 years of discussion, race-immigration is still not integrated into the regular decision-making processes of the British political system. As Milnor and Franklin point out, 'an issue so explosive that it achieves a high degree of popular saliency without achieving a high degree of integration into the decision-making system is one capable of paralysing the political system and throwing it into disarray'.[61] Race-immigration has thrown the political system into disarray in the past, and could do so again.

The most important consideration in any major change of race-immigration is how to reconcile white and coloured to each other socially, economically and politically better than has been done previously. The politics of race-immigration is highly dependent upon mutual perception. If both whites and non-whites can be induced to feel secure and hopeful about their positions, a greater degree of racial harmony is more likely. The histories of multi-ethnic political systems, do not however, provide ready answers for this problem.[62]

As people in the United Kingdom become accustomed to living with the multi-racial and multi-cultural reality, race-immigration may become a more manageable political issue. But, inter-ethnic hostility could develop to the point where it represents an acute challenge to the political system. The way British politicians have handled this issue fully justifies the description offered by James G. Christoph: 'A system that acts as much on the basis of understandings – unarticulated, unstructured, implicit responses to new situations – does not encourage bold solutions or positive action.'[63]

NOTES

1. Legislation designed to control immigration, however, will be explicitly distinguished from race relations acts attempting to guarantee civil rights for coloured United Kingdom residents.
2. Nicholas Deakin, 'The British Nationality Act of 1948: A Brief Study in the Political Mythology of Race Relations', *Race*, XI (July 1969) 77–83.

3. Nicholas Deakin, 'The Politics of the Commonwealth Immigrants Bill', *Political Quarterly*, XXXIX (Jan–Mar 1968) 25–45.
4. E. J. B. Rose *et al.*, *Colour and Citizenship* (London: Oxford University Press, 1969) pp. 224–5.
5. R. H. S. Crossman, *The Diaries of a Cabinet Minister*, vol. I (London: Hamish Hamilton and Jonathan Cape, 1976) p. 299.
6. R. H. S. Crossman, 'Understanding the Profusion of Shrinking Violets', *The Times*, 6 Sep 1972.
7. David Butler and Donald Stokes, *Political Change in Britain*, 2nd ed. (London: Macmillan, 1974) pp. 303–8; R. W. Johnson and Douglas Schoen, 'The "Powell Effect": or How One Man Can Win', *New Society* 22 July 1976, pp. 168–72; Douglas E. Schoen, *Enoch Powell and the Powellites* (New York: St Martin's Press, 1977); Donley T. Studlar, 'Policy Voting in Britain: The Colored Immigration Issue in the 1964, 1966, and 1970 General Elections', *American Political Science Review*, LXXII (Mar 1978) 46–64.
8. David Butler and Dennis Kavanagh, *The British General Election of February, 1974* (London: Macmillan, 1974); David Butler and Dennis Kavanagh, *The British General Election of October, 1974* (London: Macmillan, 1975); A. D. Fox, 'Attitudes to Immigration: A Comparison of Data from the 1970 and 1974 General Election Surveys', *New Community*, IV (Summer 1975) 167–78; Community Relations Commission, Reference and Technical Services Division, *Participation of Ethnic Minorities in the October General Election, 1974* (London: Community Relations Commission, 1975).
9. Crossman, in *The Times*, 6 Sep 1972; Derek Humphrey and Michael Ward, *Passports and Politics* (Harmondsworth: Penguin, 1974); Donley T. Studlar, 'British Public Opinion, Colour Issues, and Enoch Powell: A Longitudinal Analysis', *British Journal of Political Science*, IV (July 1974) 371–81.
10. Ira Katznelson, *Black Men, White Cities* (London: Oxford University Press, 1973).
11. David Butler and Anthony King, *The British General Election of 1964* (London: Macmillan, 1965) p. 143; Nicholas Deakin (ed.), *Colour and the British Electorate, 1964* (London: Pall Mall Press, 1965).
12. William Deedes, *Race Without Rancour* (London: Conservative Political Centre, 1968); Crossman, in *The Times*, 6 Sep 1972; Katznelson, *Black Men, White Cities*; Alan Brier and Barry Axford, 'The Theme of Race in British Social and Political Research', in Ivor Crewe (ed.), *British Political Sociology Yearbook*, vol. II: *The Politics of Race* (New York: John Wiley, 1975) pp. 2–25.
13. Paul Foot, *Immigration and Race in British Politics* (Harmondsworth: Penguin, 1965).
14. J. D. B. Miller, *The Commonwealth in the World*, 3rd ed. (Cambridge, Mass.: Harvard University Press, 1967) p. 20; Richard Rose, *Politics in England*, 2nd ed. (Boston, Mass: Little, Brown, 1974) p. 15.
15. Anthony H. Birch, ch. 4 above. Although Birch refers specifically to the 1950s when he uses these terms, they seem to apply to a broader time span as well.
16. David Goldsworthy, *Colonial Issues in British Politics, 1945–1961* (London: Oxford University Press, 1971); J. E. S. Fawcett, 'British Nationality and the Commonwealth', *The Round Table*, no. 250 (1973) 262.
17. Studlar, in *British Journal of Political Science*, IV.
18. Daniel Lawrence, *Black Migrants, White Natives* (Cambridge: Cambridge University Press, 1974) pp. 54–6.

19. Donley T. Studlar, 'Social Context and Attitudes Towards Coloured Immigrants', *British Journal of Sociology*, XXVIII (June 1977) 168–84.
20. Rose *et al.*, *Colour and Citizenship*, pp. 551–604; Richard T. Schaefer, 'Correlates of Racial Prejudice', in Timothy Leggatt (ed.), *Sociological Theory and Survey Research* (Beverley Hills: Sage, 1974) pp. 237–64; Donley T. Studlar, 'Religion and White Racial Attitudes in Britain', *Ethnic and Racial Studies*, I (July 1978) 306–15; Donley T. Studlar, 'Racial Attitudes in Britain: A Causal Analysis', *Ethnicity*, VI (June 1979) 107–22.
21. Diana Spearman, 'Enoch Powell's Postbag', *New Society*, 9 May 1968, pp. 667–8; Elinor B. Bachrach, '"Powellism" and Political Culture: The Impact of Race Problems on British Politics' (MA Thesis, University of Chicago, 1969); Lawrence, *Black Migrants, White Natives*; Donley T. Studlar, 'Political Culture and Racial Policy in Britain', *Patterns of Prejudice*, VIII (May–June 1974) 7–12; also in Richard Rose (ed.), *Studies in British Politics*, 3rd ed. (New York: St Martin's Press, 1976) pp. 105–14.
22. Rose, *Politics in England*, p. 30.
23. Katznelson, *Black Men, White Cities*.
24. R. Miles and A. Phizacklea, 'Class, Race, Ethnicity and Political Action', *Political Studies*, XXV (Dec 1977) 491–507.
25. Rose *et al.*, *Colour and Citizenship*, pp. 476–91.
26. See the comments of Richard Rose in the next chapter.
27. W. R. Bohning, *The Migration of Workers in the United Kingdom and the European Community* (London: Oxford University Press, 1972) p. 133.
28. Alan Marsh, 'Who Hates the Blacks?', *New Society*, 23 Sep 1976, pp. 649–52; Alan Little and David Kohler, 'Do We Hate the Blacks?, *New Society*, 27 Jan 1977, pp. 184–5; Community Relations Commission, Reference Division, *Some of My Best Friends . . .* (London: Community Relations Commission, 1976).
29. Keith Hindell, 'The Genesis of the Race Relations Bill', *Political Quarterly*, XXXVI (Oct–Dec 1965) 25–45; Louis Kushnick, 'The Race Bill Battle', *New Society*, 27 June 1968, pp. 943–4; Rose *et al.*, *Colour and Citizenship*, pp. 511–33.
30. Hindell, in *Political Quarterly*, XXXVI; Richard Boston, 'How the Immigrants Act Was Passed', *New Society*, 28 Mar 1968, pp. 448–52; Hannan Rose, 'The Immigration Act 1971: A Case Study in the Work of Parliament', *Parliamentary Affairs*, XXVI (Winter 1972–3) 69–91; Katznelson, *Black Men, White Cities*, p. 135; Humphry and Ward, *Passports and Politics*; Philip Norton, 'Intra-Party Dissent in the House of Commons: A Case Study – The Immigration Rules, 1972', *Parliamentary Affairs*, XXIX (Autumn 1976) 404–20.
31. Katznelson, *Black Men, White Cities*, p. 125.
32. Cynthia Enloe, *Ethnic Conflict and Political Development* (Boston, Mass.: Little, Brown, 1973) pp. 81–2.
33. Personal interview, June 1973.
34. Studlar, in *British Journal of Political Science*, IV; Robert King and Michael Wood, 'The Support for Enoch Powell', in Crewe, *British Political Sociology Yearbook*, vol. II, pp. 239–62; Johnson and Schoen, in *American Political Science Review*, LXXII; Schoen, *Enoch Powel and the Powellites*.
35. R. H. S. Crossman, *The Diaries of a Cabinet Minister*, vol. II (London: Hamish Hamilton and Jonathan Cape, 1976) pp. 675, 733–4.
36. Personal interview, June 1973.

37. Ronald Butt, *The Power of Parliament*, 2nd ed. (London: Constable, 1969) p. 280.
38. Boston, in *New Society*, 28 Mar 1968; Butt, *The Power of Parliament*; Norton, in *Parliamentary Affairs*, XXIX.
39. Marsh, in *New Society*, 23 Sep 1976; Studlar, in *British Journal of Sociology*, XXVIII; Stuart Weir, 'Youngsters in the Front Line', *New Society*, 27 Apr 1978, pp. 189–93; Studlar, in *Ethnicity*, VI.
40. Lawrence, *Black Migrants, White Natives*; Anne-Marie Phizacklea, 'A Sense of Political Efficacy: A Comparison of Black and White Adolescents', in Crewe, *British Political Sociology Yearbook*, vol. II, pp. 123–54; Miles and Phizacklea, in *Political Studies*, XXV; Gary Freeman, 'Immigrant Labor and Working-Class Politics: The French and British Experience', *Comparative Politics*, XI (Oct 1978) 24–41.
41. Richard Rose and Derek Urwin, 'Social Cohesion, Political Parties and Strains in Regimes', *Comparative Political Studies*, II (Apr 1969) 7–67; Dankwart Rustow, 'Transitions to Democracy: Toward a Dynamic Model', *Comparative Politics*, II (Apr 1970) 337–63; Richard Rose, *Governing without Consensus: An Irish Perspective* (London: Faber, 1971); Studlar, in *Patterns of Prejudice*, VIII; Donley T. Studlar, 'Ethnicity and the Policy Process in Western Europe', paper presented at meeting of Southern Political Science Association, New Orleans, 1977.
42. Rose and Urwin, in *Comparative Political Studies*, II; Richard Rose, *The United Kingdom as a Multinational State*, University of Strathclyde Survey Research Centre Occasional Paper no. 6 (Glasgow, 1970) pp. 11–21.
43. Rose and Urwin, in *Comparative Political Studies*, II, 37–41.
44. Rustow, in *Comparative Politics*, II, 360.
45. T. Alexander Smith, 'Toward a Comparative Theory of the Policy-Process', *Comparative Politics*, I (July 1969) 498–515, and *The Comparative Policy Process* (Santa Barbara, Calif.: ABC-Clio, 1975).
46. Ibid., p. 93. Smith actually calls these 'emotive–symbolic' issues, but they seem indistinguishable from what Rose and Urwin call 'communal' issues.
47. Studlar, 'Ethnicity and the Policy Process'; Donley T. Studlar, 'British Immigration Policy', in Ronald E. Krane (ed.), *International Labor Migration in Europe*, (New York: Praeger Special Studies, 1979) 109.
48. Smith, in *Comparative Politics*, I, 512.
49. Muhammed Anwar, 'Young Asians Between Two Cultures', *New Society*, 16 Dec 1976, pp. 563–5.
50. Lawrence, *Black Migrants, White Natives*, pp. 159–60.
51. Marsh, in *New Society*, 23 Sep 1976; Weir, ibid., 27 Apr 1978.
52. Schoen, *Enoch Powell and the Powellites*.
53. Cited in Joanna Mack, 'A Question of Race', *New Society*, 5 Jan 1978, pp. 8–9.
54. 'Race and Teachers: The School Councils Study', *New Society*, 16 Feb 1978, pp. 366–8.
55. Enloe, *Ethnic Conflict and Political Development*, pp. 59–60.
56. Studlar, in *Patterns of Prejudice*, VIII, 57.
57. Lawrence, *Black Migrants, White Natives*, p. 56.
58. Rose, *Politics in England*, pp. 29–30.
59. W. W. Daniel, *Racial Discrimination in England* (Harmondsworth: Penguin,

1968); David J. Smith, *The Facts of Racial Disadvantage* (London: Political and Economic Planning, 1976).

60. Sir Leslie Scarman, 'Minority Rights in a Plural Society' *New Community*, VI (Summer 1978) 248–52.
61. Andrew J. Milnor and Mark N. Franklin, 'Patterns of Opposition Behaviour in Modern Legislatures', in Allan Kornberg (ed.), *Legislatures in Comparative Perspective* (New York: David McKay, 1972) p. 441.
62. Walker Connor, 'The Politics of Ethnonationalism', *Journal of International Affairs*, XXVII, no. 1 (1973) 1–21.
63. James G. Christoph, 'Consensus and Cleavage in British Political Ideology', *American Political Science Review*, LIX (Sep 1965) 642.

8 From Steady State to Fluid State: the United Kingdom Today*

Richard Rose

The status quo is not an option.

Government dictum about devolution, 1975

The United Kingdom is a product of accident rather than design. It is, as its name declares, a union of domains once formerly subject to a multiplicity of monarchs. The accident of dynastic succession joined Wales with England in the sixteenth century, and Scotland and England in 1603. For a century thereafter, the Crown was tri-partite, with separate domains in England, Scotland and Ireland. If formal claims are taken into account, the Crown was quadri-partite, still claiming to rule France. The United Kingdom was not created until the union of Great Britain and Ireland in 1801, and its present boundaries date only from the resolution of Irish troubles in the aftermath of the First World War. Like the succession states created at Versailles, the United Kingdom is a relatively young state, and a multi-national state as well.

The constitution of a United Kingdom from a congeries of jurisdictions – 'Scotto-Anglican', predominantly Celtic, and a diversity of marcher and marginal societies – is a study that belongs to historians, for it is a story that climaxes centuries ago. It is also a story that has yet to be told. Authorities such as A. J. P. Taylor and J. G. A. Pocock differ only in arguing whether the history of this 'Atlantic archipelago' needs to be written.[1]

A millennium of history provides a traditional rationale for the belief: 'There'll always be an England'. But no such justification can be provided for anything as contingent as the United Kingdom, the state of which England is a part. Any state that consists of one and one-fifth islands can hardly be described as a natural geographical entity. Nor is this state a focal point of

* This paper has been prepared as part of a study of the Political Structure of the United Kingdom, financed by Social Science Research Council Grant HR/4689. Richard Parry has been particularly helpful in systematically searching Hansard and other rarely read HMSO documents to see what has been left unsaid about the United Kingdom.

communal identity. There are people who think of themselves as English, Scots, Welsh, Irish and even a few Britons, but there is no community of 'Ukes' within the United Kingdom.

The Royal Commission on the Constitution showed the characteristic Westminster hesitancy to make simple, clearcut statements about the territorial scope of the Constitution. The Prime Minister's charge asked it to examine 'the several countries, nations and regions of the United Kingdom'. In its report, the Commission rightly emphasised that neither the sentiments of loyalty to the Crown nor citizenship were unique to its residents. In reviewing the achievements of union, the Commission laid emphasis upon achievements outside the British isles in the Empire and Commonwealth. The distinctiveness of the Kingdom was defined by representation in the Westminster Parliament. It concluded with a two-cheers-for-the-United Kingdom (or three cheers for Great Britain) judgment that 'the story of the United Kingdom has thus been, at least in the larger island, a success story'.[2]

The authority of the United Kingdom is as it is. This is a traditional rather than a rational explanation. There is an element of mystery to it, defying analysis in simple means-end or cost-benefit terms. Authority did not arise from a rational calculation by an enlightened despot or by a Constituent Assembly in which a group of individuals deliberated about a written Constitution according to some more or less clear general ideas. The Crown can only be explained as a historical accident, like an Oxford townscape that congenially juxtaposes buildings in different styles as much as 400 years apart in age. The mystery is confirmed by the so-called practical politician's justification – 'It works' – even if those who work it do not fully understand why it does.[3]

The purpose of this paper is to make explicit tacit understandings underpinning the steady state United Kingdom, and to consider what has happened to them in the fluid state of the United Kingdom in the 1970s. The focus here is upon political structure, that is, political institutions, values and relationships, rather than social, psychological and economic relationships. Even if changes in the United Kingdom could be reduced to explanation by non-political factors, it would nonetheless be necessary to identify the political institutions forced to change. Attention is concentrated upon the centre of political life at Westminster, for if the centre fails to hold, peripheral politics is necessarily transformed.

To understand how the United Kingdom is changing, we must first understand what it is. The initial portion of this essay elucidates what the unwritten Constitution leaves vague about the territorial scope of the Crown. The second section examines the territorial management of the steady state United Kingdom up to the disruption of the civil rights movement in Northern Ireland, and the surge in Nationalist voting in Scotland and Wales. Westminster's response – the destabilisation of the United Kingdom – is the subject of the third section. The concluding section emphasises the difficulties of maintaining the conventional view of the powers of the Mace, that is, the Crown-in-Parliament, when the territorial management of the United Kingdom replaces traditional mechanisms with ad hoc institutions created without thought of their contradictions or consequences.

1 The United Kingdom: A Crown of Indefinite Domain

The absence of a written Constitution has historically been considered one of the virtues of the British political system. It is said to make government more flexible, allowing the adaptation of institutions to novel circumstances without hindrance. But amending an unwritten Constitution presents difficulties; one must first decide or discover what the Constitution is before it can be amended. The difficulties are doubled when it is the constituent structure of the United Kingdom that is under scrutiny. Not only does Westminster lack any clear idea of 'the state', it also lacks a clear and consistent definition of the territory to be governed.

When constitutional lawyers discuss the Constitution, their vision is concentrated upon a single point in space, Parliament, and all the authority that is meant to flow from an Act of Parliament. Little attention is given to the territorial extent of Parliament's authority. Even though MPs represent territorial constituencies and Lords were once great landed magnates, divisions in Parliament (with the latterday exception of Ireland) tend to be along functional, not territorial lines. Standard texts on constitutional law with reason may discuss territorial features of the United Kingdom under the heading 'Commonwealth Affairs'.[4] More space is devoted to considering such small deviant cases as the Channel Islands or the Isle of Man than to a definition of the central domain to which they are exceptions.

The absence of a Constitution means that nothing, not even the territorial boundaries of the United Kingdom, can be entrenched against the passing decision of a single Parliament. Irish Unionists once thought that the 1801 Act of Union, like the Bill of Rights of 1689, had 'the solemnity of fundamental law far beyond the pretensions of ordinary legislation'.[5] They were to learn that force was the fundamental law determining their fate. Ulstermen who used force to remain within the United Kingdom believed that the 1949 Ireland Act assured Northern Ireland's territorial integrity, but this seemingly firm guarantee was rendered a nullity by the abolition of Stormont in 1972. Whether the Articles of Union, joining Scotland and England in a single Parliament in 1707, are entrenched or capable of unilateral abrogation by Scotland is moot. In the characteristically evasive words of a Law Lord asked to rule on an alleged breach of the Treaty of Union, there may be acts that are 'unlawful but non-justiciable'.[6]

The concept of 'nation' or 'community' cannot be used to give a territorial identity to the United Kingdom. The primary identifications of the peoples of the United Kingdom are multiple, contrasting and accordion-like, contracting and expanding to cover territories far smaller *or* larger than the United Kingdom. Most Scots, Welsh and Ulster people do not identify themselves first as British, but with their immediate national setting. One loyalty that extends beyond these boundaries is that of class, creating a *landsmannschaft* that can be international. But 'racial' identifications can divide the United Kingdom, as in the Royal Commission on the Constitution's reference to 'the Scots – an intelligent and hard-working race', or in pejorative references to the 'racial' inferiority of all 32 counties of Irish. The concept of race can extend westwards to unity with kith and kin in the antipodes, or eastwards to reject alien races at some point between Calais and Suez.[7]

By contrast with Continental countries such as Germany and Italy, the United Kingdom is not the product of a nineteenth century nationalist upsurge of sentiment backed by force of arms. Nor, more to the point, has government ever seen its task as that of 'making' a nation, as absolutist monarchs and generals in the mould of Napoleon have done in France. Yet there has been a *prima facie* need for 'nation-building', *if the nation be defined as Britain*, for a congeries of communities only in part European, and in part linked to Celtic civilisations different from the Europe of Rome and Charlemagne.[8] Yet the ideal of a common, politically enforced basis for political unity was most spectacularly rejected in the acceptance of different state (*sic*) religions within the United Kingdom. At no time has the government of Great Britain or the United Kingdom sought to make its domain a 'nation-state'. By not doing so, it was able to avoid the crucial analytic questions: – Is the nation England or Britain? And what is the difference between these two symbolic references?

The political identity of the United Kingdom today is that of a multinational state. The United Kingdom is not the homeland of a *Volk*; it is a historic political institution. As such, it can display all the anomalies of historical accidents without further rationalisation. Monmouthshire has been moved back and forth between Wales and England by parliamentary fiat, or it can alternate between the two depending upon specific functions of government. A jurisdiction such as Northern Ireland, six of the historic nine counties of the Province of Ulster, can be created by Act of Parliament too. In Scotland, 'Scottish only' and 'GB' ministries serve the same citizens for different purposes, and devolution proposals would intensify this duality.

Confusion of identity is compounded by the absence of a unique and distinctive United Kingdom nationality or citizenship. Until 1948, a British subject could be any resident of the Empire and Commonwealth: 'a person belonging to any country of the Commonwealth who is a subject of the King'.[9] The 1948 British Nationality Act created the status of citizenship, dividing British subjects into two categories, those who were citizens of the United Kingdom *or* its still numerous colonies; and those who were citizens of an independent Commonwealth country. Both native-born United Kingdom residents and subjects from the most remote parts of the

Commonwealth and Empire had a common right to enter the United Kingdom and to vote in British elections. Successive Commonwealth Immigration Acts from 1962 have restricted the right of some British subjects to enter the United Kingdom and, in the case of East African Asians, restricted entry by British citizens as well. In 1971 legislation added a further complicating concept: patrial citizens of the United Kingdom and Colonies, i.e. Commonwealth citizens with one parent born in the United Kingdom. United Kingdom citizenship today most nearly equates with the status of British subjects who are also citizens of the United Kingdom and Colonies plus Commonwealth citizens who can claim one parent who was a British-born British subject. With a fine disregard for matching state and citizenship (let alone more restrictive definitions of nationalism), the 1975 Devolution White Paper proposed that members of the Scottish or Welsh Assembly should be 21 years of age and 'a British subject or a citizen of the Republic of Ireland'.[10]

The Crown, in the impersonal legal sense, is the central concept upon which the government of the United Kingdom rests. The government is Her Majesty's Government, and is authorised by royal commission confirmed by Parliament. Government institutions and civil servants exercise their authority in the name of the Crown. Those who reside within the United Kingdom, as well as hundreds of millions elsewhere in the Commonwealth, are subjects of the Crown. Where lawyers in other countries would use the word Constitution, British writers can refer to the Crown to represent 'the sum total of governmental powers'.[11]

The Crown is an idea, not a territory. Like postage stamps, the Crown has no place name. Like the unwritten Constitution, the Crown is a useful political concept *because* it is nebulous. Like a Sultan in seclusion, the Crown is always out of sight. Political authority resides in those who act in the name of the Crown. The forms by which the Crown rules are multiple, ranging from parliamentary institutions to the most unrepresentative of colonial institutions. To describe the government of the United Kingdom as that of the Crown does not stipulate how the Crown rules, or that the Crown should rule all parts of its Kingdom – for example, England and Northern Ireland – the same.

The Crown is a landless concept. It is not derived from any primordial ties to a single piece of territory. Given the German roots of so much of their family tree, British monarchs can hardly claim to be the patriarchs of an English or British race. Unlike Parliament, each of whose members is tied to a territorial constituency, the Crown can be everywhere, yet no place in particular. The Crown is infinitely portable. In the nineteenth century, its powers were rapidly extended across the globe, and in this century, they have even more abruptly retracted. The Queen's title emphasises the indefinite extent of the Crown's domain; in a formulation of increasing vagueness, it embraces 'Great Britain and Northern Ireland and her other Realms and Territories'.

The elasticity of the United Kingdom's boundaries was unambiguously reaffirmed in 1955 by an official proposal to extend them into the Mediterranean. Malta, a Crown colony, sought a greater measure of representative government, but Westminster ruled out Dominion status, because of the island's strategic importance in the Mediterranean. In consequence, an all-party committee of British MPs endorsed a proposal that in addition to a 'Stormont-type' legislature, Malta should elect three MPs to sit in the House of Commons at Westminster, giving this island between Sicily and Tunisia as much representation as the Isle of Wight, the Scottish Western Isles and the Orkneys and Shetlands combined.[12]

The British Empire was the ultimate expression of the extent and flexibility of the Crown. While Continental European nations were defining their boundaries and identities by wars with neighbouring states, the Crown was blurring its boundaries by expansion into other Continents. Where expansion occurred by plantation, as in Ireland, North America and Australasia, ties remained even when, as in America and Ireland, political authority was rejected. Where the Crown incurred responsibility for governing alien peoples, it created a dual polity. Imperial government was first of all government by men 'on the ground', whether popularly elected, as in the old Dominions, or mediating elites whose indigenous standing and interests made them turn to British officials for support.[13] The Imperial Parliament at Westminster retained what most concerned it, the power and prestige of the defining concerns of sovereignty: diplomacy, military defence, and questions of taxes, trade and tariffs.

The Imperial idea gave territorial substance and global scope to the idea of the Crown. The idea of an Imperial Federation was an ideal that Viscount Milner described as that of lands 'bound together for the defence of their common interests and the development of a common civilisation . . . in an organic union'.[14] It also meant a turning away from the local claims of a 'little' England, or a 'not very big' Britain. In the words of Earl Russell in 1870,

> There was a time when we might have stood alone as the United Kingdom of England, Scotland and Ireland. That time has passed. We conquered and peopled Canada, we took possession of the whole of Australia, Van Dieman's Land and New Zealand. We have annexed India to the Crown. There is no going back.[15]

A century later the United Kingdom remains the central figure in a Commonwealth of heterogeneous nations, a network that, like the Crown, has no adjective to link it with any territory in particular.

Nothing more remote from the political and economic unity of the United Kingdom could be imagined than the British Empire at its zenith.

Yet the concept of Westminster as the home of the Imperial Parliament provides one key to understanding its jurisdiction within as well as outside the United Kingdom. Westminster politicians saw their position as the apex of a complex of political institutions that could and did embrace self-governing Parliaments in other continents, subordinate colonies, and institutions differently governing parts of the United Kingdom.

Devoted Imperialists were eager to remove the detail and 'trivia' of domestic governance from the Imperial Parliament at Westminster. In the words of Earl Grey, Governor-General of Canada, writing in 1909,

> Before the road is cleared for the Federation of the Empire we have to put the United Kingdom straight. The time is approaching, if it is not already here, for getting this work done . . . Provincial Legislatures of the Canadian rather than the South African type for 1. Ireland 2. Scotland 3. Wales 4. England (4. North? 5. South?) with a Federal Parliament armed with powers of disallowance sitting in London.[16]

In 1919 the House of Commons resolved that it needed to 'devote more attention to the general interests of the United Kingdom . . . and matters of common Imperial concern' and called for a scheme of 'federal devolution' of government to England, Scotland and Ireland. The next year a Speaker's Conference presented a scheme to realise federal devolution.[17]

The concurrent debates about Irish Home Rule and Imperial Federation raised many conundrums that continue to confront United Kingdom politicians today.[18] The creation of Dominions gave plenary powers of government to territories outside the home islands of the Empire, thus removing Westminster from day-to-day involvement in their governance. Political sentiment, rather than constitutional or administrative bonds, have continued to link the original self-governing Dominions with Westminster. By contrast, 'home rule' for Ireland was not to mean the grant of plenary powers to an Irish Parliament, but the transfer of a limited and specified number of powers to Dublin, with considerable administrative, legislative and financial powers remaining in Westminster. But for Ireland to have continued with Westminster representation as well as a home rule Parliament would have been unfair to other parts of the United Kingdom. Logically, the problem might have been resolved by making the whole of the United Kingdom federal, but politically there was no demand for English home rule. Westminster found it easier to create Dominions or allow colonies to become independent states than to create a scheme for Irish home rule that would overcome both logical and practical political objections. Parliament greeted the departure of Ireland from the United Kingdom in 1921 with a prolonged and thankful silence about the territorial government of the United Kingdom.

II The Territorial Management of the Steady State United Kingdom

The concept of a Crown of indefinite domain contradicts the idea of the United Kingdom as a unitary state. In practice, the contradiction is resolved in favour of territorially differentiated institutions of governance. The government of the United Kingdom is institutionally a conglomerate. Like a huge multi-product, multi-national business firm, the conglomerate operates differently in different places and in respect to different functions. The typical Cabinet department is confined in the exercise of its major powers to a part of the United Kingdom. This is as true of the Department of the Environment, primarily confined to problems of England, as it is of the Scottish, Welsh and the Northern Ireland Offices. The Treasury, the Ministry of Defence and the Foreign Office are exceptional in having a United Kingdom-wide remit. This status does not arise from a demand for uniform government within the United Kingdom but from the exigencies of international relations.

The idea of the United Kingdom as a unitary state is just that – a disembodied value – and not an administrative fact. The idea is nonetheless powerful, for all that. It could even be argued that normative consent to political unity is even more important than administrative uniformity. Variety in the practice of government may be easier to allow when there is a fundamental consensus about the unity of the Kingdom. The government of the 'steady state' United Kingdom prior to the upsurge of so-called peripheral challenges in the late 1960s combined both normative integration and administrative heterogeniety.

The authority of the Crown is aptly symbolised by the Mace. The Mace is a profoundly *non*-territorial concept; it assumes that political power can be centralised at a single central locus of sovereignty, Parliament.[19] Parliament has insisted upon doctrines incompatible with federalism. First of all, all agencies of government in the United Kingdom are accountable to Parliament. Cabinet departments, whatever their territorial character, are bound to accept decisions of the Crown-in-Parliament (i.e. Cabinet, endorsed by a majority in the House of Commons). Within Cabinet, a Scottish or Welsh Office minister may fight his department's corner in the name of Scottish or Welsh interests. But win or lose, the minister must accept what his colleagues say or resign. No Scottish, Welsh or Northern Ireland minister has ever resigned on a question of territorial politics.

Secondly, the Crown-in-Parliament has sole authority to grant and to revoke territorial powers. The career of Stormont from 1921 to 1972 emphasises both of these points, and a prominent feature in the discussions of devolved Assemblies for Scotland and Wales was the design of multiple default and over-ride powers for Westminster.

Thirdly, the powers of the Crown-in-Parliament have been in the hands of parties explicitly committed to dividing along economic rather than territorial lines. Conservative and Labour politicians have done more than ignore territorial differences; they have rejected their claim to importance, or even rejected their legitimacy as 'real' issues.[20] Party organisation has reinforced the centralising ethos of Westminster politicians.[21] Parties proposing to dissolve the United Kingdom have been regarded as 'not normal'. The profoundly majoritarian nature of Westminster politics has allowed little influence to nationalist parties choosing to seek votes in one relatively small part of the United Kingdom. In conventional Westminster parlance, the poor, the disadvantaged and the politically powerless have been the chief peripheral political groups. Their *locus classicus* was not West Belfast or the East End of Glasgow, but a short Underground ride from Westminster in the East End of London.

The ideologies of British politics have denied any territorial dimension in politics; this was left to the Irish, who were assumed to have no ideology because they were nationalists! Conventional liberal doctrines have emphasised the representation of individuals rather than classes or nations. Today, many liberals go further, wishing to emancipate individuals from the claims of national sovereignty by promoting a cosmopolitan European Community. Whitehall officials, when speaking of governing in the national interest, are clear about who is to define this interest – Whitehall knows best – but vague about the boundaries of the nation whose interest they determine. By dividing communities into middle and working class groups, class theories of representation unite each class across territorial boundaries. Similarly, pressure groups fragment communities into a multiplicity of interests, uniting each fragment with like-minded persons across a wide expanse. Distinctive territorial pressure groups, like the Welsh Language Society or Ulster para-military organisations, are beyond the pale of conventional British pressure groups.

Insofar as any territorial value is articulated in British politics, it is the centralist doctrine of territorial justice.[22] In the name of equity, all persons within the United Kingdom, regardless of where they live, are said to have a right to the same pensions, unemployment benefits, health care, and other welfare state services. The finance of local government institutionalises territorial justice. The principal determinant of how much money central government distributes to a local authority is the need of its population for local services, as indicated by housing conditions, the age structure of the population, etc. Similarly, centrally designed regional economic policies are intended to discriminate in favour of areas of high unemployment in order to give workers everywhere in Britain the same opportunity of obtaining a job, or being unemployed.

From the outside, the practice of territorial justice may appear something like pork barrel politics, for government gives extra benefits to some areas. But from within, the opposite is the case. Territorial justice is a profoundly centralising decision rule. In pursuit of the dictum that the poorest he that is in West Belfast, or the poorest she that is in Dundee shall have the same scale of benefits as the poorest he in Surrey or she in Solihull, Westminster centralises the collection and distribution of public funds, as well as setting standards and supervising how these funds are spent.

For nearly a half century, from the resolution of the Irish question to its resurrection at Westminster, the House of Commons gave supreme expression to its confidence in the indivisible integrity of the United Kingdom: it hardly discussed the subject.[23] (At times, the Stormont Parliament hardly discussed anything else.) For example, when Robert McIntyre, the first Scottish National MP, tried to secure a breakdown of war casualties giving Scottish losses separately from United Kingdom totals, the Prime Minister, Winston Churchill, pointedly refused to give it.[24]

Any Scottish or Welsh MP initially elected with Home Rule sympathies came to identify Westminster as the forum within which differences of opinion should be resolved. Nor did they use the relatively harsh economic deprivations of Scotland and Wales as an argument for reducing Westminster's influence. If anything, unemployment, especially in mining, was cited by Labour MPs as evidence of the need for moving ownership from the hands of hardfaced Scottish and Welsh coal owners to Westminster. Yet Scots, Welsh and Ulster MPs have been conscious of a dual identity absent among English members. This fact has been spoken of approvingly, as an American might claim to be a loyal Texan as well as a loyal American. Arthur Woodburn, Secretary of State for Scotland from 1947 to 1950, voiced a view characteristic of non-English MPs when he described the existence of Great Britain as 'one of the greatest domestic partnerships the world has ever seen'. When confronted by nationalist challenges, MPs such as George Lawson, a veteran Scottish Labour member, could go so far as to tell the Commons, 'there is no separate Scottish nation now. There is no separate Scottish nation as distinct from the British nation'.[25]

The justifications that MPs offered for the United Kingdom were multiple, and re-inforcing. Staunch Conservatives such as Sir Robert Boothby could praise Union as having given Scots the opportunity to 'run the British Empire for over 300 years from London'.[26] A Labour minister such as Aneurin Bevan could reject the idea of devolving powers to Wales with the argument, 'This is a constitutional impossibility.' Bevan also attacked Welsh nationalism, warning of internal divisions within Wales – 'a vast majority tyrannised over by a few Welsh-speaking people' – and by economic analysis:

> Is it not rather cruel to give the impression to the 60,000 unemployed men and women in Wales that their plight would be relieved and their distress removed by this constitutional change? It is not socialism. It is escapism. This is exactly the way in which nation after nation has been ruined in the last 25 to 30 years, trying to pretend that deep-seated economic difficulties can be removed by constitutional changes.[27]

In the 1960s, Labour MPs in Scotland and Wales argued that their areas benefited disproportionately from government economic and industrial policy. In the words of the Secretary of State for Scotland, Willie Ross, 'Scotland as a nation is in a very fruitful partnership'.[28] When the Conservative government of 1970–4 faced economic difficulties, the majority of Scottish and Welsh MPs did not demand devolution, but rather the return of a Labour government at Westminster.

Generalised values have not produced uniform government throughout the multi-national territory of the United Kingdom. Very few activities can be solely the responsibility of offices in central London. The problem of any government larger than a city-state is: how to manage its domains beyond the limits of the capital?

The territorial management of the United Kingdom is in the broadest sense an *inter*-organisational problem. Whitehall has never claimed a monopoly of directive or administrative institutions. This was most evident in the days of Empire, when indirect rule accepted that in many respects Westminster was a peripheral authority, and the slowness of communication required that many decisions be made by the man on the spot. The territorial management of the United Kingdom was also based upon local institutions and resident officials in Dublin Castle, the Lord Advocate's Office in Edinburgh and the JPs' courts of the English shires.

The crucial question here is: how have the different territorial organs of the Crown related to the Imperial Parliament? The conventional legalistic approach is to stress the superiority of Westminster. A more realistic approach is to emphasise the remoteness of Westminster from government on the ground. MPs and even more, Cabinet ministers, do not deign to concern themselves with local political matters, unlike counterparts in America, Germany, Italy or even France. Whitehall departments advise, consult, inspect and even countermand the actions of agencies delivering major services to citizens, but Whitehall is not itself the prime executive agent of government. This task is left to a host of territorial authorities, and a large and growing variety of functional institutions. To influence this action, Whitehall itself must engage in inter-organisational politics.

For centuries, as Bulpitt has shown, Westminster has been the central government of a dual polity.[29] Governing institutions on the ground have been allowed to carry on with wide latitude, as long as their actions do not lead to disruption at Westminster. In a reciprocal fashion, Westminster politicians have carried out their 'Imperial' functions free from little local concerns. Few Prime Ministers have wished to concern themselves with the mechanics of English local government, let alone Welsh, Scottish or Irish local government. Nor do local councillors wish to debate the grand points of social and political theory: they are concerned with immediate problems of granting planning permissions, siting roads, trying to balance the housing account, or carrying on a case-by-case battle with local bureaucracy. As long as each level does not disturb the other, the two can co-exist as a *stratarchy* with each stratum exercising wide discretionary powers.

In the steady state United Kingdom, Northern Ireland best reflected Bulpitt's ideal-type dual polity. Westminster retained Imperial functions, such as foreign policy, defence and taxation powers, whereas Stormont administered most government activities, including police and internal security, the services of greatest concern in Ulster and that Westminster was most anxious to be shed of. The Speaker protected Westminster from being 'dragged in' to the government of Northern Ireland by ruling that MPs could not debate transferred matters. Westminster avoided political interference in Northern Ireland by not having any resident official in the Province; its liaison official was very much part-time, being simultaneously concerned with a jumble of unrelated territories in the British Isles.[30] Westminster politicians knew what powers this arrangement lost them – and were glad to be shed of such responsibilities. In 1970, a Labour minister could compare using the one power Westminster held in law – suspension of Stormont – to 'dropping the hydrogen bomb', an act whose fallout would permanently affect whoever did it.

Scotland was governed on a mixed basis during the steady state United Kingdom. In so far as traditional issues affecting the law, the church or public morality were concerned, Scotland was an autonomous stratum. When government determined major services of the contemporary welfare state, policies have been subject to influence (and largesse) from above. Education, health, housing and social services have been administered by the Scottish Office, but must conform, especially in financial terms, to Westminster policy. Cash benefits for pensioners and the unemployed are administered by Whitehall departments. The presence of a Secretary of State for Scotland in the Cabinet has tended to bind Scotland on matters important to Westminster, while leaving the negotiation of central-local relations to Edinburgh-based Scottish Office officials. In turn they are top-tier figures trying to influence Scottish local government in a triadic relationship of Westminster, St Andrews House and Scottish town halls.[31]

For most of the steady state period, Wales did not differ in its institutions of government from England. From 1746 until 1967, the word 'England' in an Act of Parliament was deemed to include Wales. Education and religion were two traditional fields where Wales was *prima facie* distinctive from England. After mishandling Wales in the Education Act of 1902, Westminster moved with relative speed to allow greater autonomy for Wales in these fields, thus freeing it from further annoyance with distinctive Welsh interests. The creation of the Welsh Office in 1964 created a triadic relationship, in which the Welsh Office is a buffer between the Cabinet and local government in Wales.[32]

Within England, there was a time when landed MPs, in their own person and through their network of local contacts, integrated local and central government. In late twentieth century England, this is no longer the case.[33] Insofar as legal powers and money are concerned, Westminster sets the parameters for local government in England. Local authorities lack the lawful authority as well as the money to attempt what Westminster does not wish them to do. Local authorities do retain the power of administering and delivering major services in their communities; they may also frustrate Westminster by not doing what it wishes, for example, in housing or education.

Among the many features of the steady state dual polity, two are both important and familiar. The first is that the different organisations do not relate as equals; Westminster is more than *primus inter pares* in this inter-organisational network. Secondly, different parts of the steady state United Kingdom have been treated very differently; there was no general rationale for non-Westminster institutions.

Other aspects of the steady state dual polity are less noted. The first is that the system (in so far as it was a whole) rested upon customs and conventions, re-inforced by specific social and political facts. It was not integration by prefects, as in France, or by the constitutional and institutional structures of a federal state. The second was that the dual polity was not a 'zero-sum' system, in which central and local governments competed against each other. It has tended to be an Alice-in-Wonderland world in which everybody could win and all could have prizes. Thirdly, the dual polity is not a stable system. In the twentieth century it has been increasingly difficult to keep the two strata separate from each other. In the period since 1945, relationships between the top tier of government in the 'Imperial' Parliament and government on the ground have become increasingly important and intertwined. In the modern welfare state each must rely upon the other for co-operation in order to carry out the governance of the United Kingdom.

Confident that its authority was supreme, Westminster was ready to adapt institutions of the steady state United Kingdom when the vogue for re-form hit post-war Whitehall. Adaptation was intended to strengthen Westminster, sometimes making its territorial parts more dependent upon central resources, and sometimes strengthening the lower tier of the dual polity in the discharge of its primary tasks and responsibilities. No major constitutional debate was raised by the adaptation of the steady state United Kingdom institutions. The absence of controversy is evidence of the acceptance of the status quo and, from a radical nationalist position, of the small scale of change.

If one wished a catchword to describe this process of adaptation, it would be 'administrative deconcentration'. Westminster sought to ship out 'boring' or 'unimportant' concerns of government to a variety of functional and territorial bodies, such as enlarged local authorities, new functional agencies, regions of the Board of Trade, or toothless Regional Economic Planning Councils. Anything deemed important, (i.e. anything that Westminster wished to keep within its own hands) was unaffected by administrative deconcentration.

The positive impetus for change was a desire for 'good government', defined as government more efficient in the delivery of public policies. The absence of a measure of efficiency or effectiveness did not bother the authors of Royal Commission reports, or of Whitehall white papers. Nor did the diminution of the number of elected representatives or the destruction of historic and sometimes traditional communities concern them. They were not old-fashioned politicians but newstyle technocrats, for whom territory was a variable, not the political basis of allegiance.[34]

Appropriately enough, the first major structural changes affected the government of London itself, basically unaltered since its creation in 1899. Committees to reform local government were established for London in 1957, Wales in 1958, England and Scotland in 1966, and Northern Ireland in 1969, and in each case legislation followed thereafter. These reports proclaimed and enforced the doctrine of the economies of scale from the South Bank of the Thames to Snowdonia, the Minches and the Foyle.

In Wales, the greatest innovation concerned government at Westminster as well as government in Wales. The creation of the Welsh Office in 1964 introduced a Welsh Secretary into the Cabinet as well as removing from Whitehall matters that concerned Wales far more than Westminster. It left unaltered the over-riding authority of Westminster, for any Welsh Secretary of State is bound to accept collective responsibility for any and all decisions made at Westminster. The creation of the Welsh Office by the 1964 Labour government was not seen as a step toward devolution to an elected Assembly, but as an end in itself. As of 1970, Labour, the party that could expect an easy majority in any elected Welsh Assembly, could be described as 'uninterested in or antagonistic towards ideas for devolution'.[35]

In Scotland, adaptation tightened the cash nexus between the Scottish Office and Whitehall. From the 1950s, the chief problems of Scotland were diagnosed as economic; diagnosis was cast in a Unionist mould, that is to say, Scotland was said to do less well than England. Prescriptions for change were also Unionist, involving the *redistribution* of economic resources – firms, jobs and earnings – from England to Scotland, as well as the supplementation of Scottish economic resources. The Scottish Development Department was created within the Scottish Office in 1962, and in the following decade, Westminster-based regional economic policy favoured Scottish (and relatively unprosperous English) regions by a combination of incentive and disincentive measures. Aficionados of Scottish politics judged the success of these policies by the crudest of 'power' indices, namely, the extent to which public expenditure per capita in Scotland exceeded that in England. In 1964, identifiable public expenditure in Scotland was 11 per cent more per capita than in England; by 1971, the gap had risen to 17 per cent, and by 1976 to 26 per cent.[36]

In the steady state United Kingdom, Northern Ireland gained greater political autonomy. In 1949, Westminster granted Stormont the right to veto any Act of Parliament that proposed that any part of Northern Ireland was no longer to be a part of the United Kingdom. From 1956 to 1962, the Stormont Ministry of Home Affairs carried out a long and successful internal security war with the IRA, interning hundreds of suspects and with loss of lives limited to 19 persons.[37] Concurrently, Stormont used its separate legislative powers to enact 'step by step' welfare legislation in imitation of the 1945–51 Labour government and its successors. By the time that Terence O'Neill became Prime Minister in 1963, there was a growing belief that socio-economic change within the Province might accomplish what force of arms had not, namely, remove age-old differences between Protestants and Catholics, so that they, like their British neighbours, could concentrate on material well-being. (What O'Neill actually said was 'live like Protestants.')[38]

Westminster did not pursue the vain hope of directing all that was done in the name of the Crown. It controlled what it wished to keep in its hands, and shed burdens by granting powers to other institutions of the dual polity. The adaptation of institutions was sometimes intended to achieve administrative deconcentration, and sometimes centripetal in effect, as in the growth of economic and industrial policy in Scotland and Northern Ireland. The growth of the welfare state in Northern Ireland and the creation of the Welsh Office strengthened Westminster as the dominant institution in a continuing process of inter-organisational interaction. The changes that Westminster countenanced or introduced were intended to make them more perfect still. The motto of the steady state United Kingdom was, in effect, the motto of its progenitor, William of Orange: *Je maintiendrai.*

III Destabilising the Steady State

In his aptly named study of *The English Constitution*, Bagehot distinguished between two different and complementary requirements of stable, legitimate authority, the need to secure first 'the loyalty and confidence of mankind, and then employ that homage in the work of government'.[39] What Bagehot said was sufficient for a state that did not exist, namely, England. But in the United Kingdom at that time, there were also Fenians concerned with breaking, not making or maintaining the authority of the Crown.

The past half century has seen a fundamental change in the concept of what United Kingdom government is. The Crown is no longer the central idea in the phrase the Crown-in-Parliament. Today, it is the idea of the Mace of Parliament. Whereas the Crown is indefinite in its territorial scope, the Mace is extremely precise: territorial boundaries are clearly stipulated in each Act of Parliament.

From a Nationalist perspective, the passing of the doctrine of the Crown has made more difficult their task, for the Crown was infinitely flexible about the specific exercise of authority. Many Nationalists claim they do not wish 'separation' from the Crown, but rather to be under the Crown as Australia or New Zealand is, rather than as Surrey or Lancashire is today. It is only the authority of the Mace at Westminster that they wish to shed. But the doctrine of the Mace is rigid in the insistence upon the unequal authority of Westminster within the British Isles.

The first object of any group seeking fundamental change is to secure Westminster's attention. The second object is to commit Westminster to accept change in what had previously been regarded as fixed. The disruption of the United Kingdom depends as much upon the errors of commission and omission at the centre as it does upon actions elsewhere. The risk of errors or accidents is high, for constitutional change is not conventional incremental policy-making. Instead of policies of little effect being adopted with low understanding, constitutional change can result in a big impact resulting from policies framed with low understanding.[40]

To secure Westminster's attention, groups must voice demands in such ways that Westminster's calm is disturbed. The point can be proven by negative as well as positive examples. The territorial management of England was not a major issue in the 1970s because proponents of English devolution (i.e. the transfer of powers to elected regional Assemblies) have been far too weak to capture attention at Westminster. No alliance of MPs has voted against party discipline as a means of pressing for change. Nor have Yorkshire Home Rule candidates been nominated or won by-elections, let alone general election contests. The House of Commons has established regional committees on English problems, but English MPs have shown no interest in them, and they are likely to expire of ennui. When English MPs do voice territorial concerns in the Commons, they usually do not refer to the administrative regions that could be strengthened by devolution. Instead, the communities that concern MPs are smaller, and often are as particular as their own constituency.[41]

Northern Ireland represents the other extreme, seizing the attention of Westminster against Westminster's will. The short-lived civil rights campaign launched in 1968 was doubly able to attract attention. First of all, the marchers demanded British standards of government, concentrating attention upon Stormont's departures from what Westminster politicians regarded as natural, albeit uncodified rights. Secondly, the marchers, the Stormont security forces and Protestant counter-demonstrators together produced dramatic confrontations that could be filmed and reported by the world's media.

In August, 1969, British-oriented protest demonstrations reverted to traditional Irish disorder. In the Belfast riots following the barricading of the Bogside of Londonderry, the Royal Ulster Constabulary lost control and seven persons were killed. The dual polity had cracked in a most visible manner: Stormont could no longer keep its local difficulties local. Against its wishes, Westminster was forced to send in British troops to secure order.

At this juncture, Westminster had two choices: *either* to defend the established Stormont government, limiting pressures for change to those that would not disturb the dominant majority, *or* to use its superior lawful authority to reform Stormont from above or abolish it altogether. In the event, it tried each alternative in turn,and succeeded in neither.

In 1969 British troops were not only defending individual Ulstermen from violence, but also defending Stormont, the only lawful authority recognised by a Westminster Act of Parliament. Many Westminster politicians did not like this regime, and some wished it abolished. But the policy of Labour and Conservative governments until 1972 was to limit demands for reform to requests for adaptation within limits acceptable to the Unionist majority. For example, in 1970 a review of local government in Ulster could not consider proportional representation for local elections. The introduction of internment without trial under British Army auspices in August 1971 represented the logical culmination of the defence of the status quo.

When internment turned into civil war in the Province, Westminster turned from coercion to conciliation. It stopped defending Stormont, and suspended it in March, 1972. Since then, Westminster has sought to constitute a government of Northern Ireland radically different from what went before: power-sharing institutions guaranteeing executive office to Catholics as well as Prostestants. It promoted a power-sharing Executive in 1974, which collapsed when Protestant workers called a general strike, and Crown forces took no action against them in defence of Westminster's authority. It promoted a Northern Ireland Constitutional Convention in 1975–6 but rejected the majority report of the Convention, because it called for government by the customary winner-take-all Westminster system![42] Westminster has succeeded in breaking the customary form of government in Northern Ireland, but it has not succeeded in settling any form of durable government in place of Stormont.

Westminster policy toward Northern Ireland has, with the perversity of logic that the English have long shown in Ireland, been 'consistently inconsistent'. The territorial integrity of the United Kingdom has been defended by the presence of British troops, but political actions have time and again reflected an uncertainty about whether Northern Ireland *does or should* belong to Westminster. Jim Callaghan has not been the only British politician to express privately, if not publicly, the wish 'to see Ireland come together again'.[43] Both Conservative and Labour governments have been ready to parley with leaders of the IRA about the 'discharge' of their United Kingdom responsibilities.

Votes have been the force de-stabilising the steady state governance of Scotland and Wales. By-election victories by a Welsh Nationalist in 1966 and a Scottish Nationalist in 1967 led the Labour government of the day to establish a Royal Commission on the Constitution in 1969. This was a classic Whitehall stratagem for maintaining the status quo, while appearing to be doing something. By the time the Commission reported in October 1973, both the Conservative and Labour parties had no wish to introduce constitutional change, for the country's economic difficulties were a pre-emptive claim on their attention, and the Nationalist parties appeared to have been vanquished at the 1970 general election.

The February 1974 election results showed the overwhelmingly Unionist allegiance of both Scottish and Welsh voters. In Wales, the pro-union parties secured 89.3 per cent of the total vote and Plaid Cymru, while winning two seats in rural, Welsh-speaking areas, actually saw its vote *drop* from the 11.5 per cent it had taken in 1970. In Scotland, the SNP increased its vote from 11.4 to 21.9 per cent of the Scottish total, similar to the Liberal surge in England. But this also meant that 78.1 per cent of Scottish voters had cast their ballots in favour of pro-union parties.

By a fluke, the February 1974 election unexpectedly made the seven Scottish Nationalist and two Welsh Nationalist MPs relevant to the calculus of party government at Westminster, for neither major party held a majority. Edward Heath might even be said to have lost control of Downing Street in Northern Ireland, for the disruption of the steady state there cost the Conservatives their customary support by 11 Ulster Unionist MPs.

The Prime Minister had two choices – either to re-affirm support for the established system of territorial management, as he had done time and again previously, or to pledge a major departure from the status quo. In the event, Harold Wilson decided that only the promise of 'something big' would safeguard Labour against further Nationalist erosion of Labour's vote. Fortified by unpublished Scottish public opinion surveys indicating the apparent electoral attractiveness of introducing constitutional change,[44] the Prime Minister pledged the creation of a directly elected Assembly for Scotland, and for Wales as well.

From Mr Wilson's perspective, the pledge worked. Labour won the October, 1974 election, literally without a seat to spare. It did not lose a single seat to the Scottish Nationalists, notwithstanding the 8.5 per cent increase in the SNP vote, and the SNP's capture of four seats from the Conservatives. Labour lost one seat to Plaid Cymru, but Plaid's 10.8 per cent share of the vote was lower than its 1970 figure.

Labour's victory at the October 1974 general election presented the government with a new problem: it had abandoned its defence of the status quo form of territorial management, but it had by no means abandoned its objections to proposals for Constitutional change.[45] The government's strategic objective was clear: to do nothing that would detract from powers that Westminster wished to keep at Westminster. To maintain the appearance that nothing would affect Westminster seriously, it adopted the rhetoric of reform for the sake of 'good government'. The impetus for change came from parties demanding self-government. But, as Nicholas Mansergh had pointed out long ago, 'No scheme of devolution is likely to satisfy a demand for self-government prompted by national sentiment or to solve a problem in political sovereignty by a proposal for better government. They provide an object lesson in confused political thinking.'[46]

The November 1975 White Paper – *Our Changing Democracy: Devolution to Scotland and Wales* – bore the imprint of its creation by interdepartmental consultation among affected Whitehall departments. In consequence, it emphasised a multiplicity of administrative and legislative devices to protect the interests of Whitehall departments against possible encroachment by Scottish and Welsh Assemblies and, if necessary, over-ride their actions. From a Scottish or Welsh perspective, the White Paper was not so much hamstrung as hamfisted. A simple explanation for the government's approach was offered by the Political Correspondent of the *Observer*, Alan Watkins:

> I have yet to meet a single minister who actively and positively wants devolution at all. Instead, a variety of justifications or explanations is produced; that the alternative is the complete loss of Scotland to the Labour Party, even to Britain; that it is useless to argue with the inevitable; that the party entered into a rash commitment which cannot now be escaped; that events acquire their own momentum.[47]

As parliamentary circumstances changed, the Labour government's policy became highly unstable. A Devolution Bill was stopped on 22 February 1977 by the failure of a government motion to guillotine a debate on a Bill that had attracted intense filibustering. Of approximately 220 Labour MPs without a government post, 43 voted against the guillotine or abstained. The government put the goodwill of its parliamentary party – rebels and all – ahead of its pledge to create devolved Assemblies and the Bill was abandoned.

A month later, the Labour government once again made devolution an over-riding commitment, when the Liberals demanded this as a price for a pact sustaining Labour in office for another session. When the very survival of the Labour government was immediately at stake, Labour rebels proved ready to accept a guillotine. Devolution Acts for Scotland and Wales received the Royal Assent on 31 July 1978. Yet so hesitant was Parliament's acceptance of devolution, that a referendum was forced upon an unwilling government, with a novel clause requiring that a pro-devolution majority receive at least 40 per cent of the total eligible electorate to constitute proper popular endorsement.

Devolution referenda on 1 March 1979 confirmed the strength of Unionist sentiment outside Westminster. In Wales, 80 per cent of voters rejected devolution; the 40 per cent rule was met, for 47 per cent of those eligible to vote were opposed.In Scotland, the electorate split. Among those voting, there was a majority of 52 per cent in favour of devolution. But this constituted only 33 per cent of those deemed eligible to vote. The Labour government thought this insufficient to justify implementing the Act forthwith; it did not expect all its own MPs to vote once again for an Act that did not have the wide support claimed. The vote against devolution in Scotland and, even more in Wales, was specially noteworthy since in each nation three of the four political parties asked their supporters to vote for it.

Appropriately enough, the Labour government's failure to bring the Devolution Act forward for a prompt post-referendum parliamentary vote led to its own downfall on a motion of no confidence moved by the Scottish National Party. The 3 May 1979 general election results supported the arguments of anti-devolutionists that there was no inelectuable pressure for changing forms of government. The Scottish National Party lost 9 of its 11 MPs, and its vote dropped to 17.3 per cent of the Scottish total. In Wales, Plaid Cymru lost 1 of its 3 MPs, its vote fell by 2.7 per cent and the vote of the Conservatives shot up by 8.2 per cent. Having promoted devolution in the belief that this was the only way to assure its electoral security, Labour found that its efforts to change the United Kingdom were against the clearly expressed wishes of the people of Wales, and divided rather than united voters in Scotland.

IV Cracking the Cake of Custom

Ordinary people do not require a rationale for political allegiance; what Bagehot called the 'cake of custom' can suffice. For most of the time since 1921, the institutions of the United Kingdom governance have been sustained by inertia. Political authority was unchallenged, and the arguments advanced on their behalf unreflective.

To examine customary institutions is to disturb them. The United Kingdom was in a steady state in the 1950s because no questions were asked about its existence. In the 1960s its stability began to be disturbed. The Royal Commission on the Constitution, by the variety and incoherence of its recommendations for change, demonstrated how difficult it is to come to any agreed conclusions about constitutional change. The 1974–9 Labour government declared that 'the status quo is not an option'; the very act of proposing devolution made the customary authority of the Scottish Office part of the status quo ante. Conservative as well as Labour politicians have promoted schemes for reforming what they had previously accepted without thinking. Northern Ireland is a standing reminder that destroying steady state institutions is far easier than establishing something positive in their aftermath.

The vacuum is most apparent in Northern Ireland, which today lacks the *sine qua non* of a state, namely a single authority that can effectively claim a monopoly of coercive force. The Crown supports British and Ulster security forces, but the Province supports Loyalist and Republican forces as well. Northern Ireland is governed by *temporary* direct rule, that is, by an Act of Parliament that requires annual renewal. Successive Northern Ireland secretaries announce their intention to let this lapse provided that Ulster people can agree among themselves about a system of government.

But this agreement is not forthcoming. The Protestant majority wishes to remain British, but divides on whether British rule is best maintained by avoiding the return of a locally elected Assembly, or by the re-creation of a devolved government at Stormont. The chief Catholic party, the Social Democratic and Labour party, wants a power-sharing local Assembly in which it is guaranteed a permanent place. It also wishes Northern Ireland to forge stronger links with the Republic as a prelude to its withdrawal from the United Kingdom to join a united Ireland. Given such mutually exclusive goals, both communities opt for direct rule as the lesser evil. The immediate cause of instability is the opposition of British public opinion to indefinite direct rule.[48]

Divisions within Wales are a bulwark of strength for United Kingdom sentiment. Language, the most distinctive mark of culture, divides the Principality into two unequal parts, of which the English-speaking is by far the larger. The net effect of devolution and the 1979 referendum has been to mobilise Anglophone supporters of the integration of Wales in the conventional Whitehall manner.

The continued erosion of Welsh-speaking is a source of instability, for it forces the supporters of Welsh Nationalism to review their priorities. If Plaid Cymru is to have any chance of electoral success, it must play down the Welsh language in order to compete for votes. But if it did this and succeeded, then in the words of the party secretary, it 'would have run its course like the Labour party without achieving anything'.[49] Moreover, the decline of the language would likely continue to extinction. The Plaid could concentrate its efforts upon winning control of local government in Welsh-speaking parts of Wales, and create a redoubt for the language there. Alternatively, promoters of the Welsh language may conclude that 'to try to do things constitutionally has got them nowhere', and instead, in the words of Plaid Cymru founder Saunders Lewis, 'look for leadership to prisons, which breed honesty, not to Westminster'.[50]

In Scotland, the events of 1979 have produced confusion. Scots disagree among themselves about the significance of the 1 March referendum result: 26 per cent believe it meant the Assembly should be established; 33 per cent saw it as an endorsement of the idea but by an insufficient margin to justify establishing an Assembly; and 30 per cent said the Noes won and the Assembly should be scrapped. An Opinion Research Centre survey undertaken shortly before the 1979 general election also found that 60 per cent wished the government to come up with new plans for an Assembly, and 40 per cent wished an Assembly with more powers than Parliament has been willing to endorse.[51]

Political parties in Scotland fairly reflect Scottish public opinion: they are divided internally, as well as differing from each other about Scotland's future governance. Only the Scottish National Party is committed to campaign for constitutional change, and it demands far more than devolution. The major British parties run the risk, if they campaign for major institutional change, of alienating some of their Unionist supporters, and equally, estranging themselves from their London-based leaders, who do not need to think about changing Scotland's government as long as Scots continue to return pro-British rather than SNP MPs to Westminster.

England, the silent partner in the United Kingdom, has immediately gained most from events of 1979. The implicit premise of the Devolution Acts was that they would only concern Scotland and Wales 'without side-effects for those living in the rest of the United Kingdom'[52] (i.e. 46 million English, and 1.5 million Ulster people). But no serious analyst of the measures accepted that Westminster could escape 'scot free' from the effects of Devolution, and English MPs and English interests (in so far as they can be disentangled from those of the Imperial Parliament) would inevitably have been affected, if only by the inefficiency of the resulting complexities. While the parties did not explicitly seek to mobilise English opinion against devolution, the negative reaction was there to be revealed by opinion polls.[53] The defeat of devolution means that English voters, and even more English MPs, do not now need to give immediate or continuing attention to the government of non-English parts of the United Kingdom. They can consider government policies as equally 'British' or 'English', and *not* have to have a special policy for Wales and Scotland.

The Westminster Parliament itself no longer stands four square behind the principle of defending the territorial integrity of the United Kingdom, and its citizens therein. The obvious party interest in the devolution debate for Scotland and Wales was a reminder that politicians may put party before *patrie*. Even stronger evidence of the contraction of Westminster's responsibilities has been given in Northern Ireland, where British policy has been to conduct a war of containment, that is, containing violence within the Northern Ireland portion of the United Kingdom. In late 1971, Reginald Maudling, then responsible at Westminster for the Province, told a press conference that he thought the Provisional IRA would 'not be defeated, not completely eliminated, but have their violence reduced to an acceptable level'. Eight years later, in response to an election campaign press conference question about Ulster, William Whitelaw, soon to succeed to the post of English Home Secretary, spoke of his 'determination to prevent violence in this part of the United Kingdom'.[54] Roy Jenkins, as Labour Home Secretary, betrayed concern for security within Great Britain without regard to Northern Ireland, by introducing the Prevention of Terrorism Act, 1974, which gives Westminster the power to deport suspected terrorists from Great Britain to what is regarded as the most expendable part of the United Kingdom. Whereas no government has asserted that Scotland or Wales should remain part of the United Kingdom as long as (and only as long as) a majority wish to do so, accepting Northern Ireland's unilateral right to secession is a shibboleth of British policy.

The great change in United Kingdom politics in the past generation is that the continued unity of the territories of the Crown can not be taken for granted. Whether this is viewed as progress or decline depends upon political persuasion. To a confirmed Unionist, it is clearly decline. A Nationalist will see the waning of Westminster's strength as evidence of progress toward independence. Those who are not committed to either position may ask: What is gained by change? The question is starkest in Northern Ireland, where 2000 people have died in a three-cornered fight about the disruption or maintenance of the United Kingdom.

In a broader historical perspective, the question is different: whether the structure of the United Kingdom is unending or whether, as Pocock suggests:

> Future historians may find themselves writing of a 'Unionist' or even a 'British' period in the history of the peoples inhabiting the Atlantic archipelago, and locating it between a date in the thirteenth, the seventeenth or the nineteenth century, and a date in the twentieth or the twenty-first.[55]

NOTES

1. See, J. G. A. Pocock, 'British History: A Plea for a New Subject', *Journal of Modern History*, XLVII (Dec 1975) 603.
2. *Royal Commission on the Constitution, 1969–1973* (often referred to as the Kilbrandon Commission), Cmnd no. 5460 (London: HMSO, 1973) vol. I, especially paras 60 ff.
3. Justification by effectiveness is ultimately derived from a conflict theory of history, and the origins of the United Kingdom do not refute this. Gianfranco Poggi, *The Development of the Modern State* (London: Hutchinson, 1978) pp. 6 ff.
4. See, S. A. de Smith, *Constitutional and Administrative Law* (Harmondsworth: Penguin, 1971), ch. 30; E. C. S. Wade and A. W. Bradley, *Constitutional Law*, 8th ed. (London: Longman, 1970) chs 30–3, 'The British Commonwealth'.
5. Oliver MacDonagh, *Ireland: The Union and its Aftermath* (London: Allen & Unwin, 1977) p. 13.
6. Lord Cooper in *MacCormick* v. *Lord Advocate*, 1953 *SC* 396. More generally, see J. D. B. Mitchell, *Constitutional Law* (Edinburgh: W. Green, 1964).
7. See, Richard Rose, 'The United Kingdom as a Multi-National State', in R. Rose (ed.), *Studies in British Politics*, 3rd ed. (London: Macmillan Press, 1976) p. 127; Ian Budge and D. W. Urwin, *Scottish Political Behaviour* (London: Longman, 1966) ch. 9; L. P. Curtis, *Anglo-Saxons and Celts* (University of Bridgeport and New York University Press, 1968, for the Conference on British Studies); *Royal Commission on the Constitution*, para. 2.
8. Cf. the comments on European states building nations in Poggi, *Development of the Modern State*, pp. 95 ff; and J. G. A. Pocock's precisely titled *The Limits and Divisions of British History* (University of Strathclyde Studies in Public Policy no. 31, Glasgow, 1979).

9. J. Chuter Ede, Home Secretary, House of Commons *Hansard*, vol. 453, col. 386 (7 July 1948).
10. *Our Changing Democracy: Devolution to Scotland and Wales*, Cmnd no. 6348 (London: HMSO, 1975) p. 61.
11. E. C. S. Wade and A. W. Bradley, *Constitutional Law*, p. 171.
12. See Malta Round Table Conference 1955, *Report*, Cmd no. 9657 (London: HMSO, 1955).
13. See Ronald Robinson, 'Non-European Foundations of European Imperialism: Sketch for a Theory of Collaboration', in Roger Owen and Bob Sutcliffe (eds), *Studies in the Theory of Imperialism* (London: Longman, 1972) pp. 117–40.
14. Quoted in A. P. Thornton, *The Imperial Idea and its Enemies* (London: Macmillan, 1959) p. 80.
15. Quoted by Nicholas Mansergh, *The Commonwealth Experience* (London: Weidenfeld and Nicolson, 1969) p. vi.
16. J. E. Kendle, 'The Round Table Movement and "Home Rule All Round"', *Historical Journal*, XI (1968) 334.
17. See Chairman's letter of transmittal in *Conference on Devolution*, Cmd no. 692 (London: HMSO, 1920).
18. For a clear and pointed statement of parallels, see Vernon Bogdanor, *Devolution* (London: Oxford University Press, 1979) ch. 2.
19. For a further development of these points, see Richard Rose, 'The United Kingdom as an Intellectual Puzzle', in Dean Jaensch (ed.), *The Politics of New Federalism* (Adelaide: Australasian Political Studies Association, 1977) pp. 22 ff.
20. For example, Samuel Beer's wide-ranging study, *Modern British Politics* (London: Faber & Faber, 1965) contains no index references to Scotland, Wales or Ireland.
21. See Richard Rose, *The Problem of Party Government* (London: Macmillan Press, 1974) 148–58; David J. Wilson, *Power and Party Bureaucracy in Britain* (Farnborough, Hants: Saxon House, 1975).
22. See Bleddyn Davies, *Social Needs and Resources in Local Services* (London: Michael Joseph, 1968).
23. For further evidence of the weakness of nationalisms then, see Alan Butt Philip, *The Welsh Question* (Cardiff: University of Wales Press, 1975) ch. 1; H. J. Hanham, *Scottish Nationalism* (London: Faber & Faber, 1969) chs 6–8; Michael Farrell, *Northern Ireland: The Orange State* (London: Pluto Press, 1976) chs 5–6.
24. See House of Commons *Hansard*, vol. 411, col. 688 (5 June 1945). Such figures were provided for patriotic Ulstermen; see J. W. Blake, *Northern Ireland in the Second World War* (Belfast: HMSO, 1956) p. 535n.
25. For Woodburn's statement, see House of Commons *Hansard*, vol. 469, col. 2098 (16 Nov 1949); for Lawson, ibid., vol. 777, col. 1790 (14 Feb 1969.
26. Ibid., vol. 472, col. 623 (10 Mar 1950).
27. Ibid., vol. 428, col. 405 (28 Oct 1946).
28. Ibid., vol. 777, col. 391 (5 Feb 1969). For an illustration drawn from within English experience, see J. K. Friend, J. M. Power and C. J. L. Yewlett, *Public Planning: The Inter-Corporate Dimension* (London: Tavistock, 1974).
29. See Jim Bulpitt, 'The Making of the United Kingdom', *Parliamentary Affairs*, XXXI (1978) 180, and other unpublished papers from his book in progress. On the related concept of stratarchy, see S. J. Eldersveld, *Political Parties: A Behavioral Analysis* (Chicago: Rand McNally, 1964).

30. On the legal basis, see Harry Calvert, *Constitutional Law in Northern Ireland* (London and Belfast: Stevens and Northern Ireland Legal Quarterly, 1968), and on Westminster, James Callaghan, *A House Divided: The Dilemma of Northern Ireland* (London: Collins, 1973) pp. 2 ff.
31. See, e.g. James G. Kellas, *The Scottish Political System* (Cambridge: University Press, 1973), George Pottinger, *The Secretaries of State of Scotland, 1926–76* (Edinburgh: Scottish Academic Press, 1979) and various papers published as *Studies in Public Policy* by the Centre for the Study of Public Policy at the University of Strathclyde.
32. See P. J. Madgwick and Mari James, *Government by Consultation: the Case of Wales*, Strathclyde Studies in Public Policy no. 47 (Glasgow, 1979).
33. Fortunately, there are two pairs of books studying change, the first concerning Cheshire: J. M. Lee, *Social Leaders and Public Persons* (Oxford: Clarendon Press, 1963), and J. M. Lee, B. Wood, B. Solomon and P. Walton, *The Scope of Local Initiative: A Study of Cheshire County Council 1961–1974* (London: Martin Robertson, 1974). On Banbury, see Margaret Stacey, *Tradition and Change* (London: Oxford University Press, 1963) and *Power, Persistence and Change* (London: Routledge & Kegan Paul, 1975).
34. For a discussion of a Europe-wide phenomenon of technocratic change, see Jack Brand, 'Reforming Local Government: Sweden and England Compared', in R. Rose (ed.), *The Dynamics of Public Policy: A Comparative Analysis* (London: Sage, 1976) pp. 35–56.
35. See Philip, *The Welsh Question*, p. 293. Note also J. Barry Jones and Michael Keating, *The British Labour Party as a Centralising Force*, Strathclyde Studies in Public Policy no. 32 (Glasgow, 1979).
36. See Ian McAllister, Richard Parry and Richard Rose, *United Kingdom Rankings*, Strathclyde Studies in Public Policy no. 44 (Glasgow, 1979) Table 17.
37. For two grudging tributes to Stormont's effectiveness against the IRA, see Michael Farrell, *Northern Ireland*, ch. 9, and J. Bowyer Bell, *The Secret Army* (London: Sphere, 1972) ch. 16.
38. Richard Rose, *Governing Without Consensus* (London: Faber & Faber, 1971), p. 301. On social legislation, see R. J. Lawrence, *The Government of Northern Ireland: Public Finance and Public Services, 1921–1964* (Oxford: Clarendon Press, 1965).
39. W. Bagehot, *The English Constitution*, World's Classics edn (London: Oxford University Press, 1955) p. 4.
40. Cf. David Braybrooke and C. E. Lindblom, *A Strategy of Decision* (New York: Free Press, 1963) ch. 4.
41. See R. L. Borthwick, 'When the Short Cut May Be a Blind Alley: The Standing Committee on Regional Affairs', *Parliamentary Affairs*, XXXI (1978) 201–9; John F. McDonald *The Lack of Political Identity in English Regions: Evidence from MPs*, Strathclyde Studies in Public Policy no. 33 (Glasgow, 1979).
42. On the Constitutional Convention, see Richard Rose, *Northern Ireland: A Time of Choice* (London: Macmillan Press, 1976). On the remoteness of Westminster authority in Northern Ireland, see Robert Fisk, *The Point of No Return* (London: Andre Deutsch, 1975).
43. Callaghan, *A House Divided*, p. 187.
44. On public opinion in this period see Richard Rose and Ian McAllister, *United Kingdom Facts* (London: Macmillan Press, 1980) ch. 5.
45. Defensiveness is found everywhere in *Devolution within the United Kingdom:*

Some Alternatives for Discussion (London: HMSO, Office of the Lord President of the Council, June 1974); *Democracy and Devolution: Proposals for Scotland and Wales*, Cmnd no. 5732 (London: HMSO, Sep 1974), and *Our Changing Democracy*. For accounts by interested parties of the debate within the Labour movement at the time, see Tam Dalyell, *Devolution: The End of Britain?* (London: Jonathan Cape, 1977), and David Heald, *Making Devolution Work* (London: Young Fabian Pamphlet no. 43, 1976).

46. Nicholas Mansergh, *The Government of Northern Ireland: A Study in Devolution* (London: Allen & Unwin, 1936) p. 16.
47. Quoted in Dalyell, *Devolution*, p. 41. Cf. a view from the opposite perspective: H. M. Drucker, *Breakaway: The Scottish Labour Party* (Edinburgh: EUSPB, 1978).
48. See Richard Rose, Ian McAllister and Peter Mair, *Is There a Concurring Majority about Northern Ireland?*, University of Strathclyde Studies in Public Policy no. 22 (Glasgow, 1978).
49. Quoted by Phillip M. Rawkins, '"The Incidental Hero": The Nationalist Vision and Self-Imposed Limits to Political Advance in Industrial South Wales' (Sociology of Wales Seminar on Ethnonationalism, Cardiff, Aug 1978).
50. Cf. Phil Williams, 'Welsh: A Formula for Survival', *Welsh Nation*, Aug 1978, pp. 4–5; 'Cymdeithas at the Crossroads', *Western Mail*, 27 Mar 1979; 'Bitter Attack on Plaid by Founder', *The Observer*, 15 Apr 1979; 'Plaid to Seek Cause of Worst Poll Results', *Western Mail*, 8 May 1979.
51. See 'Support for Rethink on Devolution', *The Scotsman*, 26 Apr 1979.
52. *Devolution: the English Dimension* (London: HMSO, 1976) para. 23. Note also, Lewis A. Gunn, 'Devolution: A Scottish View', *Political Quarterly*, XLVIII (1977) 129–39. More generally, see Bogdanor, *Devolution*; chs 7–8.
53. Richard Rose, 'Assembly – English Noes and Scottish Ayes', *Glasgow Herald*, 26 Oct 1978.
54. The Maudling quotation is from David McKittrick, 'Reggie's Biggest Contribution to North were his Blunders', *Irish Times* (14 Feb 1979) and the Whitelaw quote from the author's press conference notes. See also the contents of a Northern Ireland Ministry of Defence report, as summarised in, for example, *The Observer*, 13 May 1979.
55. Pocock, in *Journal of Modern History*, XLVII, 603.

Index

Ady, P. H., 108n
Allen, G. C., 32, 38n
Allison, Lincoln, 25n
Amateurism
  attitude with long history, 11–12
  in management, 10, 12, 22n
Amery, L. S., 82, 89, 93n
Anwar, Muhammed, 127n
An Approach to Industrial Strategy (Cmnd. 6315), 33
Apter, David, 74, 92n
Arnold, Matthew, 13, 24n
Asquith, Herbert, 82
Attlee, Clement, 75, 78
Axford, Barry, 125n

Bachrach, Elinor B., 126n
Bacon, R., 31, 38n
Bagehot, Walter, 81, 92n, 143, 153n
Balance of payments, 97–8
  effect of North Sea oil, 35
  in 1970s, 102
  post-war crisis, 97
Baldwin, Stanley, 74, 80, 82
Ball, R. J., 37n
Balogh, Thomas, 7, 21n
Barnett, Corelli, 11, 23n
Baumol, William Jack, 31
Beckerman, Wilfrid, 29
Beer, Samuel, 152n
Bell, Daniel, 21n
Bell, J. Bowyer, 153n
Benn, Anthony Wedgwood, 78
Bevan, Aneurin, 78, 138
Beveridge, Sir William, 39, 43, 52
Beveridge Report, 44, 55n
Bevins, Reginald, 81, 92n
Biffen, John, 81
Birch, Anthony, 52–72, 72n, 125n
Birchenough, Henry, 23n
Black, J., 108n
Blackaby, F. T., 37
Blake, David, 108n
Blake, J. W., 152n
Blue Streak missile, 84
Bogdanor, Vernon, 152n, 154n
Bohning, W. R., 126n
Bonar Law, Andrew, 80, 81, 82
Booth, Albert, 78
Boothby, Sir Robert, 138
Borthwick, R. L., 153n
Boston, Richard, 126n, 127n
Boycotts, as means of pressure on governments, 105
Bradley, A. W., 151n
Brand, Jack, 153n
Braybrooke, David, 153n
Brier, Alan, 125n
'British disease', 1, 4, 20n
  explanations, 29–32
  seen as an old phenomenon, 11
  symptoms, 27–9
British Empire
  extension of Crown's boundaries, 134
  racial structure, 115
British Leyland subsidies, 66
British Motor Corporation, 66
British Nationality Act (1948), 112
Brittan, Samuel, 6, 9, 21n, 22n, 99, 108n
Brodrick, George, 11, 23n
Brookings Institution report, 23n, 95
Brown, George (Lord George-Brown), 22n, 78
Budge, Ian, 151n
Bulpitt, Jim, 139, 152n
Burke, Edmund, 14
Burnet, Alastair, 10, 22n
Burtt, Everett J., 109n
Business cycle, correlation with growth, 29
Butler, David, 80n, 92n, 93n, 125n

Butt, Ronald, 119, 127n

Cabinet
  concentration of formal power, 73
  social and educational status of members, 77–81
  subordinate to Crown-in-Parliament, 136
Cairncross, Sir Alex, 22n
Calhoun, John, 91
Callaghan, James, 78, 115, 145, 153n
Calvert, Harry, 153n
Campbell-Bannerman, Sir Henry, 82
Car industry mergers, 66
Castle, Barbara, 79
Caves, Richard, 96, 107n, 108n
Censorship, abolition by commercialism, 16
Central Policy Review Staff, 85
Chamberlain, Joseph, 74, 90
Chamberlain, Neville, 80
Channel Tunnel, 66
Chapman, Brian, 2, 7, 62–3, 72n
Chapman, Richard, 63, 72n
Character, national, 9, 23n
Charles, Rodger, 56n
Checkland, S. G., 23n
Christoph, James G., 124, 128n
Churchill, Sir Winston, 74, 80
Chuter Ede, J., 152n
Citizenship
  definition as central problem for race policy, 121
  problems of definition, 117
  rights, 132–3
Civil service
  changes in recruitment and training, 64–5
  influence on government policies, 65
  Oxbridge predominance, 61–2, 72n
  reform, 61–5
  training of recruits, 62–3
Civil Service College, 64–5
Civil Service Department, 63
Clay Cross (Derbyshire), 69–70
Clegg, Hugh, 53, 56n
Clyde shipyards, 66, 69
Clynes, John Robert, 79
Cobham, David, 103, 109n
Cole, G. D. H., 2, 14, 19n
Cole, W. A., 108n
Coleridge, Samuel Taylor, 14
Committee on Policy Optimisation: Report (Cmnd. 7148), 37n
Commonwealth, independence of white dominions, 116
  see also British Empire
Conan, A. R., 99, 108n
Concorde, 66
Connor, Walker, 128n
Conservative Party
  policies of 1960s, 85
  rejection of UK territorial differences, 137
  small change in social composition, 79–83
Constitution of the United Kingdom
  accidental nature, 130
  advantages of unwritten status, 131
  see also Royal Commission on the Constitution
Consumption, 10, 96
Cooper, Richard, 108n
Corner, D. C., 99, 108n
Cost-push theory of inflation, 102, 103
Craftsmanship, destruction by technology, 16
Cripps, Sir Stafford, 78
Croome, Honor, 109n
Crosland, Anthony, 2, 9, 19n, 20n, 79
Crossman, Richard, 9, 19n, 65, 72n, 78, 87, 93n, 113, 125n, 126n
Crouch, Colin, 109n
Crown
  as centre of government, 133
  change of emphasis, 143
  territorially vague, 133
Crown-in-Parliament concept, 136–7
Cultural reasons for decline, 9–12
Culyer, A. J., 56n
Cunliffe, Marcus, 3
Currency devaluation, 87, 97
Curtis, L. P., 151n

Dalton, Hugh, 78
Dalyell, Tam, 154n
Daniel, W. W., 127n
Davies, Bleddyn, 152n
Deakin, Nicholas, 72n, 124n, 125n
Deane, Phyllis, 108n

Decline of Britain, 1–4
Decolonisation by United Kingdom, 60
Deedes, William, 125n
Defence expenditure overseas, 100
Dell, Edmund, 79
Demand-pull theory of inflation, 102
Democracies, inherent economic weaknesses, 6
Denison, Edward F., 23n, 104, 109n
Department of Economic Affairs, 61, 85
de Smith, S. A., 151n
Devolution issue, 71, 133, 135, 146–7
  referendum, 147
'Direct action' groups, 69
  territorial interests, 137
Diseases, changes in prevalence, 46
Disposable income, 41
Disraeli, Benjamin, 80
Distribution of Income and Wealth, Royal Commission: Report, 55n
Dixon, R., 38n
Donnison, David, 43, 55n
Donovan Commission, 109n
Dorfman, Gerald, 56n
Douglas, James, 72n
Douglas-Home, Sir Alec, 80, 85
Drucker, H. M., 154n

Earnings, inequalities, 41–2
East of Suez policy, 100–1
Economic aid to overseas countries, 99
Economic growth, 4–5, 20–1n
  comparative rates, 18, 60–1, 96, 102
  detrimental to quality of life, 13
  National Plan, 61
  not generally seen as important, 11, 25n, 37n
Economy
  decline: as a result of government policies, 5, 8
  government controls, 50
  international comparisons, 4–5, 12, 27–9
  restructuring, 36
  seen as main area of national decline, 3–4
  see also 'British disease'
Eden, Sir Antony, 80
Education, 45–6
  graduate MPs, 76
  Robbins Committee, 61
Einzig, Paul, 9, 22n
Eldersveld, S. J., 152n
Electoral reform, 68
Eliot, T. S., 14, 15, 25n
Eltis, W., 31, 38n
England
  effect of devolution, 150
  home rule movements, 144
'English disease' *see* 'British disease'
Enloe, Cynthia, 126n, 127n
European Economic Community
  Britain's first approach, 61, 84
  challenge to traditional leadership patterns, 74
  effect of membership on government, 71
  'entry at any price' approach, 99
  importance of members' economic prosperity, 26
Exports
  labour costs as determinant, 30–1
  post-war expansion, 97–8

Fabian politics, 59, 67
Fairlie, Henry, 2–3, 20n
Farrell, Michael, 152n, 153n
Fawcett, J. E. S., 125n
Ferris, Paul, 109n
Finer, S. E., 22n, 72n
Fiscal policies, 29
Fisher, Nigel, 92n
Fisk, Robert, 153n
Foot, Paul, 125n
Fores, Michael, 23n
Forester, Tom, 25n
Fox, A. D., 125n
Franklin, Mark N.L., 124, 128n
Fraser, Ian, 23n
Freeman, Gary, 127n
Friend, J. K., 152n
Full employment
  as a function of the welfare state, 49, 50
  commitment of main political parties, 83
  1944 White Paper, 95
  see also Unemployment
Fulton Report, 21n, 63–5, 86

Gaitskell, Hugh, 75, 78, 87–8
Galbraith, J. K., 2
General Elections
  swing away from main parties in 1974, 70
  tendency of electorate to abstain, 70
  weakening of class voting, 82
Gilmour, Ian, 21n, 93n
Goldsmith, Edward, 17, 25n
Goldsworthy, David, 125n
Goldthorpe, John, 93n
Gordon, Michael, 21n
Gordon-Walker, Patrick, 78, 113
Governing class, 73
Government
  advantages not enjoyed in other countries, 58
  attempt to open up process, 65, 89
  centred upon Crown, 133
  challenges to authority, 94
  enquiries into efficiency, 86
  imbalance between public expectation and actual performance, 69
  increasing dynamism in 1960s, 85
  institutions sustained by inertia, 148
  interventionism, 86
  policy, 32–5, 38n
    advisers, 65
  preoccupation with short-term solutions, 35
  public disenchantment, 57
  reforms countering reactions against, 68
  repeal of predecessor's actions, 59
  reshuffling of departments, 66–7, 85
  result of decline in two main parties, 73
  territorial emphasis, 136
  see also Political leadership
Grant, Wyn, 22n
Great Power status, 20n
Green Papers, 65
Grey, Earl, 135
Grove, J. W., 110n
Gunn, Lewis A., 154n
Guttsman, W. L., 80, 92n
Gwyn, William B., 1–25, 68

Hailsham, Lord, 92n
Haines, Joe, 65, 72n
Halsey, A. H., 48, 56n
Hanham, H. J., 152n
Harris, Jose, 56
Harris, Ralph, 8, 22n
Hattersley, Roy, 79
Hayek, F. A., 8, 22n
Heald, David, 154n
Healey, Dennis, 79
Health care, 46–7; *see also* National Health Service
Heath, Edward, 75, 81, 84–5, 87, 114
Heclo, Hugh, 39–56, 58, 63, 72n
Hill, Sir Charles, 81, 92n
Hindell, Keith, 126n
Hobson, John A., 15, 24n
Holtermann, Sally, 55n
Home-ownership, 44
  council house sales, 54
Hospitals, industrial action in, 70
House improvement grants, 45, 55n
House of Lords, reconstruction, 7–8
Households, definition of, 55
Hudson Institute, 9, 20n
  Report, 23n
Humanism, anti-industrial tradition, 15
Humphrey, Derek, 125n
Hutchinson, T. W., 24n
Hyam, Ronald, 108n

Imlah, Albert, H., 97, 108n
Immigrant population
  as pool of labour, 113
  assumption of assimilation, 123
  concentration in London and Midlands, 113
  differentiating between subjects and citizens, 116–17
  proportion of UK population, 111
  'second generation', 122
  statistical data collection poor, 123
Immigration
  central problems, 121
  connection with race relations, 112
  control: Conservative proposals, 67, 114–15
    early legislation, 113
  public hostility, 60
Immigration Control Acts, 118

Import controls, 97
Imports, proportion to home sales, 27
Income policies, 11
Indian Army, 100
Indian independence, effect on defence East of Suez, 100
Industrial relations
  attempts to control, 53
  exclusion from government economic policy, 50
  government intervention, 86
    TUC action against, 69
  1979 Conservative manifesto, 54
Industrial Relations Act (1971), trade union response, 105
Industrial Revolution, social and environmental effects, 13
Industry
  anti-industry tradition, 14–15
  efficiency at company level, 34
  inefficient use of labour and capital, 12, 22n
  middle-class prejudice against careers in, 10, 32
  policies to promote efficiency, 34
Inflation
  increases after 1973, 67
  promoting 'British disease', 4, 27
  rates, 4, 67, 95–6, 102
Inglehart, Richard, 25n
Institute of Economic Affairs, 8, 22n
Institutionalised care, 44, 55n
Investment, correlation with growth, 29–30
Ireland
  home rule issue, 135
  see also Northern Ireland

Jackson, D., 109n
Jay, Douglas, 78
Jay, Peter, 6, 20n, 21n
Jenkins, Roy, 79, 92n, 150
Jennings, W. Ivor, 110n
Johnson, R. W., 92n, 125n
Jones, J. Barry, 153n
Joseph, Sir Keith, 8, 22n

Kahn, Richard Ferdinand, Lord, 109n
Kaldor, Nicholas, 9, 30, 37n, 38n
Katznelson, Ira, 114, 118, 125n
Kavanagh, Dennis, 58, 72n, 73–93, 92n, 93n, 125n, 126n
Keating, Michael, 153n
Keehn, Norman H., 22
Kellas, James G., 153n
Kendle, J. E., 152n
Kenyan Asians, 113–14, 119
Keynes, John Maynard, 42, 55n
Keynesian economics, 9, 38n, 52
  dominant in 1950s, 59
  loss of public confidence, 67
Kilbrandon Commission, *see* Royal Commission on the Constitution
Kincaid, J. C., 55n
King, Anthony, 69, 72n, 93n, 125n
King, Robert, 126n
Koestler, Arthur, 5, 9, 20n, 22n
Kohler, David, 126n
Korean war, 95, 98
Krause, Lawrence, 108n
Kushnick, Louis, 126n

Labour Party
  changes in social composition, 76–9
  rejection of UK territorial differences, 137
  Wilson's tactics to hold together, 87–8
Labour supply, 31
Landsberg, Hans H., 25n
Laski, Harold J., 12, 23n
Lavers, R. J., 56n
Lawrence, Daniel, 125n, 126n, 127n
Lawrence, R. J., 153n
Lawson, George, 138
Leavis, F. R., 14–15, 24n
Lee, J. M., 153n
Leisure, 11
Levine, A. L., 109n
Liberal principles
  applied to individual representation, 137
  prevalence in 1950s, 59–60
Lindblom, C. E., 153n
Little, Alan, 126n
Living standards, post-war rises, 44
Lloyd George, David, 74–5
Local government
  control from central government, 58
  finance, 137

Local government *(contd.)*
  parameters set by Westminster, 140–1
  reform, 142
Lomax, David, 99, 108n
London, local government reform, 142
Lord, Alan, 38n
Low, Sidney, 83, 93n

McAllister, Ian, 153n, 154n
Macdonagh, Oliver, 151n
McDonald, John F., 153n
MacDonald, Ramsay, 74
Mace, 143
  as symbol of the Crown, 136
  importance of concept, 144
McFadzean, Sir Frank, 22n
Machines, effect on man's self-perception, 16
McIntosh, Sir Ronald, 38n
McIntyre, Robert, 138
Mack, Joanna, 127n
McKenzie, R. T., 81, 92n
Mackintosh, John, 7, 22n
McKittrick, David, 154n
Macmillan, Harold, 75, 80, 90
MacRae, Donald, 2, 10, 20n, 22n
Maddison, Angus, 108n
Madge, Nicola, 55n
Madgwick, P. J., 153n
Mair, Peter, 154n
Malta
  Round Table Conference (1955), 152n
  seeks representative government, 134
Malthus, Thomas Robert, 13
Management
  amateurism, 10, 12, 22n
  constraints imposed by trade unions, 32
  middle class prejudice against careers in, 10, 32
  workers' suspicions of, 10
Mansergh, Nicholas, 146, 152n, 154n
Marsh, Alan, 126n, 127n
Marshall, Alfred, 104
Marshall, T. H., 39
Marshall Aid, 97
Marxists, 5
Mason, Roy, 78
Maudling, Reginald, 150
Mauser, W. A. P., 108n
Means-tested benefits, 43
Meritocracy, 74, 78–81
Meyer, F. V., 99, 108n
Miles, R., 126n, 127n
Mill, John Stuart, 15, 37n, 105
Miller, J. D. B., 125n
Milner, Viscount, 134
Milnor, Andrew J., 124, 128n
Miners' strikes, 106–7
Mishan, Ezra, 15–17, 25n
Mitchell, J. D. B., 151n
Modernisation in 1960s, 87
Monetary policies, 29
Moran, Michael, 56n, 109n, 110n
Morris, Alfred, 72n
Morris, William, 14
Morrison, Herbert, 78
Mortgage tax relief schemes, 45
Mosley, Sir Oswald, 90
Mowat, C. L., 92n
Muller, W. D., 92n
Multi-racial society, 116, 121
Musgrave, Richard and Peggy, 95

Nairn, Tom, 20n
National Economic Development Council, 34, 61
National Front, 114, 122–3
National Health Service, 46, 70
National Incomes Commission, 61
National insurance, 43
Nationalisation, acceptance by both main parties, 83
Nationalist parties, 70, 137–8, 145–6
  ground lost in 1979 Election, 148
Nicholson, Max, 21n
Nordlinger, Eric, 92n
North Sea oil
  economic effects on take-home pay, 71
  revenue from tax on profits, 36
  solution of balance of payments problems, 35
Northern Ireland, 131
  civil rights movement, 144–5
  example of dual polity, 140
  no single visible authority, 148
  Stormont: abolition (1972), 131, 144–5

operation, 142–3
Norton, Philip, 126n

Official Secrets Act, 65
Oil crisis, effect on economic policy-making, 35
see also North Sea oil
Olson, Mancur, 25n, 105
Opie, Roger, 99
Orme, Stan, 78
Orwell, George, 14
Overcrowding, 45
Over-manning, 104–5
Overseas lobby, 99

Paish, F. W., 108n
Panić, M., 103, 107n, 108n, 109n
Panitch, Leo, 56n, 109n
Parker, J. E. S., 99, 108n
Parkin, Michael, 38n, 103, 109n
Parliament
and Constitution, 131, 136
relationship to colonial governments, 135
relationship with local institutions, 139
Parliamentary parties
discipline, 57
withdrawal of public support, 70
Parry, Richard, 129n, 153n
Patrial citizens, 133
Peacock, Alan, 26–38, 38n, 56n
Peters, B. Guy, 68, 72n
Phelps Brown, E. H., 12, 23n, 103, 104, 109n
Philip, Allan Butt, 152n
Phillips, Godfrey, 151n, 152n
Phizacklea, A., 126n, 127n
Picketing, 69
Pinto-Duschinsky, Michael, 80, 92n
Playfair, Lyon, 12, 23n
Pocock, J. G. A., 129, 151, 151n, 154n
Poggi, Gianfranco, 151n
Polanyi, G., 55n
Policy advisers, 65
Political aspects of economic decline, 6, 29
Political institutions, 73
Political leadership
changes in social background, 74–7
changes in style, 74, 83–9, 90
comparison of Wilson and Heath, 88–9
introduction of elections, 82
length of apprenticeships, 90
Political strikes, 105–6
Pollution, 15, 45
Pottinger, George, 153n
Poverty, definitions of, 55n
Powell, Enoch, 90, 114, 115, 118–19
Power, J. M., 152n
Premium Bond system, 42
Prices, 21n, 95
Productivity
influence of trade unions, 104
slow rate of expansion, 12, 30
Proportional representation, 68
Public assistance, 43
Public enquiries, disruption by protestors, 70
Public expenditure
attempts to curb, 71
in Scotland, 142
share of GDP, 31
Public housing, 44, 45
Public investment, 66
Public sector employment, 31
increase in growth, 52
Putnam, Robert, 93n
Putting Britain Right Ahead, 85

Quality of life
affected by economic growth, 13
indicators in *Social Trends*, 27
Snow–Leavis controversy, 14–15, 24n

Race relations in political process, 118, 119, 122
legal protection of civil rights, 124, 124n
not 'normal' part of political process, 118
Race Relations Acts, 113, 118
Racial change in society, 111
Racial equality, not easily accepted, 115
Radcliffe Committee, 99
Raison, Timothy, 107
Rawkins, Phillip M., 154n

Rees, Merlyn, 79, 92n.
Referenda, 74
Religious faith, destroyed by science and technology, 16
Restrictive practices, 104–5
Ricardo, David, 13
Ricketts, Martin, 38n
Robbins Committee on Higher Education, 61
Roberts, Ben, 109n
Robertson, D. H., 99
Robinson, Joan, 108n
Robinson, Ronald, 152n
Rodgers, William, 79
Rose, E. J. B., 125n
Rose, Hannan, 126n
Rose, Richard, 7, 12, 21n, 24n, 68, 72n, 92n, 116, 120, 126n, 127n, 129–54, 151n, 152n, 154n
Ross, Willie, 139
Roth, Andrew, 92n
Rothenstein, Sir John, 63n, 72n
Royal Commission on the Constitution, 130, 145–6, 148, 151n
Russell, Earl, 134
Rustow, Dankwart, 127n
Rutter, Michael, 55n

Sampson, Anthony, 84, 93n
Scarman, Sir Leslie, 128n
Schaefer, Richard T., 126n
Schoen, Douglas, 125n, 127n
Schumacher, E. F., 17, 25n
Schumpeter, Joseph, 6, 21n, 51, 56n, 81, 92n
Scotland
  divided on wish for constitutional reform, 149–50
  economic ties with Westminster, 142
  system of government, 140
Security, of workers, 10–11
Self, Peter, 93n
Semmel, B., 92n
Sewill, Brendan, 7, 22n
Shanks, Michael, 11, 20n, 22n
Sheriff, Peta, 72n
Shils, Edward, 19n
Shore, Peter, 79
Sickness and invalidity benefits, 43
Signposts for the Sixties, 85
Silver, A., 81, 92n
Sisson, C. H., 72n
Smith, T. Alexander, 121, 127n
Smoke control zones, 45
Snow, C. P., 14–15, 24n
Social class
  educational differences, 46
  health differences, 47, 56n
  housing differences, 45
  party differences in Parliament, 76–7
  providing 'governing class', 73
  race relations made analogous with, 119
  transcending national barriers, 132
'Social contract', 51
Social justice, acting against economic growth, 11
Social policy
  hopes of 1940s, 39
  not extended to labour relations, 50–1
  perpetual attempts at correction, 54
  territorial justice, 137–8
  undermined by sectional interests, 48
  see also Welfare state
Socialism, 2
Society
  agricultural *v*. industrial, 14
  multi-racial, 116, 121
Solomon, B., 153n
Southey, Robert, 14
Spearman, Diana, 126n
Squatters, 70
Stacey, Frank, 72n
Stacey, Margaret, 153n
Stokes, Donald, 125n
Stormont, *see* Northern Ireland
Stout, D. R., 38n
Strikes, political, 105–6
Studlar, Donley T., 111–28, 125n, 126n, 127n
Subsidies, 36
Suez crisis (1956), 60, 84
Supplementary benefits, 43

Tawney, R. H., 14
Taxation
  avoidance and evasion, 69
  of profits on North Sea oil, 36

Taxation *(contd.)*
opportunities to reduce, 36
reform, 11
Taylor, A. J. P., 129
Technological change, resulting in anxiety, 16
Thatcher, Margaret, 81, 91, 115–16
Thirlwall, A. P., 38n
Thornton, A. P., 152n
Titmuss, Richard, 9, 39, 42
Toynbee, Arnold, 7, 22n
Trade, decline in share of world trade, 4, 27
Trade unions
actions in times of full employment, 6
challenges to authority, 103–4
constraints on managerial practices, 32
effect on industry, 23n
exemptions from tortious liability, 22n
extent of responsibility for decline, 94
governments' avoidance of control, 50–1
monetarists' view of, 103
not influenced by government, 7
wage settlements negotiated in 1970s, 102–3
Training
civil servants, 64–5
inadequacies, 10, 32
Transport, destruction of areas of natural beauty, 16
Treasury
influence reduced, 61
overall control function, 58
Trilling, Lionel, 24n
Turner, H. A., 109n

Ugandan Asians, 114
Unemployment
among black youths, 122
growth in, 4, 27, 67, 95, 101
promoting 'British disease', 3
see also Full employment
Unemployment benefit, 43
United Kingdom
as centre of Commonwealth, 134
boundaries ambiguous, 134
not a unitary state, 136
political identity, 132
political development, 129
Unservile State Group, 56n
Urwin, Derek, 120, 127n, 151n

Varley, Eric, 78
Verdoorn's Law, 30–1

Wade, E. C. S., 151n, 152n
Wage settlements, in 1970s, 102–3
Wales
effect of Welsh Office on Westminster, 142
language question, 149
system of government, 140
Walton, P., 153n
Ward, Michael, 125n
Wealth
comparative decline, 4–5
distribution of, 41
Weintraub, Sidney, 109n
Weir, Stuart, 127n
Welch, Colin, 9, 22n
Welfare benefits, keeping up with price rises, 41
Welfare state
basis of decline, 49
changing public attitudes, 52–3
commitment of main political parties, 83
defining areas of responsibility, 49–50
initial dependence on government, 49
post-war stagnation, 40
unsatisfactory development, 39–40
see also Social policy
Wertheimer, Egon, 92n
Whitelaw, William, 150
Whiting, Alan, 37
Widows' benefits, 43
Wildavsky, Aaron, 58, 63n, 72n
Wilkinson, F., 109n
Williams, Alan, 56n
Williams, Phil, 154n
Williams, Raymond, 14, 24n
Wilson, David J., 152n
Wilson, Harold, 75, 79, 84, 86, 90, 93n, 146
Wood, B., 153n
Wood, J. B., 55n
Wood, Michael, 126n
Woodburn, Arthur, 138

Wootton, Graham, 94–110, 107n, 109n, 110n
Workers
  suspicion of managers, 10
  see also Labour supply
Worswick, David, 96, 108n

Yewlett, C. J. L., 152n
Young, Michael, 92n
Youngson, A. J., 108n